THE PERVERSITY OF POETRY

DINO FRANCO FELLUGA

THE PERVERSITY OF POETRY

Romantic Ideology and the Popular Male Poet of Genius

STATE UNIVERSITY OF NEW YORK PRESS

Published by
State University of New York Press
Albany

Printed in the United States of America

For information, address the State University of New York Press, 90 State Street, Suite 700, Albany, NY 12207

Production, Laurie Searl
Marketing, Anne M. Valentine

Library of Congress Cataloging-in-Publication Data

Felluga, Dino Franco, 1966–
The perversity of poetry : romantic ideology and the popular male poet of genius / Dino Franco Felluga.
p. cm.
Includes bibliographical references (p.) and index.
ISBN 0-7914-6299-4 (alk. paper) — ISBN 0-7914-6300-1 (pbk. : alk. paper)
1. English poetry—Male authors—History and criticism. 2. Byron, George Gordon Byron, Baron, 1788–1824—Appreciation. 3. Popular literature—Great Britain—History and criticism. 4. English poetry—19th century—History and criticism. 5. Scott, Walter, Sir, 1771–1832—Poetic works. 6. Scott, Walter, Sir, 1771–1832—Appreciation. 7. Creation (Literary, artistic, etc.) 8. Romanticism—Great Britain. 9. Masculinity in literature. 10. Genius in literature. 11. Men in literature. I. Title.
PR590.F45 2004
821'.7099286—dc22 2004042986

10 9 8 7 6 5 4 3 2 1

per Virgilio e Silvia

CONTENTS

Acknowledgments ix

Abbreviations xi

Introduction 1

1 Diagnosing Genius: The Tropic Body and the Constitution of the Man of Letters 13

2 Romanticism's Last Minstrel: Scott, Ideological Fetishes, and the Technology of the Book 33

3 Byron's Spectropoetics and Revolution 71

4 Poetry and Pathology 105

Coda: Tennyson's *Idylls,* Pure Poetry, and the Market 143

Notes 163

Works Cited 183

Index 199

ACKNOWLEDGMENTS

One thing that this book about the isolated and perverse Romantic poet has taught me is that writing may be somewhat perverse—it may even be slightly melancholic—but it is never truly solitary. This study has been written with and for many wonderful people—the genii of this book on Romantic genius. The book has also partaken of the genii loci of a number of places over the space of its composition, from Santa Barbara to Calgary to Stanford to West Lafayette, Indiana. I will never be able to return the gifts I have received; to name as I do here is but to trace the lineaments of a love and friendship beyond words.

My greatest debt of gratitude goes to Alan Liu, Garrett Stewart, Regenia Gagnier, and Barbara Gelpi, four critics who have been my inspirations in all things having to do with my career and my intellectual development. I am deeply indebted to a number of others: to Cory Davies, A. C. Hamilton, John Matthews, and Clive Thomson for their guidance early in my career; to Julie Carlson, Richard Corum, Richard Helgerson, Paul Hernadi, Hayden White, and Muriel Zimmerman for their generosity and inspiration during my time at UCSB; to Victor Ramraj and Fred Wah for their guidance and support while I was at the University of Calgary; to Jay Fliegelman, Maureen Harkin, Suvir Kaul, Joss Marsh, Robert Polhemus, David Riggs, and Jennifer Summit who aided and inspired me during my time at Stanford; to Ann Astell, Geraldine Friedman, Shaun Hughes, Beate Allert, Nancy Peterson, and Siobhan Somerville who helped me with my project during my time at Purdue; and to UCSB's Interdisciplinary Humanities Center, the University of Calgary's Institute for the Humanities, the Social Sciences and Humanities Research Council of Canada, and the Purdue Research Foundation for funding my work. I would also like to give special thanks to those scholars who have read and generously commented on portions of my book or offered advice and help in its final stages: Steven Bruhm, Jason Camlot, Joseph Childers, Richard Dienst, Michael Eberle-Sinatra, Andrew Elfenbein, Ghislaine McDayter, Arkady Plotnitsky, Kathy

Psomiades, Tilottama Rajan, Cannon Schmitt, Karen Swann, Herbert Tucker, and my two superb readers at SUNY. An earlier version of the Coda appeared as "Tennyson's *Idylls*, Pure Poetry, and the Market" in *SEL: Studies in English Literature* 37: 4 (Autumn 1997). A short section of chapter 3 and of chapter 4 appeared in *European Romantic Review* (of the Taylor and Francis group at http://www.tandf.co.uk). Respectively, those were published as "'With a most voiceless thought': Byron and the Radicalism of Textual Culture," *ERR* 8 (Winter 2000); and "The Fetish-Logic of Bourgeois Subjectivity, or, the Truth the Romantic Poet Reveals about the Victorian Novel" *ERR* 14: 2 (April 2003). Some material from chapter 4 appeared in "Novel Poetry: Transgressing the Law of Genre" in *Victorian Poetry* 41: 4 (Winter 2003). I thank those journals for permitting me to reprint that material here. Finally, my thanks go out to the graduate students in my Byron class at Purdue, who patiently bore with my Byron obsession in fall of 2001.

My closest reader and my strongest critic in every stage of this project has been Emily Allen. Her genius and her gifts (in both senses) have most inspired me. She is my support and my guide in all things. The true heroes of this book on the metrical romance are my parents, who worked so hard and sacrificed so much for their children, and whose story reads like a romance of the New World. They have given me everything they could and I dedicate this book to them.

ABBREVIATIONS

When possible, I have attempted to quote periodical reviews from extant collections in order to make it easier for the reader to locate the original article. In order to avoid the repetition of bibliographical matter, I will follow the following abbreviations for these collections.

BC	*Byron: The Critical Heritage*. Ed. Andrew Rutherford. New York: Barnes and Noble, 1970.
BI	*Byron: Interviews and Recollections*. Ed. Norman Page. New Jersey: Humanities Press, 1985.
RR	*The Romantics Reviewed: Contemporary Reviews of British Romantic Writers*. Part B. 5 vols. Ed. Donald H. Reiman. New York: Garland, 1972.
T	*Tennyson: The Critical Heritage*. Ed. John Jump. London: Routledge, 1967.
VP	*The Victorian Poet: Poetics and Persona*. Ed. Joseph Bristow. London: Croom Helm, 1987.
VS	*Victorian Scrutinies: Reviews of Poetry, 1830–1870*. Ed. Isobel Armstrong. London: Athlone, 1972.

INTRODUCTION

> *who* was ever altered by a poem?
>
> —Byron, *Letters*

Nineteenth-century critics expressed with cries of alarm what was for W. H. Auden by 1939 a mere statement of fact: "poetry makes nothing happen." The lines that follow this statement in Auden's famous poem, "In Memory of W. B. Yeats," speak to a number of the concerns in this book:

> For poetry makes nothing happen: it survives
> In the valley of its making where executives
> Would never want to tamper, flows on south
> From ranches of isolation and the busy griefs. (36–39)

What this study explores is the cultural background, the literary prehistory for what was by Auden's day already cliché—the poet's isolation, poetry's inefficacy, its opposition to political economy, its self-creating and self-involved autonomy, and its association with strong emotion. From the retrospective of poetry's marginalization in the twentieth century, many studies follow Auden's lead and read canonical nineteenth-century poetry as always already ineffective, elitist, self-involved, as caught up in what Jerome McGann has termed "Romantic ideology"; however, as this book illustrates, the slow devolvement of poetry into the cliché of inefficacy was a gradual, uneven, and highly contested development in the period. Poetry did not, in other words, go quietly into high culture's good night.

This book focuses on three things associated with poetry in the Romantic and early Victorian period that complicate the attribution of high-cultural inefficacy to the poetic enterprise: popularity, politics, and pathology. Sir Walter Scott and Lord Byron serve as the dialectical foci for such a study precisely because of their unprecedented popularity in the period, and, indeed, one of the topics I will seek to clarify is the relationship of Scott's and Byron's verse romances to the market and print technologies of their age. This book also argues that both Scott and Byron had an effect on the political fabric of the Romantic period, albeit an effect that was undercut by a medico-moral rhetoric of health and perversity not only applied to both poets but also *invited* by both poets in order to screen or figure their political messages. What is so interesting about these two fantastically popular poets, who were consistently and pervasively juxtaposed as the two opposing possibilities for the future of poetry, is that they not only spoke to an emergent mass market and influenced opposing political groups but also invited their own marginalization by playing into a medical rhetoric about poetical geniuses that would eventually ensure their dismissal by Victorian critics. Following Scott's own lead, Romantic and Victorian critics continually represented Scott's poetry as a panacea for a modern world overtaken by new principles of utilitarianism, capitalism, industrialism, and democracy. Following Byron's lead, those same critics tended to represent Byron's poetry as a disease in the heart of the social order or as a contagious pandemic leading to various pathological symptoms, particularly those arising from the sexual perversity of Byron's body and corpus. Through such "treatment" of these exemplary poet figures, the figuration of poets in general was translated from the register of politics to that of medicine and sexuality. Alfred Lord Tennyson, who is the subject of the book's Coda, represents a Victorian negotiation and sublation of the dialectical opposition represented by Scott and Byron.

This book posits that the two positions figured for poetry in Scott and Byron are, in fact, strictly homologous: both serve, in the end, to push the poetic enterprise to the margins of the social body, be it as cure or as curse, thus opening the way for the eventual dominance of the realist novel; however, both of these fantasized possibilities for poetry obscure the fact that Scott and Byron not only facilitated the emergence of a mass market through the unprecedented dissemination of their work but also participated actively in the political struggles of their time period, much more so than is usually acknowledged: Scott through his counterrevolutionary opposition to radicalism and his orchestration of a new legitimating ideology of medievalism for George IV; Byron through his positing of a principle of justice and revolutionary opposition in his poetry, a principle that inspired a host of disparate radical groups. The shift to a rhetoric of health served, one might say, to cure Romantic poetry of its earlier association with both the mass market and revolutionary politics, leaving us with nothing but the purified figure of McGann's Romantic ideology.

Of particular interest in this shift is that we can also witness the self-legitimization of the literary critic, who used the very medical rhetoric formerly applied to the bodily constitution of the scholar and the man of letters—who in the eighteenth century were believed to suffer from all sorts of bodily and mental ills—in order to reconstitute the critic as medic. This new physician of culture borrowed the increasingly specialized terminology of the doctor, the alienist, and the scientist, in order to exculpate himself from the charge of disease and to charge himself with maintaining the mental and bodily health of a new reading public. By examining such rhetorical strategies, this book contributes to a growing body of work on the relation between Romantic literature and medicine, filling in the still largely unexplored issue of poetry's pathologization in the period.[1] The notions of genius, the melancholic, and the Satanic hero will occupy me throughout since the interrelated concepts illustrate how closely intertwined were the notions of the revolutionary and the valetudinary for the nineteenth-century poet. As we will see, the melancholic Satanic hero of revolutionary opposition quickly devolved over the course of the nineteenth century into patient zero: the source, according to the criticism, of various ills threatening both the social body of Britain and the individual body of the private reader.

To be more precise, the literary "specialist" reduced the ideological power of Romantic poetry in two related ways: he posited the notion of an ideal or pure or, in Scott's case, uncorrupted because archaic poetry outside or at a temporal remove from the concerns of the quotidian, a characterization that was often connected to a rhetoric of panacea, or he recast poetry as variously perverse, leading to a host of diseases threatening the body politic. The response to Scott's poetry is exemplary of the first strategy; the response to Byron's poetry of the latter. In either case, poetry was reimagined as on the margins of the social body, be it as injected cure or infecting disease. It is a position from which poetry has sought to extricate itself ever since.

One symptom of poetry's marginalization is that criticism no longer takes seriously the poetic form that throughout the nineteenth century captured the ear of a mass audience: the verse romance. The prose romance has recently begun to garner a great deal of interest in literary scholarship; a number of notable studies have now explored the important influence of the romance on the rise of the novel, especially Michael McKeon's *The Origins of the English Novel*, Ian Duncan's *Modern Romance and the Transformations of the Novel*, and Miranda Burgess's *British Fiction and the Production of Social Order*. However, the role of the *metrical* romance in these debates has been largely ignored, despite the centrality of such poems in the market dynamics of the Romantic period and despite the crucial role of Romantic ideology as counterdiscourse to the definition and formation of the Victorian bourgeois subject.

Today, the romance as form is popularly associated with the emotional escapism of what Gillian Beer calls "sub-literature": adolescent fantasy stories, Hallmark sentimentalism, and Harlequin soft-core pornography; however, the fact is that in the nineteenth century the romance was able to run the ideological gamut from the nostalgic conservatism of Scott to the melancholic radicalism of Byron to what has been termed the subversive reactionary position of Tennyson. The romance succeeded in introducing "romantic" poetry to an emergent mass market, speaking to readers across class lines and ideological perspectives; it inspired revolutionaries in some manifestations, quieted the masses in others. Indeed, the romance appeared to speak directly to the age even when it did so through the anachronisms of medievalism and, as a result, the form concerned itself with a number of issues that seem to have little to do with our contemporary notions of "romance": fantasies of empire, allegories of textual production, forms of ideological critique, theories of justice, and the threat of revolution.

Scott, Byron, and Tennyson are central figures for this study precisely because of the popularity of their romances and, hence, the influence of these poets on the age, an influence that far surpassed that of the other now-canonical poets that critics generally associate with Romanticism and the Victorian period. Indeed, as far as the *Romantic* public was concerned, Scott and Byron *were* the main poets of the period and the romance form was the dominant genre, just as for the Victorians Tennyson was the representative poet of the age and his *Idylls of the King* one of his greatest accomplishments. And yet, the romance poetry of Byron, Scott, and Tennyson is not as well represented in contemporary scholarship as the lyric poetry of William Wordsworth, Samuel Coleridge, John Keats, and Percy Shelley or the dramatic monologues and short lyrics of the Victorian period. Although Scott scholarship has been driven by numerous superb studies of Scott's novels, the poetical romances, which were so fantastically influential in the period, are still largely ignored. Byron scholarship has been picking up steam over the last few years, thanks to a new willingness to take Byron's philosophy and aesthetics seriously; however, it is also true that, as James Chandler recently put it in his *England in 1819*, "We are still early in the Byron revival," and criticism has still to explore some of the more difficult aesthetic and ideological questions raised by Byron's poetry (388). Tennyson scholarship has also been less than vigorous over the last decade, largely due to the publishing industry's tendency to prefer books on the Victorian novel rather than Victorian poetry (with the exception, perhaps, of the Decadents).

This book not only focuses on the most popular poetical romances of the nineteenth century, thus seeking to clarify their relation to an emergent mass market and mass readership, but it also helps to explain how it was that the romance was gradually dismissed as a serious generic form over the course of that century. How was it that the romantic and particularly the romance came to be associated with impotent, adolescent fantasy rather than with the revolutionary ideals posited by Byron or, as David Duff has recently argued, by Shelley? What this book attempts to trace, in other words, is a *semantic* transformation of the *romantic*—from the adult pursuit of revolutionaries often inspired by the romance form into the adolescent pursuit of the voluptuary concerned only with romance.

That transformation is exemplified in my very title, *The Perversity of Poetry*. Semantically, "perversity" suggests the rhetorical as well as historical shift I examine: from the nineteenth-century definition, which is akin to "subversion" ("turning aside from truth or right" [OED]) to the more common contemporary usage ("a disorder of sexual behavior in which satisfaction is sought through channels other than those of normal heterosexual intercourse" [OED]). On the one hand, this book explores the subversive potential of Lord Byron's poetry, its threatening effectiveness among disparate groups dissatisfied with the emergent ideologies of mass-market capitalism and bourgeois domesticity (those hegemonic versions of "truth or right"). On the other hand, the book illustrates how various late Romantic and Victorian critics sought to neutralize the most radical Romantic poets by associating verse in general with adolescent sexual perversity, which in turn tied poetry to the pathologies that were believed to arise from onanistic desire. The book explores, in other words, how Romantic subversion quickly came to be read by the Victorians as somatic perversion (in the modern sense).

This book is interested, then, in disentangling what was in the nineteenth century a vibrant, heterogeneous, widely read, and serious form from that form's eventual degeneration into adolescent fantasy. That degeneration can perhaps best be understood in terms of Karl Marx's notion of "simple abstraction" as Michael McKeon reemploys that term for "a dialectical theory of genre." As McKeon argues, "'The Novel' must be understood as what Marx calls a 'simple abstraction,' a deceptively monolithic category that encloses a complex historical process" (20). Rather than explore the novel, I will concern myself with the term that McKeon himself sometimes reduces into an overly simple abstraction in his study, what he dubs "romance idealism."[2] As I will show, a considerable ideological complexity is hidden by our tendency to read "romance idealism" as a monolithic rather than properly dialectical category. That complexity is exemplified in the opposing uses for the romance adopted by Scott and Byron, the two poles of my dialectic, as well as in the conflicted, subversive reactionary form of romance later adopted by Tennyson in the *Idylls of the King*.

At the same time, I distinguish my analysis of generic change from certain branches of Marxist theory by contesting McKeon's claim that "[i]t is first of all not method but history that is dialectical" (420). My point will be, on the contrary, that the dialectic is very much a methodological tool employed by the poets and critics of the period themselves for the purpose of reducing generic complexity to the more easily perceived playing field of an agonistic battle. In other words, the dialectical model served an ideological function for nineteenth-century poets and critics, who manipulated the complex cultural field of the age in both self-conscious and self-mystifying ways. The ultimate goal of positing a dialectical opposition between Scott and Byron, especially when critics rethought that dialectic in terms of a rhetoric of health and pathology, was precisely the obfuscation of these poets' means of production and their political influence on their age, two issues that this book seeks to take seriously once again.

METHODOLOGY AND IDEOLOGY

To argue that "poetry makes nothing happen" is to subscribe to the aestheticization and consequent marginalization of the cultural realm that the nineteenth century invents and that I propose as one of the objects of this study's investigation.[3] This book argues, then, for the materiality of ideological formation, which is to say that I reject the separation between a discursive realm of thought and the material realm of social existence. Following the Marx-inflected psychoanalysis of Slavoj Žižek, this book contends that "reality" itself can only be conceived discursively. "Ideology is not an illusionary, false representation of reality," Žižek has argued, "but (social) *reality it-self* [*sic*] based upon an illusion, structured by an illusion" ("Truth" 211). By the same token, discursive formulations cannot be understood outside of material effects. The analysis of the criticism of the period is a perfect example since we see in the effort to establish the genre of literary criticism a questioning of existing, material social relations and the establishment of foundations for emergent social formations (the periodical review system, the modern university system, a new system of scholarly book production and distribution) that made possible the very materiality of the book you are reading right now, not to mention material aspects of the world in which we live: the fragmentation of the work force into specialized spheres of production; the institutional mechanisms that instantiate a separation between "high" and "pop" cultural productions; the cordoning off of the university intellectual and a concomitant anti-intellectualism in culture at large; and so on. The ways that nineteenth-century critics came to make sense of the social and cultural world would lead—necessarily lead—to material effects. In this, I also follow Ernesto Laclau and Chantalle Mouffe, who argue that

> [s]ynonymy, metonymy, metaphor are not forms of thought that add a second sense to a primary, constitutive literality of social relations; instead, they are part of the primary terrain itself in which the social is constituted. Rejection of the thought/reality dichotomy must go together with a rethinking and interpenetration of the categories which have until now been considered exclusive of one or the other. (110)

In the chapters that follow, I propose to analyze this interpenetration by examining the material effects of "master-tropes," the dominant fantasy constructions that allowed nineteenth-century critics to make sense of not only poetry and the romance but also their own historical reality. An analysis of the master-tropes of the period can help us to understand better the subtle changes occurring in the material-discursive reality that was nineteenth-century Britain.

My argument will therefore at times proceed by analogy. In particular, the book will concern itself with the creation of a particular and pervasive trope: the "nervous temperament." The effect of this medical commonplace on the construction and policing of the female subject has been thoroughly explored in recent years, particularly in terms of the rise of the novel.[4] What has been often overlooked is the application of this same medical discourse to the nervous bodies of men—especially those men most commonly identified as suffering from the "nervous temperament": men of letters, men of genius, melancholics, minstrels, and masturbators.[5] This book examines the effect of this analogical alignment of nervous temperaments, an alignment that led to a conflation among the figures and, at times, to the explicit association of male poets with not only melancholic men of genius but also the newly pathologized masturbator.

The pervasive rhetoric about nerves was also used by critics to make sense of the circulatory systems of Britain as a whole, thus allowing critics to translate complex political issues into sexual and medical ones. Great Britain was reconceived in such formulations as a determinable figure analogous to the circulatory rhythms of the healthy body and mind, be it an all-inclusive English social body or the endlessly replicated, disciplined body of the solitary reader and writer. The very impossibility of this imagined consistency only drove the effort to make that body perfectly and purely representative. Even the most cursory reading of nineteenth-century reviews of novels and poetry cannot help but come across this sexualization and medicalization. The language of these periodical reviews is fraught with anxieties about desire and pathology: What is the healthy discharge of emotion in literature? How can one disseminate one's thoughts without contagion in the circulatory systems of the market? What is the proper relationship between the private reader and the public text or between the private poet and his public? The complexities of a growing literary market were thus translated into different registers than the economic, those of medicine and sexuality, with the double effect of naturalizing (as desire or bodily need) and of idealizing (into determinable figures) the demands of the consuming reader. By conceiving of the market as itself a self-contained system of energies, Romantic and early Victorian fears about the sudden proliferation of indeterminate texts and readers—about Wordsworth's "pestilential masses of ignorant population" (*Letters* 21) or Arthur Hallam's "hydra, the Reading Public" (849)—were transmuted into a hegemonic discourse about not the voracious multitude but the nineteenth-century social body.[6]

Such anxieties betrayed themselves in a language brimming with metaphor, as if the critic could, through the power of language, make his public wholesome and whole. The use of habitual, and to a large extent unnoticed, tropes thus served both to reflect and affect the period's habitus, Pierre Bourdieu's term for the prejudices a group acquires by internalizing the objective conditions of a given society.[7] An integral connection, I would argue, exists between the habitus of a hegemonic group and the detritus of language: those innocuous tropes that one normally passes over in the act of reading. Both can be said to represent the worn-down bedrock of ideological construction, that which supports one's ideological world without being noticed, that which is taken for granted although it is, in fact, produced with each performative utterance of the cliché: a "peculiar kind of nervous susceptibility seems to be the distinctive character of the poetic temperment" (John Stuart Mill 67); "pushpin is of equal value with . . . poetry" (Jeremy Bentham 843); "poetry makes nothing happen."

CHAPTER BREAKDOWN

Chapter 1 begins by setting up the major transformations that we can find in eighteenth- and nineteenth-century medicine, suggesting that we can witness a coincidence between changes in medicine and changes in literature. Both changes were being driven by an emergent mass market, against which medicine and literature sought to establish their own cultural capital. The chapter concentrates on the ways that the emergent science of "nerves" at first contributed to the general pathologization of all scholarly activity in the period (including that of the medical scientist), seeing such activities as symptomatic of civilization's unhealthy if necessary reliance on market circulation. As the eighteenth century proceeded, however, the medic increasingly sought to distinguish medical science and the genius of the outstanding scientist from both the market and the market's preferred textual product: imaginative literature, especially novels and romances. Despite the difficulties of establishing medicine as a non-market-driven institution before the Victorian rise of the hospital and the modern university, the physician thus tried to establish himself as a healthy professional scientist in a position to diagnose both the social body and its literally nerve-wracking market pursuits. As we will see, it was this earlier model of specialization that inspired the literary specialist to adopt a similar model of professionalization, including the adoption of a medical rhetoric of nerves, in order to define certain literary endeavors and a certain kind of genius as healthful while diagnosing others as inherently pathological, masturbatory, or otherwise perverse.

The second chapter turns to the extremely popular romances of Sir Walter Scott to see how Scott played to the market while safeguarding from criticism his early poetic experiments in the romance, *The Lay of the Last Minstrel* (1805), *Marmion* (1808), and *The Lady of the Lake* (1810). How, I ask, did Scott establish his poetic productions as healthy, masculine, and pure while both narrativizing poetic form and securing profits on the market? To answer that question, the chapter explores the ideological function and malleability of the romance form, illustrating how Scott employed the temporal logic of the psychoanalytical (by way of the anthropological) fetish in order to preserve the virility of the barbarous past while simultaneously acknowledging that past as forever lost. That maneuver was very much a political one, for Scott provided the British monarchy and the British government with a new ideology of self-legitimation through the fetish-logic of medievalism, an ideology that would sustain the government throughout the Victorian period. In particular, the chapter examines Scott's orchestration of King George IV's visit to Scotland, illustrating how Scott used the romance to defend the status quo and to imagine a contemporary Britain reinvigorated by the virility of its own superseded past. The periodical reviewers responded to Scott's strategies by employing a pervasive rhetoric of health, seeing Scott's genius as the masculine antidote to the effeminizing influences of the age and seeing Scott's medievalist romances as panacea for the ills of the industrial age. However, Scott's romances represent an especially telling contradiction, for Scott's fetishization of the book in his metrical romances—especially in his first, the *Lay of the Last Minstrel*—was also a defense against that other fetishization that enabled his popularity but was already threatening to spell the end of poetry's cultural supremacy: the exchangeable abstraction of the commodity form. Even while he illustrated poetry's political power and influence in the period, Scott's rhetorical maneuvers set the stage for poetry's eventual marginalization into the cultic object of the high-cultural specialist. The chapter explores, in other words, the transition Scott himself figured (and resisted) in his romances: the supplanting of what I term the Cult of the Book by the mass market's Culture of the Text.

In chapter 3, I turn to the Satanic figure who was most often contrasted to Scott's purportedly healthy form of genius: Byron. The chapter illustrates how *Childe Harold* undid Scott's fetishizing maneuvers by refusing to recreate the past, instead discussing the present as if it were already dead and buried. Byron thus countered the nostalgic mourning of Scott's romances with his own ethical stance of moral melancholia. In so doing, Byron provided a position from which people from different classes could question the values and ideological fantasies propagated by the dominant ideologies of his time. The political ramifications of this maneuver were felt throughout the nineteenth century, illustrating the ability of Romantic poetry and of Romantic ideology to "make something happen." Byron's contemporizing of the medieval also drew attention to the Culture of the Text that Scott worked so hard to resist. Through a thoroughgoing textualization of culture, Byron's romance form underscored the performative nature of all ideologies, of all claims to truth, a strategy that reworked Scott's Romantic ideology from within the very form of romance. *Childe Harold* also attempted to go beyond a mere deconstruction of existing ideologies and posited an undeconstructible idea of justice that was inextricably tied to the "textual phenomenon" and that escaped economy's fantasy of a perfect circulation without loss and without excess. Byron's critique thus opened up the possibility of an alternate way of understanding one's relation to the market, as well as an alternate vision for both the romance form and the spirit of poetry generally.

Chapter 4 illustrates how, in reaction to Byron's radicalism, the critical rhetoric that incorporated social problems as sexualized, unhealthy bodies began to characterize poets in general as effeminate, melancholy, and sickly geniuses. Complementing while departing from Andrew Elfenbein's *Romantic Genius: The Prehistory of a Homosexual Role*, the chapter explores how it was, in fact, the masturbator rather than the homosexual that served as the master-trope for the poetic sensibility of the Romantic genius, establishing a rhetoric of pathology that would, after the Oscar Wilde trials, be redirected to the homosexual. Byron's romance form and his moral melancholia, both of which were read for a time as inspiring potential and potent subversion, were thus recast as but romantic delusions and impotent perversions, respectively. The chapter also explains why after Byron the rhetoric of pathology was applied as successfully to the male poet as to the female novel reader, who, at the end of the eighteenth century, was the more common object of such sexualizing rhetoric. Much in the same way that Eve Sedgwick in *Between Men* pinpoints how homophobia serves to screen society's actual homosocial organization, I here examine how the nineteenth-century's application of masturbatory rhetoric to the Romantic poet of genius screened the masturbatory nature of what contemporary critics theorized as the bourgeois subject's and the capitalist market's supposedly balanced circulation of desires and energies.[8] Playing into and supporting the ideological strategies of the bourgeois subject, the "high" Victorian novel adopted the same fetish strategies proposed by Scott in order to define itself against what was now characterized as the adolescent diversions of romance and the convalescent perversions of the Romantic poet of genius.

The Coda addresses the paradoxical critical demands made on poetry after mid-century. Responding to the critical backlash against Byronic and hyper-Romantic, not to mention market-oriented poetry, critics called for poetry that would "tell a plain tale" yet remain distinct from the effeminizing "pulp fiction" of the popular presses. Analyzing the often ambivalent reviews of Tennyson's poems in light of criticism's double agenda, the chapter reads Tennyson's *Idylls of the King* as a response to the ensuing dialectical injunction: realize (be like the novel) but idealize (be "poetic"). The *Idylls* attempted to reconcile the contradictions inherent in the dialectic by translating fears of the literary market into an allegorical tale about gender and sexuality, but in such a way as to undercut the generic exigencies of the romance in favor of domestic and novelistic concerns. As himself a latter-day "Romantic" and the person who took over the poet laureateship from Wordsworth, Tennyson found himself in an important position with regard to the legacy of Romanticism and the romance form. The *Idylls* represents a canny Victorian negotiation of that legacy. The work became such a phenomenal success in the 1860s because it attempted to address the conflicting cultural demands of the time; indeed, for this reason the periodical reviews represented the *Idylls* as a purifying tonic for a prosaic age, thus reprising the rhetoric formerly applied to Scott. However, Tennyson's effort to obey opposing injunctions led to an exaggerated conspicuousness about his ideological project, which helps to explain why the work was so thoroughly reviled only a decade later. The Coda illustrates how the concept of "pure poetry," which influenced many critics' characterization of poetry in the Victorian period, was structurally analogous to the rhetoric of poetic perversity, and thus helped ensure poetry's marginalization over the course of the nineteenth century, ultimately setting the stage for the Decadent alignment of pure verse and the perverse.[9]

ONE

DIAGNOSING GENIUS

The Tropic Body and the Constitution of the Man of Letters

> [I]t is possible, in general, to establish that a brilliant and lively imagination requires either currently existing nervous concentrations or, at least, a disposition that is very close to their formation. This disposition itself would consequently seem to have to be regarded as a sort of illness.
>
> —Pierre-Jean-George Cabanis

BEFORE I CAN TURN TO THE RHETORICAL STRATEGIES USED BY MEN of letters to "diagnose" Scott and Byron, the two poets who were consistently seen as the opposing possibilities for poetic genius in the late Romantic period, and before I can begin to demonstrate the connection between each poet's poetry and politics, I need to clarify the historical conditions that drove critics in the Romantic period to adopt a rhetoric of health and disease in the first place. This chapter examines the medical work from approximately 1725 to 1825 that diagnosed both the reader of romance and the man of letters as subject to nervous disease. A new way of thinking about both the human and the social body came to the fore in the eighteenth century, one that then facilitated the figuration of Britain as an analyzable and diagnosable whole. In this figuration, civilization itself was seen as a sign of ill health—and learning of all sorts was thus characterized as a potentially unhealthy pursuit. To be civilized was a mark of both distinction and threatened extinction, a figuration that grew out of not only the ancient tradition of the melancholic great man but also a new rhetoric of nerves that was applied equally to the man of letters and to the woman of sensibility in the period. It is out of this conflation of traditions and tropes that the new figure of the man of genius emerged.

Although at first lauded, genius was by the end of the eighteenth century a rather fraught category, conferring both authority and infirmity.[1] By the Romantic period, the physician needed, then, to find a way to claim the authority of genius while extricating himself from the charge of disease, thus charging himself with the authority to make prognostications about the English social body at large. He did so by setting the profession of medicine against both the dispossessing emotions of the literary imagination and the possessions of a luxury market, both of which were represented as contributing to civilization's continuing corruption. The figure of the masturbator was particularly important for the emergent doctor, who pathologized this figure for the first time in the eighteenth century as a way to attack not just the sexual act but also the textual act of imaginative creation and reception. By pathologizing the imagination and its mass-market products, the late-eighteenth-century medical researcher was able to distinguish his own professional activities from those of the hack writer, though, as we will see, he was still threatened by the analogous maneuvers of the quack doctor. It was this earlier model of medical professionalization that provided the Romantic man of letters with an idea of how to create the tropic body of high "culture" (in our modern sense) out of the earlier definition of "culture": the husbandry of the human and animal body. The critic learned from the medic that the best way to safeguard his own form of genius from the charge of disease was by pathologizing both the market and the imagination.

MAKING EVERY BODY NERVOUS

For the eighteenth century, knowledge was not only power but also weakness.[2] Increasingly throughout the period, the alarm was sounded about the dangers of scientific advancement and scholarly learning. As Samuel Cheyne puts it in his influential *The English Malady* (1733), "[S]ince this present Age has made Efforts to go beyond former Times, in all the Arts of *Ingenuity*, *Invention*, *Study*, *Learning*, and all the contemplative and sedentary Professions, . . . the Organs of these Faculties being thereby worn and spoil'd, must affect and deaden the whole *System*, and lay a Foundation for the Diseases of Lowness and Weakness" (37–38).[3] Cheyne even offers himself up as characteristic example, finishing his treatise with "*The CASE of the Author*," in which he attributes his health problems and his need for a special dietary regimen to his being part of "the *thinking*, *speculative*, and *sedentary* Part of Mankind" (246). According to Cheyne, the very markers of English civilization (improved diet, wealth, education, and urbanization), coupled with adverse climatic conditions, have resulted in the epidemic spread of "nervous *Disorders*," which he attributes to "*one* third *of the Complaints of the People of* Condition *in* England" (ii).[4] Paradoxically, according to Cheyne, one of the main culprits causing civilization's frightful symptoms is the very science he is in the process of presenting to the public: "Far be it from me," he concludes, "to lessen the Value and Necessity *now*, of those *Divine Sciences*," including "*Mathematicks, Natural Philosophy, Chymistry, Anatomy, Knowledge of the Materia Medica*, and *Animal Oeconomy*," but it must also be acknowledged, he continues, that "since our *Luxury* has kept Pace with our *Knowledge*: the *Obstinacy* and *Violence*, the *Number* and *Degrees* of our *Diseases* have increased proportionally" (255). The very fruits of civilization—knowledge and luxury—thus threaten the very constitution of Britain, leading to the ever-increasing frequency of nervous complaints.

By concentrating on such "nervous *Disorders*," Cheyne was instrumental in shifting the main focus of eighteenth-century medicine from Galenic humoral pathology to what Peter Melville Logan calls a "new body . . . , one marked by its susceptibility to hysteria and a host of related nervous conditions, variously called hypochondria, spleen, vapours, lowness of spirits, melancholia, bile, excess sensibility, or, simply, nerves" (1).[5] Because of the perceived connection of this nervous condition to both aristocratic and scholastic pursuits, Logan explains, nerves even "became fashionable during the eighteenth century as a sign of social stature or of the acute sensibility associated with the disorder" (19).[6] Indeed, Cheyne's friend and printer, Samuel Richardson, popularized the notion of "nervous sensibility" for men and, especially, women through his highly influential novels of sentiment, which made a virtue of the "nervous susceptibility" that was a sign of "*natural* sensitivity and judgement" (Mullan 73). "As long as sensibility, that capacity which escapes speech," was "represented as a set of bodily symptoms," John Mullan writes, "the picture of exemplary femininity" could all too easily "be one of sickness, of physical debility," which thus became "the final proofs of feeling": "The body's collapse is the sign of virtue *in extremis*" (110).

Women had for centuries been seen as a weaker version of the male body, which helped to give authority to the new science's attribution of nervous susceptibility to women.[7] What should be noted is that the new discourse about nerves allowed the very distinct tradition of womanly weakness to come together with the equally long albeit completely *separate* tradition that associated hypochondria and/or melancholia with greater understanding and judgment in men.[8] As Aristotle asks in his *Problems*, "Why is it that all men who have become outstanding in philosophy, statesmanship, poetry or the arts are melancholic, and some to such an extent that they are infected by the diseases arising from black bile?" (155).[9] This veneration of the melancholic "great man" reached a peak in the Renaissance when Burton's popular work on melancholy reinforced the link between melancholia and outstanding mental achievement.[10] Referring to Henry Howard, the Earl of Northampton, Burton for example states that "I am of that Noblemans mind, *Melancholy advanceth mens conceipts, more then any humour whatsoever*, improves their meditations more then any strong drinke, or sacke" (1.391). So popular was this alignment in the Renaissance that Lawrence Babb titled his study of Renaissance melancholia *The Elizabethan Malady*. As Juliana Schiesari explains, "More than just the undesirable *disease* that humoral medicine had traditionally diagnosed as caused by an excess of black bile, melancholia by the time of the Renaissance had *also* come to be perceived as an eloquent form of mental disturbance—a special, albeit difficult, gift—as hierarchically superior to mere depression as were the individuals afflicted by it" (8).

This alignment of superior mental ability with bodily debility continued into the eighteenth century. Following the earlier tradition of melancholia, Richard Blackmore in 1725 explains that hypochondriacal men are "endowed with refined and elevated Parts, quick Apprehension, distinguishing Judgment, clear Reason, and great Vivacity of Imagination; and in these Perfections they are superior to the common Level of Mankind." For this reason, according to Blackmore, "the lowest Degree" of this "obstinate Disease" is "rather desirable than hurtful; and therefore no Skill or Remedies should be employed to remove it" (89–90). Understanding and judgment are facilitated by disease in such formulations, although in other versions of the relationship they are, rather, the cause of mental decay. Robert James in his *Medicinal Dictionary* (1743–45), for example, writes of "mania" that "Weakness of the Brain" is "produced by intense Application of the Mind, or too long protracted Lucubrations." He therefore states that "the Reason is Obvious, why the Literati, and Men of a studious Turn, are more Subject to Alienations of Mind than the common People," although James also includes "ingenious Men, Poets, Philosophers, and those charmed with the more deep and abstruse Parts of Mathematics and Algebra" as "subject to Melancholy."[11] In such formulations, capacity and incapacity are inextricably intertwined, so much so that it is sometimes difficult to disentangle cause from effect and vice versa. Nature and nurture both contribute to the "constitution" of what is increasingly termed the "nervous temperament" of scholars and men of letters. And "constitution" here must remain ambiguously determined: on the one hand, there is a bodily constitution or "temperament" that predisposes a person to both disease and heightened sensibility; on the other hand, certain endeavors can actively constitute a body as nervous and thus prone to disease.[12]

The significant change that occurred in the eighteenth century, a change that facilitated this collapse of cause and effect, was that Aristotle's humoral theory of melancholia was slowly but surely replaced by a model based instead on nerves. One result of this shift in medical thinking was that for the first time medics began to "treat" both women and thinkers in the same way, a development that of course made thinkers and men of letters, well, *nervous*. Indeed, women of leisure and scholarly men were thus implicitly aligned, so much so that the discourse yoking mental ability to physical debility began to get written nationally: Cheyne's English Malady or, as Blackmore terms it in 1725, "the *English* Spleen" (v).[13] As early as 1723, we can find William Stukeley writing that "the modish disease call'd the vapors . . . does most frequently attack scholars and persons of the soft sex most eminent for wit and good sense" (Mullan 208). Blackmore in 1725 attributes the traditionally male condition of hypochondria to "the Tenderness and Delicacy of the nervous Fibres" (28), thus using the very same language applied to women of nervous susceptibility; in fact, after referring to the greater mental ability of hypochondriacal men, he explains that "many Hysterick Women owe their good Sense, ready Wit, and lively Fancy, to the like Fountain" (90). The reason for this, he explains, is that both hypochondria and hysteria "are of the same Species"; women suffer from more symptoms because of "a more soft, tender, and delicate Texture of the Nerves," but "this proves no Difference in their Nature and essential Properties" (96). William Smith in *A Dissertation upon the Nerves* (1768) similarly refuses to distinguish between the spleen and vapours: "[T]he symptoms and causes are the same" though "we call the same disease vapours in women, and spleen in men" (149). Smith also associates weak nerves *in general* with mental ability, thus foregoing any distinction based on gender: "People of weak nerves are generally quick thinkers, from the delicacy of their sensitive organs" (191). Collapsing cause and effect, he goes on to conclude that "all study is pernicious and hurtful" (191). Of particular note for this alignment of weak nerves and mental ability is the work of the celebrated Swiss doctor, Samuel Auguste David Tissot, who not only popularized the notion of nervous disease in his *Traité des nerfs et de leurs maladies* (1778–80) but in two well-regarded and widely translated tracts also pinpointed both "people of fashion" and "literary and sedentary persons" (*les gens de lettres*) as particularly susceptible to such disease.[14]

A result of such work is that a number of previously incommensurable activities could be posited as equally dangerous to the constitution because of their perceived impact on a person's nervous system. At first, one of the greatest dangers was seen to arise from the reading of novels and romances, particularly among women and the young, whose especially "susceptible" or "irritable" or "excitable" nervous systems were believed to be adversely affected by the passions elicited by the reading of idealizing and "exciting" narratives.[15] Critics were thus able to re-forge essentializing differences between men and women despite a rhetoric of nervousness that threatened to align the two genders. As Thomas Clarkson puts it in 1806, women are especially in danger "on account of the greater delicacy of their constitutions," making them "the more susceptible of such impressions" (134). In particular, critics and medics worried about masturbation as the most dangerous potential result of such reading. The connection of masturbation to romance- and novel-reading has been well documented and can be found throughout the medical and critical essays of the period.[16] Romantic reviews and medical tracts constructed such reading as a dangerous form of auto-sensuality that distracted the feminized reader from the proper discharge of duty. As Thomas Beddoes, for example, writes of "circulating-library literature," in a section of his *Hygëia* where he discusses female masturbation, "The sensations, to which all these melting tales immediately give rise, and the voluptuous reveries, which they leave behind, may, without injustice, be regarded, as a part of the concealed fountains, from which the NILE of female unhealthiness derives its origin" (1.4.45). Clarkson states with authority that "music and novels have done more to produce the sickly countenances and nervous habits of our highly educated females, than any other causes that can be assigned" (135n). Aligning the excessive stimulus or excitement of reading with torpor, Clarkson explains that "[t]he excess of stimulus on the mind from the interesting and melting tales, that are peculiar to novels, affects the organs of the body, and relaxes the tone of the nerves" (135n). According to the new science of nerves, the passions elicited by such reading practices disturbed the nervous system in such a way as to lead to a plethora of diseases, including madness, moral depravity, and early death.

What has been less frequently noted due to criticism's tendency to focus on women and novels when it turns to such medical work is the fact that a number of male figures soon became just as commonly associated with nervous complaints: the melancholic, the man of letters, and the figure that would grow out of the ancient discourse of the melancholic great man, the man of genius. Throughout the last quarter of the eighteenth century and well into the nineteenth century, these three characters were most frequently associated with the nervous temperament in men. The fourth figure that needs once again to be added to this group of nervous bodies is that of the diseased masturbator, who, like the man of genius, was a creation of the eighteenth century and the new discourse of nervous sensibility.[17] Despite the relative newness of onanism as pathology, the male masturbator was quickly associated with the other three nervous male bodies already mentioned; indeed, it should be noted that anti-onanist tracts were particularly concerned with the effect of this practice on men.[18]

Melancholy was seen as both a result and a cause of masturbation from the earliest anti-onanist tracts onward. In fact, we can trace the association all the way back to Aristotle, who states that "the melancholic are usually lustful" because they suffer from a surfeit of breath or air (159). As proof, he gives the example of childhood masturbation: "Even before they can emit semen boys, when they are near to the age of puberty, derive pleasure through lust by rubbing the privates; this pleasure is clearly due to the breath passing through the channels through which the moisture is afterwards conveyed" (161). The alignment appeared again in the medical tracts of the eighteenth and nineteenth centuries. As Tissot, for example, argues in his widely disseminated and frequently quoted work, *On Onanism; or, a Treatise upon the Disorders Produced by Masturbation* (1760), melancholy is at once the predisposing cause and the inevitable effect of masturbation.[19] Tissot's wisdom was then repeated by the many anti-onanist tracts that followed in his wake.[20]

The man of letters was also in the eighteenth and nineteenth centuries perceived at times as prone to the "solitary vice"—a perception driven not by ancient medical commonplaces but, rather, the new discourse of nerves. As Tissot writes in his essay on *les gens de lettres*, addressing the reader directly, "For which of you, that has been addicted to a studious life, has not often found, after intense thought, that the innermost part of the brain has been affected by a troublesome heat, and intense pain, such as the muscles feel when fatigued with long labour?" (*Three Essays* 2.13). Thomas Trotter explains in *A View of the Nervous Temperament* (1807) that "[f]ew men attached to literary pursuits are active, strong and athletic" because "[a]ll the secretions, and their excretories, fall into inaction from want of muscular motion" until "the whole nervous system sinks into listlessness and inactivity" (38–39): "The mind itself, by pursuing one train of thought, and poring too long over the same subject, becomes torpid to external agents: and an undue mental exertion seems to subtract from the body much of that stimulation which is required for many operations in the animal economy, particularly what belongs to emotion and passion" (39). It was a short step from this nervous exhaustion to the same nervous exhaustion attributed to masturbation. As Tissot explains in his *Onanism*,

> Nothing so much weakens as that continual bent of the mind, ever occupied with the same object. The masturbator, entirely devoted to his filthy meditations, is subject to the same disorders as the man of letters, who fixes his attention upon a single question; and it is rare that this excess does not cause harm. (*Three Essays* 3.66–67)[21]

Pierre-Jean-George Cabanis takes this comment yet one step further in 1796 when he argues that "[m]en of letters, thinkers, artists, in a word all the men whose nerves and brains receive many impressions or combine many ideas, are very much subject to nocturnal emissions that are very disturbing to them" (1.136).[22]

Given this logic, a number of medical tracts began to surmise that the heightened nervous sensibility of the man of genius predisposed him, like the man of letters, to the worst sorts of sexual perversions. Even Joseph Warton's early work, *An Essay on the Genius and Writings of Pope* (1756), which valorized the "pure poetry" of the true genius, admits that "[t]he same temperament, and the same sensibility that makes a poet or a painter, will be apt to make a man a lover and a debauchee" (1.106). This commonplace was repeated in various Romantic works. Beddoes, for example, writes in 1802 that "[g]enius, in virtue of its sensibility, eagerly pursues the first pleasures of excess; and in virtue of the same sensibility, receives more injury than mediocrity" (1.1.79–80). The entry for "masturbation" in Fournier and Béguin's 1819 *Dictionnaire des sciences médicales* remarks upon the fact that "[t]he excessive development of nervous sensibility . . . is the source of so many laudable actions and so many vices"; it "gives birth to the most admirable productions of genius, or to those shapeless works that attest to the force and deviations of the imagination" (Rosario, "Phantastical" 110). The most popular anti-onanist tract of the Romantic period in Britain, Samuel Solomon's *A Guide to Health* (1796), argues that "[g]enius often throws the nerves into convulsions" and is therefore "more liable to disorders of the nerves" (27). Solomon also pinpoints those "leading a studious or sedentary life" as particularly prone to "nervous disorders." Once such nervous diseases establish themselves in the student or the man of genius, he explains in the following paragraph, "the mind is more exposed to the transient impression of depraved or whimsical ideas, than in a state of health" (28).[23]

It is out of this conflation of nervous figures that the periodical reviewers and essay writers of the *nineteenth* century attempted to extricate the man of letters. Before I can turn to the maneuvers of specific men of letters in the following chapters, I need to clarify both the predominant metaphorical ideas constructing this nervous body and the ways that medical scholars themselves sought to separate their own endeavors from the very diseases they attributed to scholarly pursuits.

ENGLAND'S TROPIC BODY

The nervous system provided medical writers with a central metaphorical model that allowed them to treat of the human body, mind, and even soul as a single system of forces or energies. This is not to say that these new medical theorists did not borrow certain tropes from ancient medicine. Indeed, Tissot quotes Galen consistently throughout his various tracts and begins his *Essay on Diseases Incidental to Literary and Sedentary Persons* with a eulogy to that ancient humoural pathologist. What did occur is that the new medical model took the ancient theory of humours, which concerned itself with the proper balancing of the body's fluids (blood, phlegm, choler, and black bile), and reapplied the principles of fluidic balance and humoural temperament to the nervous body.

In 1725, Blackmore characterizes this shift as a "great Revolution" against "the Authority of *Aristotle*, who had gained an empire of vast Extent and long Duration over the Schools and Colleges of Knowledge." Asserting his "natural Right to the free Exercise of Reason, upon an impartial Examination of Things," Blackmore imagines himself throwing "off the Yoke of Servitude and Aristotelian Bigotry" (ix–x). Blackmore nonetheless supports the principle of fluidic balance, imagining "that the Distempers that affect the Head, the system of the Nerves and the 'Animal Spirits, all proceed from the depraved serous Streams, that irritate and provoke the nervous Fibres, and drive the Spirits into Disorder and Confusion" (xii). Cabanis at the other end of the century similarly dismisses the ancients as "lost . . . in visions" (1.59), but preserves their notion of the temperaments, including the idea that the healthiest body is one "formed of the four [humours] in equal parts, the TEMPERATE TEMPERAMENT par excellence" (1.58). Cabanis however sees nervous sensibility as the principle that unites the various organs and energies of the body: "[T]he difference of the temperaments depends above all on the difference of the centers of sensibility, on the relations of force or weakness, and on the sympathic communications of various organs" (1.62). Cabanis goes on to understand this interrelation in terms of the nervous system and the notion of sympathy, which he then quickly ties to ethics and the sociability of man, concluding that "it will easily be felt to what extent the progress in the science of physical man can contribute to the general perfecting of the human species" (1.71).[24]

What allowed for this easy translation from the animal economy of the patient to the political economy of the nation was the malleability of nervous fluid or energy as structuring principle. At issue was the medium by which the nerves were believed to communicate to the body's various systems as well as between the internal self and the external world. Some of the contenders included electricity (especially in the theories of Luigi Galvani) and some sort of fluid, or a combination of the two, an "electric fluid" (1.10), as Erasmus Darwin puts it in 1794, following Galvani.[25] As Alexander Crichton, for example, writes in his 1798 *An Inquiry into the Nature and Origin of Mental Derangement*, "We have had reason to believe that the medium, by means of which all impressions *ab externo*, are conveyed to the mind, and all those arising in the mind are communicated to the various parts of the body, is a peculiar fluid secreted, or at least formed in the medullary substance of the nerves" (168). Others were content to assume a principle of "communication" without determining the exact nature of the medium. As Robert Whytt writes in his *Observations on the Nature, Causes, and Cure of Those Disorders which Are Commonly Called Nervous, Hypochondriac, or Hysteric* (1764), "[A]ltho' the minute structure of the nerves, the nature of their fluid, and those conditions on which depend their powers of feeling . . . lie much beyond our reach; yet we know certainly, that the nerves are endued with feeling . . . and [I] have thought it better to stop short here, than to amuse myself or others with subtile speculations concerning matters that are involved in the greatest obscurity" (Logan 18). As late as 1834, Sylvester Graham explains in a *Lecture to Young Men* that

> [p]hysiologists have indulged in a great deal of conjecture and speculation concerning the "animal spirits—nervous fluid—vital electricity," &c. &c., but as yet, it is all conjecture and speculation. We know that, by some means or other, the influence of the will, is conveyed through certain nerves, to the organs of voluntary motion . . . and that vital energy is distributed through certain other nerves, from the general and particular centers of action, to the several organs, for the supply of their functional powers:—and we know, too, that in the functional exercise of the genital organs, something very analogous to electricity or galvanism, diffuses a peculiar and powerful excitement, and sensation, throughout the whole nervous system. Now, whether these vital effects are produced by means of nervous fluid or spirit, or something still more subtile [*sic*] and intangible,—or by some other means; human research and investigation have not ascertained, and perhaps never will. (23–24)

Medical texts of the period commonly dealt not with a micro- or otherwise scopic body but, rather, with a tropic body—an imagined "nervous system" of circulatory "communication," of bodily "feeling," and of fluidic balance.[26] They dealt, in other words, with a new mode of and model for understanding one's susceptibility to both the world and one's own internal passions and energies.

According to this model, the result of extreme emotion, mental labor, and nervous excitability was not only physical but also mental deterioration. Indeed, a number of pathological concerns were seen as interrelated in the medical tracts of the period: physiological disease, moral disorder, and mental distress.[27] Such a conflation of medical, theological, and psychological domains was quite common in the scientific literature of both the eighteenth and nineteenth centuries thanks to the notion of an all-pervasive "nervous energy" or "vital force" that unified all the sensitivities of the human system. One thinks, for example, of the Victorian reformers' rallying cry, *mens sana in corpore sano*. Tissot puts it this way: "We have . . . seen the strict union there is between the body and soul; it is evident how much the well being of the first depends upon the latter" (*Three Essays* 3.107). And yet, Tissot must admit that he has not in fact "seen" the union, for the medium of communication between the body and the soul is unknown: "We are equally ignorant of the nature of spirit, and the nature of matter; but we know that these two parts of man are so intimately united, that all the change which the one undergoes is felt by the other" (*Three Essays* 3.61). In such a speculative rather than speculable union, the mind, the soul, and the body were linked by the same system of nervous fluids or energies, so that, as soon as someone began to be represented as somehow "unbalanced" or "overexcitable," he or she was often quickly diagnosed as at once invalid, immoral, and insane.

By the Romantic period, the emphasis was laid particularly on the importance of a proper balance of nervous energies, which was sometimes superimposed on and reconciled with an emergent medical discourse of pathology that pinpointed disease in specific tissues and organs. According to Cabanis, for example, the very notion of "temperament," which was discussed by some of the most influential medical writers of the period, entails a certain preponderance and therefore imbalance of one organ over the others. The concern with specific organs did not keep Cabanis from imagining a general system of nervous balance. Indeed, he explained that the perfectly healthy temperament may well be "a veritable abstraction, a purely ideal model," since it requires a "perfect equilibrium" that will generally not survive "the bad habits of life" (1.305). The diseases of individual organs result, in other words, from some imbalance in the all-encompassing nervous system. Despite his putative concern with localized disease, Cabanis thus conflated nature and nurture, cause and effect, which in turn facilitated the translation of his terms to and his diagnosis of the body politic.

The notion of an imperfectly balanced system of energies or fluids came to predominate the medical work of the Romantic period because of the influence and celebrity of not only French medicine but also Edinburgh's medical school, which was associated with such influential medical writers as William Cullen, John Brown, Trotter, Benjamin Rush, and Beddoes.[28] These writers were particularly interested in exploring the notion of nervous balance and temperament. John Brown's *Elements of Medicine* was perhaps the most literal and programmatic expression of this principle, which he managed to reduce to a mathematical chart: "[O]ne degree of exciting power applied takes off one degree of excitability, and every subsequent degree impairs the excitability in a proportion exactly equal to its degree of force" (99n). As Hermione de Almeida paraphrases Brown's influential if controversial thesis about the balancing of a body's nervous energies, "[A] principle of excitability . . . had to be maintained in even supply in the animated body. Too little excitement presaged loss of energy and death from debility. But too much excitability worked the body at too high a pitch; it produced a state of *overwrought intensity* (false energy) that masked imminent, deathly exhaustion" (281).[29] Brown is a particularly interesting figure given his influence on the Romantic poets through Coleridge's friend, Beddoes (who wrote the biographical preface to Brown's *Elements of Medicine*, the 1804 translation of the original Latin text). Beddoes echoes Brown when, for example, he writes: "Life is not to be raised into a bright blaze that shall go instantly out. It never is more languid towards the last than with those, who labour to force it into extraordinary vividness" (1.4.93).[30]

G. J. Barker-Benfield has termed this nineteenth-century concern with the careful balancing of all one's vital energies the "spermatic economy." According to such a paradigm, any excessive amount of emotion or activity had to be strictly regulated. One of the greatest dangers of all, according to many science journals, came from sexual activity, leading to an easy equation between sexuality and pathology; however, from the beginning, the danger was closely associated with the passions of the imagination, which helps to explain why masturbation was suddenly seen as particularly noxious and why such literary pursuits as novel and romance reading became associated with this activity. For example, according to Tissot, the real danger came not so much from ejaculation as from the predominance of desire over natural want:

> We subject ourselves to want without being in want; and such is the case of masturbators. It is imagination, habit, and not nature that importune them. They drain nature both of that which is necessary, and also of that which she herself would have taken care to dispose of. (*Three Essays* 3.65–66)

Jean-Jacques Rousseau, who corresponded frequently with Tissot following their first meeting in June 1762, infamously echoed these same sentiments in his own *Confessions*, which he began composing in 1766. Writing of his first masturbatory experiences, he confesses:

> Soon I . . . learned that dangerous means of cheating Nature [*ce dangereux supplément*], which leads in young men of my temperament to various kinds of excesses, that eventually imperil their health, their strength, and sometimes their lives. This vice, which shame and timidity find so

> convenient, has a particular attraction for lively imaginations. It allows them to dispose, so to speak, of the whole female sex at their will, and to make any beauty who tempts them serve their pleasure without the need of first obtaining her consent. Seduced by this fatal advantage, I set about destroying the sturdy constitution which Nature had restored to me. (108–109)[31]

Immanuel Kant was similarly careful to associate what he considered the crime of masturbation specifically with the creative powers of the imagination. As he states in a section of the 1785 *Metaphysics of Morals*, entitled "defiling oneself by lust," "Lust is called unnatural if one is aroused to it not by a real object but by his imagining it, so that he himself creates one, contrapurposively; for in this way imagination brings forth a desire contrary to nature's end" (*Practical Philosophy* 549).[32] By 1796, Cabanis was able to state that "[w]e know, *so well that we cannot doubt it*, that the exhaustion that follows the pleasures of love depends much less on the material losses that accompany them, than on the voluptuous impressions that are inherent in them" (1.145; my italics). Indeed, he gives as further proof the fact that "the efforts of the imagination or of meditation . . . do not cause less lassitude than the most enervating pleasures or the most difficult tasks" (1.145).

The reason why it was so easy for anti-onanist rhetoric to pinpoint the imagination as primary culprit is because, according to the medical tracts, the real danger came not simply from the loss of semen but from the loss of one's "nervous energy" or "vital power." According to Graham, for example, the physical threat arises not from "the acme of coition and producing an emission of semen, and the convulsive paroxysms which attend it" but, rather, "this peculiar *excitement*, or *vital stimulation*," which "produces general debility, morbid irritability and sympathy, and all the consequent train of evils which result" (24). Like Tissot, Rousseau, Kant, and many others before him, Graham is therefore able to pinpoint the imagination as the true cause of nervous complaints:

> Hence, therefore, sexual desire, cherished by the mind and dwelt on by the imagination, not only increases the excitability and peculiar sensibility of the genital organs themselves, but always throws an influence, equal to the intensity of the affection, over the whole nervous domain;—disturbing all the function depending on the nerves for vital energy . . . and, if this excitement is frequently repeated, or long continued, it inevitably induces an increased degree of irritability and debility, and relaxation generally throughout the nervous and muscular tissues, and especially the nerves of organic life. And, hence, those lascivious day-dreams, and *amorous reveries*, in which young people too generally,—and especially the idle, and the voluptuous, and the sedentary, and the nervous,—are exceedingly apt to indulge, are often

> the sources of general debility, effeminacy, disordered functions, and permanent disease, and even premature death, without the actual exercise of the genital organs! Indeed! This unchastity of thought—this *adultery of the mind*, is the beginning of immeasurable evil to the human family. (25)

What is important to note is that even in the anti-onanist tracts, the greatest danger was seen to be not coition but cognition, a fact that facilitated the cross-pollination of clichés, tropes, and commonplaces between the domains of science and literature.[33] According to this way of thinking, excitability was, in fact, but a prelude to morbid relaxation, the obverse conditions of a "disturbed and unequally balanced system" in this psychosomatic rather than merely spermatic economy.

QUACKS, HACKS, AND THE MAD SCIENTIST

One problem with this rhetoric of nervous excitability, particularly as it was applied to onanism, was that, even as medical practitioners claimed an ever-greater knowledge of empirical and anatomical technique, the tropic nature of the general model made the concern with nervousness prey to an ever-burgeoning market in quackery, as Graham's traffic in, yes, Graham crackers and Graham flour attests. (They were attributed with the power to heal all sorts of nervous complaints, including the diseases arising from masturbation.) Perhaps the best example in Britain was Samuel Solomon, whose *Guide to Health* supposedly went to sixty-five editions between approximately 1796 and 1815. Solomon in fact offers market sale as the principle of his own legitimacy, stating in the preface to the fifty-third edition that "The Guide to Health having already passed through fifty-three editions, and still continuing to sell with unprecedented rapidity, precludes the necessity of apologizing for the re-publication of a work, which has been found so extensively useful" (v). Indeed, he goes on to defend even the cost of advertising in newspapers as *proof* of his cure's effectiveness:

> It requires the *strongest* conviction of their *intrinsic* worth and physical excellence, by *long* and *great experience*, to induce an inventor or proprietor of any medicine to incur the serious and certain expence of making it known by ADVERTISEMENTS; an expence [*sic*] of no less than FIVE THOUSAND pounds annually to Dr. Solomon, and which *a very great and general demand* can *alone defray*, and which nothing short of fatuity could induce any one to enter upon without such previous conviction; for it were of small avail to enter upon the talk and expence of making known that remedy, *whose merit will not support its character* when known. (xiii–xiv)

Solomon offers market sale as evidence of effectiveness and his own medicine as a challenge to the professional doctor, adding: "Happy it is for this country, that *every* SCIENCE is *open to every one* who shall choose to explore it: and thrice happy are its people, that the STUDY OF PHYSIC is *not restrained* to those alone, who have passed through various ceremonies" (xii).

The strange circular structure of Solomon's apology recasts profit as proof and market dissemination as the path to Britain's general health. Indeed, this conflation of market and bodily circulation is brought to perfect alignment when we read that Solomon's miracle cure, the Cordial Balm of Gilead, is in fact made of "*Gold! pure virgin gold*!" (36). Coleridge himself provides us with the name for this ideological operation, fetishization, though he offers it in the anthropological rather than Marxist sense: "The account given by Stavorinus of the Chinese *Xylo*mancer at Batavia may serve for the model of all the children of Superstition, from the African Fetisch-worshipper or Oboe-wi~~ch~~tch to the Purchaser of Dr Solomon's Balm of Gilead, or King George's State-Lottery Ticket" (*Notebooks* 3.4015). Marx would build on this anthropological sense to read the operation whereby commodities take on a power of their own, making us forget the labor-power behind their production; in the commodity fetish, we allow ourselves to believe in the power of a thing (money) whereas the real power lies in people (social relations, labor power, etc.). The State-Lottery is, in fact, a perfect example since exchange-value is here completely separated from the individual's labor-power or even a given commodity's use-value; the lottery is driven, to put it crudely, by the people's belief in the power of money. An analogous fetish-logic is at work in Solomon, except that we are seeing a different sort of exploitation than the kind Marx had in mind: Solomon capitalizes, rather, upon the public's fear that the very luxuries and purchases made possible by a capitalist market expose to disease anyone with money to spend on commodities (in other words, luxury kills). Solomon claims to feed back to the public not the filthy lucre of commodity exchange but the purifying change effected by pure virgin gold. The fraudulent relation between a quack and his duped consumer is thus magically transformed into the power of the real thing: both gold standard and name-brand cure.

This literalization of market *consumption* (purchase and drink pure gold to protect yourself from impure market purchases) underscores the importance of credence to an economy of credits and debits: we must believe in the fiction, the fetish of money's virtù for the capitalist system to work, even in the simple act of monetary exchange. One of the issues this book will explore in the following chapters is the fetish-logic of market exchange, how, on the one hand, this logic structured both the bourgeois understanding of capitalist circulation and the romance strategies of Scott; how Byron's poetry, on the other hand, threatened that logic on the level of both content and form. Dr Solomon's Balm of Gilead and King George's State-Lottery Ticket were aligned by Coleridge because they both relied on the consumer's willingness to believe in their power. As Jacques Derrida puts it, regarding money's reliance on the consumer's willingness to believe, "as long as one can *count with and on cash money* to produce effects . . . , as long as money passes for (real) money, it is simply not different from the money that, perhaps, it counterfeits" (*Given Time* 153). The danger for the emergent professionalization of medicine was that the doctor's own cures could all too easily be exposed as the same sort of counterfeit: a psychosomatic placebo that preyed on and cured all malaise by faith. The real power to cure lay with the people and their ideological fantasies; it did not inhere in a doctor's placebo nor did it inhere in the gilded pill (or potion) of pelf.[34]

By the same token, so to speak, the doctor could all too easily be exposed as a competitor for clients and profit on the open market. Indeed, Solomon himself must open his opus by acknowledging how easily his own sham could in turn be shammed:

> Doctor Solomon having received authentic information that his "Guide to Health" has been pirated, and that many spurious copies are in circulation in a very incomplete manner, feels it a duty he owes to himself and the public, as the most effectual mode of suppressing the sale of these spurious copies, to sign his name on each book with a pen; and further to guard against forgery, to annex a fac simile, that unless his signature corresponds therewith, the public may be assured they are attempted to be imposed upon.
>
> *This is a genuine copy.* (xvii)
>
> [signature and facsimile of "S Solomon MD" follows]

As if he were preparing the way for Derrida's "Signature, Event, Context," Solomon thus gets caught in a circuit of copies and reiterations, which he tries to arrest by way of signature, imprimatur (the facsimile as right to print), attestation (an affadavit of authenticity sworn by Thomas Golightly before "his Majesty's Justices of the Peace" [253]), and matriculation (Solomon not only signed as MD but included a copy of his diploma with each bottle of the Balm of Gilead [253]).

What is so fascinating about Solomon is that he replicated the very strategies employed by the doctors of the time to establish their own professional credentials as separate from market concerns. Starting with Tissot's attack against *Onania* in the opening of his *Onanism*, numerous respectable doctors felt the need either to begin or conclude their medical tracts with an unveiling of the counterfeit, especially when it came to the issue of masturbation.[35] It is also true that they laid claim to an ever more anatomical, empirical, and chemical understanding of the body's workings; however, although there were real advances in medical science during this time period, there was very little improvement in medical practice.[36] In addition, medicine often spoke most authoritatively about precisely those things it could not, in fact, prove: the pathology of masturbation, the balancing of nervous energies, and the various physiological temperaments. In large part, it was a *tropological* discourse about nerves that convinced the public of their need for cure.[37]

In addition to the concern about the quack market in medicine, the very insistence that the professional doctor (as opposed to the commercial charlatan) brought greater study and mental acuity to bear on the question of nervous disorders paradoxically forced the physician to acknowledge his own sedentary research *into* disease as potentially productive *of* it. As we enter the Romantic period, then, we also find "professional" medical texts distinguishing their own brand of scholarly pursuits as healthy even while they continued to pathologize the work of other scholarly figures, particularly the man of letters.

It is perhaps more than a coincidence, for example, that Tissot, the most popular and respected onanopathologist of the eighteenth century, who helped to cement the connection between melancholia and masturbation, was also one of the most prominent physicians of the period warning against the traditional association of study—including, of course, medical study—with the melancholic temperament. As he states in his work, *On Diseases Incidental to Literary and Sedentary Persons*,

> It has indeed been observed, that this species of melancholy in some measure promotes learning, by increasing the penetration; for, whilst melancholy men are intent upon one idea only, the mind contemplates this object alone, and considers it on every side; nor is it distracted by other pursuits. But however proceeded to this pitch of madness, as to desire to purchase an increase of discernment at such a price [*sic*]? Of what advantage is science without health? He knows too much, who is rendered unhappy by his knowledge. (*Three Essays* 2.32)

This pathologization of the melancholic temperament was soon picked up by influential British medical tracts as well, particularly John Haslam's 1809 *Observations on Madness and Melancholy*, the expanded edition of his 1798 *Observations on Insanity*:

> As the terms Mania and Melancholia, are in general use, and serve to distinguish the forms under which insanity is exhibited, there can be no objection to retain them; but I would strongly oppose their being considered as opposite diseases. In both there is an equal derangement. On dissection, the state of the brain does not shew [*sic*] any appearances peculiar to melancholia; nor is the treatment, which I have observed most successful, different from that which is employed in mania. (36–37)[38]

One result of the rise of psychology at the end of the eighteenth century was that genius and melancholia increasingly became the objects of pathologizing investigation. Before the Romantic period, albeit with some exceptions, tracts on insanity tended to make a clear distinction between debilitating disease or mania, on the one hand, and the melancholic temperament, on the other, a fact that is at once acknowledged and rejected by Haslam. Haslam's claims were in turn quoted by numerous other medical writers of the period.

So much is Haslam intent on giving no quarter to the melancholic that he feels obliged to dissociate genius and scholarly pursuits altogether from the pathology of melancholy:

> It has also been considered, that intellectual labour frequently becomes a cause of insanity; that those, who are in the habit of exercising the faculty of thought, for the perfection and preservation of the reason of others, are thereby in danger of losing their own. We hear much of this, from those who have copiously treated of this disease, without the toil of practical remark; whose heads become bewildered by the gentlest exercise, and to whom the recreation of thinking becomes the exciting cause of stupidity or delirium. These persons enumemerate [*sic*], among the exciting causes of delirium, "Too great, or too long continued exertion of the mental faculties, as in the delirium which often succeeds long continued and abstract calculation; and the deliria to which men of genius are peculiarly subject." (217–18)

Because of melancholia's pathologization at the hands of the emergent discipline of psychology at the turn of the nineteenth century, Haslam desires, in other words, to protect respectable scholars and geniuses, such as himself, from the charge—formerly the distinction—of melancholia. Indeed, Haslam states facetiously: "What is meant by the deliria, to which men of genius are peculiarly subject, I am unable, from a want of sufficient genius and delirium, to comprehend" (120).

And yet, Haslam is more than happy to associate the work of the *imagination* with incipient mental disease: "It is well understood, that a want of rational employment is a very successful mode of courting delirium; that an indulgence in those reveries which keep the imagination on the wing, and imprison the understanding, is likely to promote it" (220). Haslam thus falls short of excluding *literary genius* from the melancholic diagnosis. Instead, he makes a distinction between empirical investigation and the flights of the imagination, in this way safeguarding his own enterprise from the charge of disease.

Johann Christoph Spurzheim, one of the most influential of the new phrenologists, concurs in his *Observations on the Deranged Manifestations of the Mind, or Insanity* (1817):

> In melancholy the patients, sometimes for years, are given up to their fate; they are considered as fanciful and imaginary. It is, however, a

> great fault on the part of the friends, and even of physicians, not to consider the deranged imagination as the effect of a bodily cause. The advances of the disease, which produce melancholy, are insidious and imperceptible, and after a long duration the removal of the cause must be more difficult. (148–49)

According to Spurzheim, the worst dangers are "nervous sensibility and imagination," as well as "luxury and refinement," all of which increase the number and variety of diseases that predispose the mind to insanity because they lead the mind to "romantic or ideal notions of the world, hence disappointment in finding the world as it is, and not as it ought to be according to fanciful dreams" (*Observations* 118). The potentially revolutionary desire to improve the world—aligned here specifically with the romance tradition—is thus recast as impotent adolescent fantasy. Although Spurzheim follows the eighteenth-century commonplace that "[a] too intense application of the intellectual faculties, deep thought, incessant study during day or night, may equally lead to the derangement of the mental operations," he is also careful to associate diseased genius with the creative imagination rather than with empirical investigation: "Among scientific professions, however, with respect to insanity, it may be observed that those whose occupations naturally excite the feelings at the same time, such as priests, poets, advocates, actors, musicians, painters, sculptors, are more disposed to insanity than those who study geometry, mathematics, and natural philosophy in general" (*Observations* 118).

Spurzheim thus corroborates the conclusions of Philippe Pinel in his influential *Traité médico-philosophique sur l'aliénation mentale ou la manie* (1801), also cited by both Haslam and Beddoes: Pinel found in the registers of the Bicêtre insane asylum

> a great many monks and priests, as also a great many country people, who had been driven beside themselves by horrid pictures of futurity;—several artists, as sculptors, painters, and musicians;—some versifiers, in extacies with their own productions;—a pretty considerable number of advocates and attorneys;—but there does not appear the name of a single person, accustomed to the habitual exercise of his intellectual faculties;—not one naturalist, or natural philosopher of ability;—not a chemist or geometrician. (Beddoes 3.10.25–26)[39]

Such medical works offer an equation between "nervous sensibility and imagination," which in turn condemns those professions that most excited the feelings associated with "nervous susceptibility." Although Tissot, Beddoes, and Spurzheim all argue that intense study inevitably leads to the exhaustion of the nervous system, they thus safeguard themselves and their own studies from the charge of disease.

My focus on medicine in this chapter serves to underline a point that is easily forgotten after the medical profession's successful assumption of cultural capital in the modern age: before the rise of the hospital and the modern university system, medicine and literature had to compete on the open market against quacks and hacks, respectively, often finding innovative ways to establish cultural capital in advance of the institutional, disciplinary supports we now take for granted. After all, it is only in recent history that medical *science* has been able to transform its own etymology: no longer knowledge in general but its own separate discipline with its own specialized institutions. As late as the Romantic period, scientific texts offered themselves to the public in the form of verse: Erasmus Darwin's *The Botanic Garden* (1791) and *The Temple of Nature* (1803), two influential texts that went through a number of editions and influenced many Romantic poets.[40] The rise of the periodical review in the Romantic period similarly broke down disciplinary distinctions, so that we can find reviews and discussions of scientific texts next to, say, reviews of Wordsworth.[41] Indeed, the same terminology infected, as it were, both medical and literary-critical reviews, as we will see. Even the education of physicians at Cambridge and Oxford consisted not of medical training, as we understand it, but "a six years' course in a wide range of subjects, followed by a slightly longer period devoted to a literary study of the classical medical authors" (Jewson 374).[42]

In fact, it has only been in the last century that the surgeon has completely overcome his earlier association with manual labor. Until 1745, surgeons were lumped together with barbers in the Company of Barber-Surgeons before creating their own separate corporation. The modern-day hospital and medical school, which institutionalized our contemporary split between general practitioners and medical specialists, were not properly established until the Victorian period, so that the Romantic period was a time of confusion. As M. Jeanne Peterson explains, "Before the passage of the Medical Act in 1858, the organizational structure of the medical profession was in a state of near-chaos" (*Medical* 5). For one, medicine had to overcome the class distinctions that, in the eighteenth century and still nominally if not functionally in the Romantic period, separated the upper-class, Oxbridge-trained physician from the surgeon and apothecary, who were considered to be of a much lower status before the growth of the hospital system. Physicians, surgeons, and apothecaries each had their own medical corporation, each offering separate examinations and certifications: The Royal College of Physicians; the Company of Surgeons, which became the Royal College of Surgeons of London in 1800; and the Worshipful Society of Apothecaries. In the Romantic period, these distinctions were rapidly breaking down as physicians rethought the wisdom of their training and surgeons increasingly took on the roles of both physician and apothecary to compete for middle-class patients who were ever more interested in and able to pay for medical care. Before the implementation of an institutional support for surgery and pharmacy, however, the research doctor was often reliant on alternative forms of income (for instance, teaching, general practice, or the market in medical books) and on alternative forms of legitimacy (knowledge of Latin, a classical education, and upper-class contacts).

We must also keep in mind that medicine and literature were, in the Romantic period, experiencing a rather similar transformation. In the eighteenth century, both literature and medicine still largely relied on a patronage system; both enterprises were in a position of servility before the aristocratic classes that paid for them.[43] By the Victorian period, both would rely instead on institutional systems for legitimacy and support: the hospital for medicine; the public university for both. In between, which is to say throughout the Romantic period, we witness the fraught battle to extricate literature and medicine from a vulgar market upon which they both to some extent relied after the collapse of the patronage system.[44]

It will be the task of the following chapters to think through the effects of these changes on, specifically, the "constitution" of both the man of letters and the popular male poet of genius. Literary criticism faced a number of difficulties at the moment of its emergence, for the Romantic critic—before the rise of the modern university system—had to distinguish himself from the vulgar market upon which he relied, while disentangling himself from a rhetoric of pathology that had been consistently applied to the man of letters over the course of the eighteenth century. As we will see in the chapters that follow, the solution for many critics was to co-opt the very profession of physician that had formerly pathologized the scholar in order to diagnose the health of a body politic that these men of letters saw as threatened by the encroaching diseases of a mass market. In so doing, such critics legitimized the emergent notion of high culture and facilitated the rise of a new class of critic, thus setting the stage for the establishment of the university intellectual later in the nineteenth century.

TWO

ROMANTICISM'S LAST MINSTREL

Scott, Ideological Fetishes, and the Technology of the Book

> Lord Byron and Sir Walter Scott are among writers now living the two, who would carry away a majority of suffrages as the greatest geniuses of the age . . . . In their poetry, in their prose, in their politics, and in their tempers, no two men can be more unlike.
>
> —William Hazlitt

WHEN HE DECIDED TO TURN TO THE ROMANCE FORM IN HIS 1805 *Lay of the Last Minstrel*, just a few years after Wordsworth attacked the "degrading thirst after outrageous stimulation" fed by "idle and extravagant stories in verse" (*Prose* 1.128–30), Scott was engaging a rather embattled generic form. And yet, over the next few years, Scott managed to turn the rhetoric of nervous sensibility and disease completely around, claiming for himself and for his metrical romances a rhetoric of manly and invigorating health. Reviewers followed suit, making use of the very pathologization of civilization that we saw in the medical tracts of the eighteenth century in order to claim for the chivalric romance the ability to reinvigorate a society driven to idleness and effeminacy by the luxuries and advances made possible by the rise of capitalist "culture."

By presenting his romances as healthy antidotes to the political troubles of his age, Scott set up the medieval past as an uncorrupted principle of health in a society made soft by the market-driven luxuries of British civilization. In so doing, however, Scott also acknowledged that past *as* past, persisting only in his own invigorating fictions. Scott's orchestration of King George IV's visit to Edinburgh, which Scott organized in 1822 and which I will address as the most obviously politicized extension of the ideology found in Scott's metrical romances, proceeded by a similar methodology: Scott provided the British monarch with a powerful form of self-legitimation and self-invigoration in the fictional traditions Scott created; however, those traditions were, at the same time, acknowledged as both superseded and fictionalized, thus at once facilitating and undercutting both Sir Walter's and King George's political influence.

This chapter, then, makes two apparently competing arguments: on the one hand, I wish to take seriously John Gibson Lockhart's statement that Scott's "services, direct and indirect, toward repressing the revolutionary propensities of his age were vast—far beyond the comprehension of vulgar politicians" (Alice Chandler 48–49); on the other hand, I wish to explore how the rhetoric of health employed by reviewers and Scott himself to describe his poetical romances and his fantasized medievalism served to obfuscate and, ultimately, undercut Scott's political influence.

The key to this situation lies in the same logic of the fetish I explored in the last chapter with regard to Solomon's *Guide to Health*. In addition to the anthropological and Marxist fetish already discussed, this chapter explores a third psychoanalytical version of the fetish that structured the fantasies of the emergent bourgeois subject in the nineteenth century, allowing contradictory claims to stand together in Scott's fictionalized version of medieval tradition. Following Octave Mannoni's influential article, "*Je sais bien mais quand-même*," we can express the logic of this psychoanalytical fetish as follows: I know very well that these medievalist fantasies are not real but, nonetheless, I will act as if I believed.[1] This logic at once allowed those medievalist fantasies to assume political influence and ensured that no one ultimately took Scott's influence with regard to those ideological fantasies seriously. The same fetish-logic that drove the romance fantasy of King George's visit to Edinburgh, particularly the king's donning of Highland garb at the Holyrood Levee, also drove Scott's earlier reaction to the transformations beginning to occur in the production, marketing, and dissemination of texts. Scott, as this chapter illustrates, used the romance as a bulwark against change, as a means to familiarize the past and harmonize the present. He also attempted to reinvest his works with both the power of the minstrel's voice and the aura of the magical book, thus combating—while never succeeding to eradicate—the effects of mass production. In so doing, Scott established a principle of uncorrupted health in a fantasy of precapitalist totemic magic that was *at the same time* acknowledged as impossible in and superseded by the industrial present.

Before this chapter can turn to Scott's dressing of King George and his redressing of the market in books, however, I need to clarify how it was that Scott managed to escape the ills attributed to both genius and the writing of imaginative works, especially works of romance, at a time when both were under fire. As we will see, Scott *invited* critics to apply a rhetoric of health to his market products, thus providing critics with a way to legitimize his particular form of the popular romance as healthy, pure, and somehow above market concerns. In so doing, Scott established his legitimacy and his influence on the age but he also contributed to the rarefication of poetry into the cultic object of the literary specialist. Scott thus set the stage for poetry's anticipated supersession: in more ways than one, then, Scott adopted his own scripted role as last minstrel.

THE EXCEPTIONAL GENIUS

According to Scott's introduction to the 1830 publication of the *Lay*, the question of health was uppermost in Scott's mind when he turned to the writing of romances in 1805. Indeed, the extended insistence on his own health in that introduction would appear rather odd without an understanding of the ways contemporary medical tracts and reviewers consistently pathologized not only the reading of romances but also the man of letters and the man of genius. From the retrospect of 1830, Scott may even have felt the need to protect himself from the pathologization of the male poet that was not fully instantiated until Byron usurped Scott's "reign" (Walter Scott, *Poetical* 157) between 1812 and Byron's early death in 1824.[2] Indeed, in his introduction to *Rokeby* Scott repeats the Byronic stereotype I will explore in chapter 4: "For his own misfortune, perhaps, *but certainly to the high increase of his poetical character*, nature had mixed in Lord Byron's system those passions which agitate the human heart with most violence, and which may be said to have hurried his bright career to an early close" (*Poetical* 230; my italics). Writing of Byron in his journal in 1825, Scott repeats this sentiment: "These two peculiarities of extreme suspicion and love of mischief are both shades of the malady which certainly tinctured some part of the character of this mighty genius and, *without some tendency towards which, genius—I mean that kind which depends on the imaginative power—perhaps cannot exist to great extent*" (9; my italics). In any case, twenty-five years after the *Lay*'s initial publication, Scott still felt the need in the new introduction to defend himself from having turned to the "precarious resources of literature" (*Poetical* 86) rather than the profession of law, "which might have been deemed by many the wiser alternative" (*Poetical* 42).

Scott did not fail to outline the dangers that faced such a choice. He mentions both the charge of *genus irritabile vatum* (*Poetical* 42) and the "irritability of men of genius," citing "the many humiliating instances in which men of the greatest genius have, to avenge some pitiful quarrel, made themselves ridiculous during their lives, to become the still more degraded objects of pity to future times" (*Poetical* 42). He also mentions the problems faced by men of letters who confine themselves to "the desk and the library." Such an undue concentration on "literary pursuits" can only "be compared," Scott explains, "to the injudicious conduct of one who pampers himself with cordial and luscious draughts, until he is unable to endure wholesome bitters" (*Poetical* 42). By contrast, Scott claims to have "resolved to stick by the society of my *commis*, instead of seeking that of a more literary cast, and to maintain my general interest in what was going on around me" (*Poetical* 42). He also denies himself the title of genius in order to escape its associated "weaknesses of temper": "Upon the whole, as I had no pretensions to the genius of the distinguished persons who had fallen into such errors, I concluded there could be no occasion for imitating them in their mistakes, or what I considered as such; and, in adopting literary pursuits as the principal occupation of my future life, I resolved, if possible, to avoid those weaknesses of temper which seemed to have most easily beset my more celebrated predecessors" (*Poetical* 42).

What is more, Scott suggests that his turn to literary pursuits was actually a way for him to maintain both his own uncommon good health and the good health of Britain as a whole. Given that Scott here discusses his turn to what had previously been characterized as the diseased form of romance, what Trotter in 1807 calls "one of the greatest causes of [those] nervous disorders" (89) accounting for two-thirds of the maladies of England (xvii), the passage is worth quoting at some length:

> I ought to have mentioned, that since my fourteenth or fifteenth year, my health, originally delicate, had become extremely robust. From infancy I had laboured under the infirmity of a severe lameness, but, as I believe is usually the case with men of spirit who suffer under personal inconveniences of this nature, I had, since the improvement of my health, in defiance of this incapacitating circumstance, distinguished myself by the endurance of toil on foot or horse-back, having often walked thirty miles a-day, and rode upwards of a hundred, without resting. In this manner I made many pleasant journeys through parts of the country then not very accessible, gaining more amusement and instruction than I have been able to acquire since I have traveled in a more commodious manner. I practiced most silvan sports also, with some success, and with great delight. But these pleasures must have been all resigned, or used with great moderation, had I determined to regain my station at the bar. It was even doubtful whether I could, with perfect character as a jurisconsult, retain a situation in a volunteer corps of cavalry, which I then held. The threats of invasion were at this time instant and menacing; the call by Britain on her children was universal, and was answered by some, who, like myself, consulted rather their desire than their ability to bear arms. My services, however, were found useful in assisting to maintain the discipline of the corps, being the point on which their constitution rendered them most amenable to military criticism. In other respects, the squadron was a fine one, consisting chiefly of handsome men, well mounted and armed at their own expense. My attention to the corps took up a good deal of time; and while it occupied many of the happiest hours of my life, it furnished an additional reason for my reluctance again to encounter the severe course of study indispensable to success in the juridical profession. (*Poetical* 42)

Disciplining the "constitution" of Britain's fighting forces ("corps" in the English sense), Scott here adopts for himself and for his own well-disciplined "robust" body ("corps" in the French sense) the martial quality of the very romances he is about to pen. The heroic romance appears to inspire Scott's own turn to the volunteer corps, a squadron "well mounted and armed *at their own expense*," which marks them as men of condition (in every sense). In other words, Scott joins the company of "handsome men," like any "stalworth knight" (*Marmion* 1.62).[3] The pastoral romance, by the same token, appears to direct Scott's adoption of sylvan pursuits; Scott thus enacts in his own life the manly hunting scenes of his fictional romances; one imagines Scott among "the sounds of silvan war" (*Lady of the Lake* 1.74) riding "Alone, but with unbated zeal" (*Lady of the Lake* 1.114). In *Marmion* Scott refers to his volunteer cavalry even within his lay, arguing that Edinburgh is still protected by her "dauntless voluntary line" (Fifth Canto, Introduction 100), although Scott also states how "gladly" he would "avert" his eyes from "Bodings, or true or false, to change/ For Fiction's fair romantic range,/ Or for tradition's dubious light" (Fifth Canto, Introduction 122–25). It is ultimately through the turn to metrical fiction, he contends, that he can hope "At once to charm, instruct, and mend," and

> With even patience to endure
> Lingering disease and painful cure,
> And boast affliction's pangs subdued
> By mild and manly fortitude. (Fifth Canto, Introduction 164, 170-73)

In such ways, the turn to romance writing as profession is triply recast as healthy pursuit: it affords Scott the time to defend the constitution of both his body and the nation; it provides the generic markers for healthiness, masculinity, and the defense of empire; and it even functions as a panacea for the political ills of the age.[4] Through the turn to poetic fiction, Scott suggests, he was able to have a direct political influence on his current moment, even as he softens that influence through a rhetoric of romance and of cure.

Scott repeats the same sorts of maneuvers in his unfinished autobiography, which later opened John Gibson Lockhart's Boswellian *Life of Scott*. Admitting the "alarm" he feels because of the present age's rage "for literary anecdote and private history," he assures the public that he himself has led "a very quiet and uniform life" (Lockhart 1), and that he therefore does not exemplify the sorts of lessons that one can glean from poets that came before him: "From the lives of some poets a most important moral lesson may doubtless be derived, and few sermons can be read with so much profit as the Memoirs of Burns, of Chatterton, or of Savage" (Lockhart 1). Citing the pathologization of the poet that I will explore in chapter 4, Scott makes it clear that he does not suffer any sort of "malady" that would warrant sermonizing: "Were I conscious of anything peculiar in my own moral character which could render such development necessary or useful, I would as readily consent to it as *I would bequeath my body to dissection, if the operation could tend to point out the nature and the means of curing any peculiar malady*" (Lockhart 1–2; my italics). At once corroborating such pathologization and presenting himself as the exception that proves the rule, Scott goes on to explain that his own "frailties, follies, or vices" are not, in fact,

> very different in number or degree from those of other men in my situation. As I have not been blessed with the talents of Burns or Chatterton, I have been happily exempted from the influence of their violent passions, exasperated by the struggle of feelings which rose up against the unjust decrees of fortune. Yet, although I cannot tell of difficulties vanquished, and distance of rank annihilated by the strength of genius, those who shall hereafter read this little Memoir may find in it some hints to be improved, for the regulation of their own minds, or the training those of others. (Lockhart 2)

Scott offers himself up not as characteristic sickly genius but as the model for the regulation and training of the reader's mind, much in the same way that Scott presented himself as the regulator of his soldiers' training in the volunteer corps, and much in the same way that he offers himself up as a model for the regulation and training of future *writers* in his introduction to the *Lay*: "I did not abandon the profession to which I had been educated, without certain prudential resolutions, which, at the risk of some egotism, I will here mention; not without the hope that they may be useful to young persons who may stand in circumstances similar to those in which I then stood" (*Poetical* 42). Rather than present himself as under "the influence" of "violent passions," Scott becomes the taskmaster ensuring the healthy constitution of future readers, writers, and citizens. We have only to follow his "quiet and uniform" example. And the evidence for his success will be found in the same place that medics and critics pinpointed the ill effects of reading romances or, later, Byronic poetry: the body under threat of death and dissection. Scott plays to the rhetoric even while he exempts himself, explaining that, except for one instance of infirmity in his youth ("the breaking of a blood vessel" [*Poetical* 39]), "I have enjoyed a state of the most robust health" (*Poetical* 40).

Given the mass of critical work on the pathologization of the novel, one might assume that Scott would be most worried about being classed among the mass-market novelists, yet his self-professed fear here and in the 1830 introduction to the *Lay* was, rather, that he would be classed with the person that he most resembled (lameness included) and whose class he, more or less, shared—Byron (as well as all the other poets that were retroactively pathologized in Byron's wake or, rather, undertow).[5] As this book argues in the next two chapters, what has been overlooked in cultural criticism's turn to the novel is the threat perceived throughout the late Romantic and Victorian periods not just from the novel but also from a certain kind of poetry, which, although generally gendered masculine, was nonetheless seen as dangerous because of its spontaneous overflows, violent passions, and commanding geniuses. Even one of the best of these cultural critics of the novel, Ina Ferris, writes that, unlike the many periodical reviews on the ill effects of novel reading, "one finds few articles entitled 'On the Depravity of Writing Poetry' " ("Trope" 20).[6] If this were true, however, how would one explain a passage such as the following from an 1821 review of *Don Juan* by William Roberts in the *British Review*?

> Unthinking youth have been enticed to sin beyond the vicious propensities of nature, plunged early into diseases and death, and sunk down to damnation in multitudes. Was it for this that poesy was endued with all those allurements that lead the mind away in pleasing captivity? Was it for this that she was furnished with so many intellectual charms, that she might seduce the heart from God, the original beauty, the most lovely of beings? Could those sweet and resistless forces of metaphor, wit, sound, and number be given that they should be ranged under the banner of the great malicious spirit, to invade the rights of heaven, and bring swift and everlasting destruction upon men? How will these allies of the nether world, the lewd and profane versifiers, stand aghast before the great Judge, when the ruin of so many souls whom they never saw shall be laid to the charge of their writings, and dreadfully requited. (*RR* 1.489–90)

The passage is all the more interesting for being a quotation attributed to the previous century, albeit one whose original I have not been able to determine. Regardless, Roberts is thus able to make a transhistorical claim for what was, in fact, a relatively new attribution of both crippling disease and Satanic subversion to certain kinds of poetry.[7] What we are being offered in such statements is precisely the *depravity of reading and writing poetry*.

Or, rather, I should say that we find in the period's criticism two competing visions for the poetic enterprise. On the one hand, we are offered poetry as "the foul inoculation of epidemic vice," filling "the moral world with disease" (*RR* 1.467), as Roberts puts it in his earlier review of *Childe Harold* IV. On the other hand, we are offered poetry as panacea, with meter not the allure of seduction and subversion but, rather, the very principle of regulation and balance. And that division was most perfectly represented for the period in the commonplace opposition between the robust, chivalric Scott and the sickly, Satanic Byron. As Bulwer-Lytton, for example, summarizes the relationship in 1838,

> Scott—if subject to occasional and severe illness, still of the most robust constitution, and the most hardy nerves: Byron—the prey to maladies, which evinced from his youth a general derangement of some of the most important organs of the human frame—not occasional, but constant—interfering with the most ordinary comforts of life and making the body itself the tormentor of the mind. (*Critical* 1.30–31)

Using language from the science of nerves outlined in chapter 1, Edward Bulwer-Lytton sets the "hardy nerves" of Scott against what physicians of the time would be most likely to term the "nervous temperament" of Byron. As Thomas Carlyle would so succinctly say of Scott, "An eminently well-conditioned man, healthy in body, healthy in soul; we will call him one of the *healthiest* of men" (*Critical* 38). "Were one to preach a Sermon on Health," Carlyle continues, "Scott ought to be the text" (*Critical* 51).

Writers even began to follow Scott's lead and offered him up as the antidote—one might say the anti-poet—to the maladies and infirmities of poetry writing and wild genius. R. R. Madden in his 1833 *Infirmities of Genius* argues that Scott is the exception that proves the rule about the *Habits and Constitutional Peculiarities of Men of Genius* (Madden's subtitle). After outlining for four hundred pages how poets of genius are prone to disease, immorality, and madness, he finishes with Sir Walter, stating that Scott had a "decided advantage over the majority of the *genus irritabile* of authors, whether of works of prose or poetry" (218), citing seventeen more examples of that majority over the next two pages. It is precisely because of the infirmities of the poet of genius, Madden explains, that "the history of a well-ordered mind, like that of Scott, is not without its lesson; and perhaps, by the encouragement of the example it offers for imitation, exhibits the advantage and the reward of mental management, of moderated enthusiasm, and of the government of imagination, as powerfully as the calamities of Cowper and the errors of Lord Byron tend to persuade their followers to avoid their errors" (204). Indeed, the very infirmities of study and imaginative writing function as testaments to Scott's fantastic physical strength: "It required, indeed, no ordinary stock of health to enable an author to resist the wear and tear of mind and body, which the incessant application to literary pursuits is productive of" (211). Madden proceeds to quote Tissot's book on the diseases of men of letters, offering Scott, once again, as the exception to the rule regarding "the dangers to which literary men expose themselves by excessive application" (223). In particular, Madden cites a passage where Tissot offers his own exception in a professor of Oriental literature that he knows: "When wearied by his mental labours it was his custom to repair his strength and spirits by exercising his body in the cultivation of his grounds, and he supported both by that gaiety of heart, that amenity of manners, which is killed in the study, and which is only maintained by communing with our fellow-men for our mutual advantage" (227). Given such passages, it becomes clearer why Scott wanted to "stick by the society of my *commis*" or, as he explains in his introduction to *Rokeby*, to work the soil of Abbotsford (*Poetical* 228–29) and "for health's sake to walk a mile or two every day before breakfast . . . upon his own land" (*Poetical* 229). Scott, presenting himself as a man of property, thus molded his own reputation in direct opposition to the sicknesses of the man of letters and to the other figure who would "carry away a majority of suffrages" as the greatest genius of the age—Byron. Nineteenth-century critics were all too willing to follow suit. Madden, for example, argues that "though there are few errors of conduct to be noticed, and still fewer physical infirmities to be connected with them, no indulgence to be demanded for the one, and no charitable feelings to be appealed to for the other, there is still a moral in the secret of [Scott's] happiness to be found in the record of his virtues, his moderated passions, and well regulated habits, which has the strong persuasion of an admirable example to recommend it in lieu of the awful lesson of a life of error and of suffering for the enforcement of a warning" (257–58). We are back to the "hints" Scott himself offered to his readers "for the regulation of their own minds, or the training those of others."

So successful was Scott's maneuver that critics began to offer novels and romances as cures in their own right for the ills of poetry writing, thus completely contradicting the pathologization of novels and romances more commonly explored by recent criticism. According to a reviewer in the *New Monthly Magazine* of 1820, Scott's novels "with their fresh spirit of health, have counteracted the workings of that blasting spell by which the genius of Lord Byron once threatened strangely to fascinate and debase the vast multitude of English readers" (543). In such formulations, Byron represents the perversion against which Scott works to reconstitute the purity of both England's men of genius and the vital principle of the nation, England's "genius" (the older sense of the term: characteristic disposition). Because of Byron, the reviewer explains, "[t]he genius of our country was thus in danger of being perverted from its purest uses to become the minister of vain philosophy, and the anatomist of polluted natures" (543). Whereas Byron rendered "our poetry 'sicklied o'er with the pale cast of thought' " (543), Scott "writes everywhere with a keen and healthful relish for all the good things of life—constantly refreshes us" (543).

William Hazlitt in his 1825 "Advice to a Schoolboy" similarly warns against "solitary reveries" (17.94) and "those sedentary studies, 'Which waste the marrow, and consume the brain' " (17.91), suggesting that "[t]he best qualifier of this theoretical *mania* and of the dreams of poets and moralists (who both treat of things as *they ought to be* and not as *they are*) is in one sense to be found in some of our own popular writers, such as our Novelists and periodical Essayists" (17.94). Hazlitt may have Scott particularly in mind, for he explains in his 1824 essay on Scott's writing:

> All is fresh, as from the hand of nature: by going a century or two back and laying the scene in a remote and uncultivated district, all becomes new and startling in the present advanced period.—Highland manners, characters, scenery, superstitions, Northern dialect and costume, the wars, the religion, and politics of the sixteenth and seventeenth centuries, give a charming and wholesome relief to the fastidious refinement and "over-laboured lassitude" of modern readers, like the effect of plunging a nervous valetudinarian into a cold-bath. The *Scotch Novels*, for this reason, are not so much admired in

> Scotland as in England. The contrast, the transition is less striking . . . . The mountain air is most bracing to our languid nerves, and it is brought us in ship-loads from the neighbourhood of Abbot's-Ford. (11.61)

The romance thus becomes itself the solution for the "languid nerves" and "over-laboured lassitude" of civilization that medical tracts warned against throughout the eighteenth and into the nineteenth century. John Scott in 1820 writes that the Waverley novels allow us to "join the course of [Scott's] lively and rapid narrative in the true spirit of the *chace* [*sic*]" and that "the scenery around is fresh and invigorating; health and manliness are made to circulate through our frames" (12). As Walter Bagehot puts it in an 1858 article on the Waverley novels, "There are no such books as [Scott's] for the sick-room, or for freshening the painful intervals of a morbid mind" (2.113).

Even before Scott turned to the novel, medical tracts started repeating the idea that certain novels could function as preservatives rather than poisons, which points to the novel's increasing success in claiming for itself a certain cultural legitimacy. Benjamin Rush in his 1812 *Medical Inquiries and Observations, upon the Diseases of the Mind* explains that "Mr. Cowper often relieved his melancholy by reading novels" (118) and that "[t]he celebrated Mr. McLaurin, the friend and contemporary of sir Isaac Newton, made it a practice to relieve his mind, when debilitated by hard study, and thereby predisposed to this disease, by reading novels and romances" (143–44). One review of Byron's *Manfred* in the *Knight Errant* later follows suit by begging leave of "persons writhing under the influence" of Byron "to recommend, as an excellent antidote . . . a few pages of Robinson Crusoe" (*RR* 3.1223). This is not to say that dire warnings about the effects of novel and romance reading did not exist throughout the nineteenth century, for the rhetoric would be aimed at any sub-form that appeared dangerous, from French to sensationalist to pornographic fiction; it is only to say that critical work on the novel has not given us the whole story and that poetry plays a much larger part in the story of literature's pathologization than has been previously suggested.

THE EMPEROR'S NEW CLOTHES

What has also been insufficiently acknowledged until recently is the influence of Scott's romance fantasies on the political fabric of his age.[8] Scott's strategy of translating political effect into medical edict so perfectly naturalized and obfuscated his ideological strategies that his influence on political ceremony was rarely taken seriously through the nineteenth and most of the twentieth century. The fact is, however, that Scott's very insistence on not being taken seriously (I am not a genius, I am only interested in my health and that of others) was precisely what helped to ensure Scott's influence through his amazing reinvigoration of the romance form, even as Scott's insistence on his good health also set the stage for his eventual marginalization. I wish here to recover the political and market influence of, specifically, Scott's *metrical* romances, which are usually ignored in favor of his novels. As in the two chapters on Byron that follow, this chapter thinks through the ideological possibilities of the metrical romance in order to uncover behind the rhetoric of health and pathology—which was applied to and invited by Scott and Byron—the relation between political economy, on the one hand, and a politics driven by economy, on the other. As the chapter will go on to illustrate, the fictional and ideological strategies critics usually locate in Scott's novels were already firmly established in the metrical romances that preceded *Waverley*. I wish thus to recover poetry's place in Great Britain's gradual accommodation of capitalist culture.

The secret to Scott's influence on that culture lies, not to phrase it too indelicately, underneath his kilt. It is perhaps best exemplified by King George IV's donning of the Royal Stewart tartan on August 17, 1822, an act that was performed for the Levee held at Holyrood in Edinburgh during the Royal Visit of that year, and which was stage-managed by none other than Scott himself. What we see in 1822 is the overtly political watershed of the more covertly political agenda that Scott first established in his metrical romances of 1805–10. The king's visit illustrates the notion of the fetish that I believe also structures Scott's metrical and prose romances, a notion that allows Scott to refresh with "wholesome bitters" a society too used to pampering itself "with cordial and luscious draughts." We have returned to the fetish-logic that we saw in Solomon's *Guide to Health* except that Scott is dealing not in "*Gold! pure virgin gold*!" but, rather, in all that is *old*, albeit still *pure* and *virgin*.

What makes King George IV's wearing of a Highland kilt so significant is its very insignificance: one more unremarkable detail in a romance-inspired pageant of state. What is easy to forget is that the wearing of kilts and other Highland garb had only been legal for thirty-nine years; from the passing of the Dress Act in 1747 to its repeal in 1783, punishment for wearing the tartan included a six-month imprisonment for the first offense and a seven-year exile to an overseas work farm for the second.[9] What lay behind such sartorial proscriptions, of course, were the very Jacobite rebellions Scott fictionalized with such success in his Waverley novels. And yet, by 1822, George IV himself donned the tartan at Scott's request. Such an act was made possible largely thanks to Scott's poetical, followed by his prose, romances, both of which sought to inject the energy and wildness of barbarity into a new fiction of empire, while simultaneously reminding the reader of his civilized distance from that very barbarity. The Royal Visit allowed Scott to literalize on the very body of the emperor his own *fiction* of state.

This emperor's new clothes served a number of purposes: as Basil Skinner suggests, it functioned as "an act of official forgiveness for the Jacobite indiscretions of 1715 and 1745" (232); as part of the pageantry of the Royal Visit, it sought to re-establish the glory of the king after the ridicule that office suffered under the madness of King George III; finally, the pageantry of ceremonial dress attempted, as John Sutherland puts it, "to bind the country's wounds, and rally the populace around its traditional governors in emotional displays of regimented unity" (257) at a time directly following the most incendiary radical violence of the nineteenth century, including the Peterloo Massacre of 1819, the Cato Street Conspiracy of 1820, and, close to home, the insurrection at Bonnymuir in April 1820.[10]

The fact that King George IV consciously sought to reinvest in the glory of kingship by way of investiture and that he did so after George III had so thoroughly discredited the kingship underlines, I think, the extent to which George IV was already effectuating a transition from a traditional form of the king's authority (the king's two bodies) to the king's new function after the Reform Act of 1832. In traditional authority, Žižek explains, the iconology of tradition maintains a connection to what we might term, echoing Walter Benjamin, the king's "aura": "The king, the judge, the president, and so on, can be personally dishonest, rotten, but when they adopt the insignia of Authority, they experience a kind of mystic transubstantiation; the judge no longer speaks as a person, it is Law itself which speaks through him" (*For They* 249). The traditional fetish, in other words, resembles the anthropological sense of the term: credulity before the totemic king.

The role of the audience in this operation is crucial and perhaps best exemplified by the child who laughs at the king's nudity in Hans Christian Andersen's tale, "The Emperor's New Clothes." Indeed, it is worth noting that *Great Britain's* emperor, though not naked at the Levee, did wear flesh-colored tights underneath his rather short kilt, which provoked a good deal of suppressed mirth. As Lady Hamilton put it, in reference to the fat king's unbecomingly short kilt, "As he is to be here for so short a time, the more we see of him the better" (Skinner 233). The danger of laughing at the king (of forcing us to acknowledge the king's ridiculousness) is that such an act threatens to undo "the very community of which we were a member. . . . by blurting out what should remain unspoken if the existing intersubjective network is to retain its consistency" (Žižek, *For They* 12). Like the child's laughter in Andersen's tale, we thus threaten to expose the purely formal operation by which the king " 'quilts' the social edifice" (Žižek, *For They* 19). Lady Hamilton and the other participants in Scott's romance of state instead followed the logic of the fetish as articulated by Mannoni, which is to say, not the anthropological but the Freudian fetish. It is this fetish-logic that would increasingly characterize the subject's relationship to political authority in the nineteenth century: I know very well (that the king is ridiculous), but nevertheless (I will act as if I believed in his kingliness, for otherwise the whole symbolic system collapses).

Scott (and, to some extent, the king himself) followed a similar strategy. Where they departed from traditional authority was in adopting the role of manipulator, in full consciousness that the purpose was to lead the populace into believing in empire so that it would stop its radical activities. As Žižek explains, "The manipulator 'knows very well' that all magic ritual is only deception—the moment of belief ('but nevertheless') is displaced, projected into the other, into the simpleton, into the object of his manipulation" (*For They* 248). Scott therefore felt no compunction in *creating traditions where they did not exist*, which in turn fed his own fictions. As Sutherland explains, Scott

> invented "traditions" as freely as anything in the plots of his novels. (One of these inventions, that the Company of Archers were the "ancient bodyguard to the Kings of Scotland," inspired his next novel, *Quentin Durward*.) (258)

Even the kilt itself has been shown to be a relatively recent invention of the eighteenth century—a product of retroactive fantasy construction, a fact acknowledged, indeed, by Scott himself;[11] and yet this fact in no way prevented Scott from adopting the costume for his vision of the king's visit. Such fantasy-constructions on the part of Scott and the other Romantic creators of both Scottish and English "tradition" would seem to threaten the very constitution of society, since such manipulations appear to uncover the fictional and artificial nature of all laws and conventions. In actuality, such maneuvers constitute the mechanism whereby the emergent capitalist culture of the nineteenth century would secure its disciplinary hold on the people. Middle-class fiction, which Scott managed to purify and legitimate in his Waverley novels, would come to structure the middle-class subject by claiming truth in fiction itself.[12] Indeed, fictional realism is exemplary of the ideological maneuver of the psychoanalytical fetish. Coleridge's definition of his romances in the *Lyrical Ballads* perfectly exemplifies this function: "[I]t was agreed, that my endeavours should be directed to persons and characters supernatural, or at least romantic; yet so as to transfer from our inward nature a human interest and a semblance of truth sufficient to procure for these shadows of imagination that willing suspension of disbelief for the moment, which constitutes poetic faith" (*Biographia* 2.6). This same "suspension of disbelief" would be adopted by the novel, and with such great effectiveness that the source in Coleridge (and the metrical romance) is often forgotten. For the reader of prose fiction, the operation is the same: I know very well that what I am reading is not true *in stricto sensu* but, nonetheless, I believe it to be "true" (for example, in the transcendent sense of nature or the spirit of the age).

What has been insufficiently acknowledged is the debt that the novel owes not just to Scott's historical but also to Scott's *metrical* romances, which first popularized for the nineteenth century this same fetish-logic. In order to set the king's visit in the context of Scott's metrical romances, I will provide an example of what I mean from *Marmion* before returning to King George's own fetishized kilt. *Marmion* represents a watershed text due to Scott's mixing of "high" history and "low" fiction in that metrical romance. The fetish-logic is established both in the story and in the surrounding discursive introduction. In the very diegesis of the tale, the fictional Marmion himself refuses to believe a tale told by his host of an Elfin Warrior who purportedly appears at a charmed mound to challenge all comers: "I would not that the prating knaves/ Had cause for saying, o'er their ale/ That I could credit such a tale" (3.546–78). And yet Marmion decides to "welcome fond credulity" (3.588) and rides "forth in silence of the night,/ As hoping half to meet a sprite" (3.581–82). When a knight does appear at the spot, Marmion falls victim to his fancy and fully becomes a dupe to his own credulity: "But I have seen, since past the Tweed,/ What much has changed my sceptic creed,/ And made me credit aught" (4.374–76). Ultimately, however, Marmion must come to understand the greater "truth" of the tale: the apparition is not only revealed to have, in fact, been Marmion's enemy, de Wilton, but Marmion is forced to recognize through the tale that he must make amends for his evil crimes. Marmion's relation to the superstitious tale, it turns out, is the same as the court's relation to Marmion's forgery, by which he attempts to destroy his rival, de Wilton. Indeed, as Nancy Goslee has argued, Marmion's evil act of forgery is, in itself, significant: Marmion's forgery "is a metaphor not only for the self-indulgence but for the opportunism involved in the writing of romance fictions, of documents that subvert the verifiability and the ethical responsibilities of history and law" (43). Scott in this metrical tale must rework the public's understanding of both the fictionality of romance and the truth of history. The difference between Marmion's forgery and Scott's is that Scott's is everywhere acknowledged *as such*. When it comes to Scott's fictions, no one is allowed to fall into credulity.

What is "true" in Scott's metrical fiction therefore lies not in any direct mimesis: both the gothic elements *and* the historical elements of the tale must be acknowledged as secondary to a yet greater lesson. When it comes to the actual historical details of Flodden Field, Scott states that "Such acts to chronicles I yield" (5.1011), advising the reader to "Go seek them there and see" (5.1012). As Scott makes clear, "Mine is a tale of Flodden Field,/ And not a history" (5.1013–14). What Scott presents as truth, rather, is a moral sense at one step removed from the historical real. As a result, chivalry itself is aligned by Scott not with the superstitions of the romance, as one might expect, but rather with the moral virtues represented by de Wilton, who is associated with "truth, as diamond pure and hard" (6.139). Indeed, one's susceptibility to being duped by fiction is itself a sign of one's moral stature, according to Scott. As Sir David of the Mount tells Marmion,

> Spotless in faith, in bosom bold,
> True son of chivalry should hold
> These midnight terrors vain;
> For seldom have such spirits power
> To harm, save in the evil hour
> When guilt we meditate within
> Or harbor unrepented sin (4.474–80)

Purity of heart and of aim in a "true son of chivalry" should, according to Scott, take the place of an overly credulous belief in gothic spirits.

Scott repeats the same maneuvers in his Introduction to the second Canto, imagining himself being momentarily taken up by his fancies as he thinks of the story of a "Wizard Priest" who is purported to have been buried at the former Chapel of Saint Mary of the Lowes. After returning to his home, Scott imagines himself pondering

> o'er some mystic lay,
> Till the wild tale had all its sway,
> And, in the bittern's distant shriek,
> I heard unearthly voices speak,
> And thought the Wizard Priest was come
> To claim again his ancient home!
> And bade my busy fancy range,
> To frame him fitting shape and strange,
> Till from the task my brow I cleared,
> And smiled to think that I had feared. (217–26)

As with Marmion, Scott argues here that only someone "whose heart is ill at ease" (233), who "loves to drown his bosom's jar/ Amid the elemental war" (235–36), would be disturbed by such a tale. The proper, healthful response, according to Scott, is to accept the tale as "but escape from fortune's strife" (228), for only in this way can we "deem each hour to musing given/ A step upon the road to heaven" (231–32). Fiction thus once again marks out the very path to truth in an ideal, moral sense. It is also in this "true" sense a principle of health in the present. As Scott explains in the introduction to the sixth Canto, "in our northern clime" still lingers "Some remnants of the good old time" (86–87) through such tales:

> And still within our valleys here
> We hold the kindred title dear,
> Even when, perchance, its far-fetched claim
> To Southron ear sounds empty name. (88–91)

Scotland's "store of literary wealth" (234), its "gossip history" (206) rather than its chronicle history, is for Scott aligned precisely with "life and health" (233) and allows Scott to illustrate how, although his great-grandsire may have "lost his land," he still "kept his beard" (106). Scott acknowledges the past as past and his fictions as fictional yet, nonetheless, or perhaps for that very reason, he claims his medievalist fictions as at once healthful, masculine, and somehow "true," a "step upon the road to heaven."

An analogous maneuver, to return to the king's kilt, was adopted by the participants in George IV's pageant of state: like Scott, they were fully conscious of the fact that they were participating in an artificial spectacle and it was *in their very acknowledgment of that artificiality* that the ideological power of the spectacle resided. Knowledge of the ceremony's artificiality, even ridiculousness, in no way prevented its successful ideological functioning; an acknowledgment of the ceremony's artificiality even served as a sign that one's heart was not "ill at ease," that one could appreciate the spectacle without taking the ideological referent (Jacobite rebellion) seriously.

The same paradox in turn applied to Scott himself as the manipulator of the king's pageant: the Wizard of the North's self-conscious prestidigitation in no way protected the manipulator from participation in the fetish-belief *even while he was conscious of its artificial nature*: "[I]f it seems as though the real 'answered' the manipulation, the distance between manipulator and manipulated is destroyed and the manipulator himself falls into credulity, begins to believe in his own deception" (Žižek, *For They* 248). Of course, Scott's pageant was fantastically successful, so much so that such medievalizing gestures would serve to constitute the monarchy for the rest of the nineteenth century, from the adoption of Arthuriana by Queen Victoria and Prince Albert to the rebuilding of the Parliament buildings along medievalist lines.[13]

What distinguished George IV's proto-Victorian ceremony of state from traditional authority, then, was the translation of the king's traditional power structure into British "culture." The operation worked only once the king's trappings were completely divested of their immediate relationship to what Foucault has termed in *Discipline and Punish* a "society of spectacle," or, to sharpen this point by way of apparent tautology, the king's kilt effected the transition from Foucault's "society of spectacle" to Guy Debord's *Society of Spectacle*.[14] In the emergent system, the iconology was emptied of the premodern violence Foucault explores in the feudal system, just as George IV was being slowly but surely emptied of direct political influence—which is also to say that the king's iconology was entering into a modern, carceral system of power relations where the constitutional rather than constitutive king merely holds the empty place of each subject's rational, self-elected participation in a simulacral culture of nationhood. Debord makes a similar point with regard to the transition from eighteenth- to nineteenth-century social life:

> All social life was by this time concentrated in the ornamented poverty of the Court—in the chintzy trappings of a bleak State administration whose apex was the "profession of the king"; and all individual historical freedom had had to consent to this sacrifice. The free play of the feudal lords' irreversible time had exhausted itself in their last, lost battles: in the Fronde, or in the Scots' uprising in support of Charles Edward. (104)

Despite this loss of a feudal power structure, the *spectacle* of power persisted in the ceremony of state, in the chintzy trappings of nationhood. And, after Scott, that culture of nationhood was spoken, almost exclusively, in medievalist romance language.

The transition from a traditional to a modern form of nationhood is especially well represented, as I have suggested, in the king's kilt. Whereas the earlier, traditional power structure answered the wearing of Highland dress with the king's punishment, the concept of a democratic social body co-opted opposition as quaint, even refreshing, cultural fantasy. In other words, power was already in the process of devolving to the people through the increasing importance of both public opinion and public credulity in the fiction of state; the king's advertising campaign—directed by Scott, the market sensation of the day—was already caught up in the proto-capitalist production of the "real thing," which is to say, as in the Coke campaign with the same slogan, the simulacrum (or the spectacle or the model) of the real.[15] Scott first established this maneuver in his metrical romances; in his later turn to prose fiction, Scott and the novelists who would follow him adopted the same strategy: real*ism* claimed to access the truth of the real through the act of fictionalizing. It was precisely this strategy that ultimately safeguarded such forms—both Scott's metrical and prose romances—from the charge of disease.

The British monarchy and, for that matter, the Highland culture of tartans and kilts could only become useful to the iconology of the modern nation-state once they were emptied out of any vestige of premodern violence, once they too became fictionalized. The king could return to Scotland with such fanfare precisely because he was not the "Butcher" Cumberland (who was the last Hanoverian to set foot on Scottish soil), just as all the Scottish participants could wear their kilts because the Highland garb had been emptied out of the violence of revolutionary insurrection. The former association with violence still signified but only as a principle of vigor and healthiness within the regulation and training of the modern, civilized subject, offering, as Hazlitt put it with regard to Scott's romances, "charming and wholesome relief to the fastidious refinement and 'over-laboured lassitude' of modern readers." Scott's fictional romances, both metrical and prosaic, helped to establish this maneuver, turning the real and bitterly fought conflicts of the past into joyful because only half-believed yet no less powerful cultural fantasy.

What is more, the form of law itself changed: no longer "Obey!" but the superego's command, "Enjoy!"—a command that applied both to the reading of entertaining fictions and to the entertainments associated with the king's visit. When it came to the king's visit, that command was spoken by none other than Scott himself in his one-shilling booklet, *Hints addressed to the Inhabitants of Edinburgh and others in prospect of His Majesty's Visit*, an instruction manual for the joyful festivities to come. Responding to the political divisions of the past years ("It is really too much to have people divided in this manner, where there is no true reason why they should be so" [8]), Scott responded by recasting a symbol of enmity into a sign of joyful celebration. Referring to the anticipated "Highland Ball," Scott writes that "[n]o gentleman is allowed to appear in anything but the ancient Highland costume" (26).[16] The very desire to transgress against the king (a Highland costume) is thus turned into the command to celebrate *en masse*. Indeed, Scott insists when discussing the Levee at Holyrood that "[t]hose who wear the Highland dress must, however, be careful to be armed in the proper Highland fashion,—steel-wrought pistols, broadsword, and dirk" (16). By turning Highland transgression into quaint Scottish culture, the former signs of violence become the proof of propriety and the proper dress of "a great entertainment" (26). As Sutherland puts it, "Thus an item of clothing for the wearing of which a Scotsman could face execution until 1782 became the uniform of Lowland gentlemen who before August 1822 would no more have thought have [*sic*] wearing a kilt than a suit of medieval armour" (258).

That the kilt is an article of dress makes the fetish function all too perfect, particularly since it is that article which screens the phallus. We should keep in mind that, in his essay on fetishism, Freud expressly resists calling the fetish a penis-substitute. He names it instead "a substitute for the woman's (mother's) phallus which the little boy once believed in and does not wish to forego" (5.199). The *skirt*, in this most precisely Freudian of ways, could thus be said to be "the vehicle both of denying and of asseverating the fact of castration" (Freud 5.203). Add to this the fact that traditional Highland dress also includes the wearing of the sporran over the penis, that the sporran is itself a purse holding that other fetish (money), and that, in Scott's day, "purse" still carried the sense either of scrotum or the female genitalia, and we find ourselves in the sort of dream logic (overdetermination, condensation, metonymy, displacement, etc.) that often marks the perceived fullness of an ideological edifice's actual and constitutive lack.[17] The further fact that the traditional tartan dress is affixed at the upper torso by a single "point de capiton," a large brooch or pin on the left shoulder, in turn provides us with the psychoanalytical name for this ideological operation: let us call it not the quilting but the kilting point.

ROMANCING THE STATE

The ways that Scott's romance of state influenced political power structures in the Romantic period become clear if we remember, as Britain certainly did, the traumatic events of the French Revolution. In 1790, Edmund Burke responded to events across the Channel by renouncing his Whiggish sympathies and adopting instead a position of nostalgic conservatism. Faced with the violence of revolutionary change, made all too real by the recent execution of Marie Antoinette, he turned in disgust from the present to lament the loss of traditional values. He turned, in fact, all the way back to the medieval period:

> Little did I dream that I should have lived to see disasters fallen upon [Marie Antoinette] in a nation of gallant men, in a nation of men of honour, and of cavaliers. I thought ten thousand swords must have leaped from their scabbards to avenge even a look that threatened her with insult. But the age of chivalry is gone. That of sophisters, economists, and calculators, has succeeded; and the glory of England is extinguished for ever. (73)

In fact, the age of chivalry was just in the process of being revived, which is precisely why Burke's statement would have struck a chord with his reading audience. Faced with two revolutions—the political one across the Channel and the industrial one at home—Britain increasingly turned to that imagined past of honor, gallantry, and stability to shore up the "glory of England" in despite of traumatic change, war, and instability. Medievalism appears to have served an apotropaic fantasy in the nineteenth century, warding off economists and sanscullotists alike in order to ensure the orderly expansion of empire. It also served as a principle of health, allowing Britain at once to envision itself as a social body (with a cultural history that included all its people rather than just its leaders) and to preserve within that body a vital power that would protect Britain from the ravages of modernity and the rise of capitalist culture. The vestiges of premodern violence could thus serve to invigorate the nation even as it was acknowledged as superseded by modernity. After all, Britain relied precisely on those sophisters, economists, and calculators to finance its chivalrous wars, to fuel its imperialist interests, and thus financially to ensure Britain's glory and strength in the nineteenth century.

The chivalric, medieval romance could successfully serve contradictory agendas because held in productive tension within its cultural fantasy were the very transitions threatening to rip apart a British empire in the throes of industrial revolution, social upheaval, and war. As this chapter has argued, what allowed ideological antagonisms, tensions, and traumas to be at once asseverated and denied in the romance is the logic of the fetish, which, as Freud argues, provides an individual with one way to address the mourning associated with trauma.[18] Faced with the traumas of their own day, many nineteenth-century critics, writers, and politicians turned to a similar logic with regard to the fantasy of medievalism: I know very well that we cannot recover a virgin time before the traumatic changes effected by the industrial or the French revolution but, nonetheless, I will believe in such a fantasy.

It is perhaps because of this fetish-function that the romance was so pervasive throughout the late eighteenth and nineteenth centuries, from the early antiquarian impulses of Percy's *Reliques* or Scott's *Minstrelsy*, to its market dissemination in various generic forms (ballads, gothic fiction, metrical romances, historical novels), to its enlistment by the Victorian period in the ideological unification of both nation and empire. Somehow, in a time of social, aesthetic, and technological upheaval, this phenomenon succeeded in speaking (although in different ways) to completely antagonistic sectors of the population and did so in such a way as to stabilize Britain's constitutional monarchy and the healthy "constitution" of Britain as a whole.

Medievalism appealed not only to those members of the aristocracy that sought legitimacy for their own status in the traditions of the past, but also to conservative middle-class reformers who felt that capitalist expansion and a new proletariat required guidance and restraint, and even to certain Radical groups who looked to medieval Britain for a time when the poor still maintained a certain degree of dignity and self-sufficiency, if not outright freedom.[19] Even William Cobbett, whose Radical publications sold in the tens of thousands in the early part of the nineteenth century, could turn to a lost feudal order as early as 1803 to legitimate his own critique of the Utilitarians: "The days of the Veres and Percies, and Cliffords, and Nevilles must return, and the glory of leading *vassals* into the *field* must once more be the responsibility of England's gentry" (Alice Chandler 62).[20] Medievalism could appeal to the Tories who desired permanent stability in the social order, to the Whigs who claimed the antiquity of British liberties through the Magna Carta (the 1215 Great Charter of English personal and political liberty), and even to those Radicals who imagined a benevolent aristocracy and an oppressed proletariat uniting in their opposition to laissez-faire economics.[21]

Medievalism discovered one of the necessary elements of the successful mass-market product: easy, pan-ideological consumption. By at once claiming to access an uncorrupted "truth" that would save the present and acknowledging itself as fictional, as mere cultural fantasy, medievalism allowed various ideological positions to claim stability not in the violent imposition of power or the bloody upheavals of revolution but in an ideology somehow sublimed into "truth, as diamond pure and hard." Even the weapons of violent rebellion were thus magically recast—as in Scott's royal spectacle of steel-wrought pistols, broadswords, and dirks—into the cultural markers of health.

Scott represented a highly influential version of this maneuver. In Scott's romance genre, both novelistic and metrical, social antagonisms were recast as the imagined resolution of ideological contradiction in Britain's own historical past, thus offering the public a fantasy of nostalgia that could sell without the former fears about naïve readers duped into mistaking the fiction for reality. The principle that managed ideological contradiction in Scott's fantasy of nostalgia and that ensured readers would not be duped by the fictions they read was the fetish in the psychoanalytical sense I have been outlining. Indeed, Žižek defines "nostalgia" precisely in terms of a split between belief and ironic distance, which thus explains the need for the "ism" in medieval*ism*: "[W]e are fascinated by the gaze of the mythic 'naïve' spectator, the one who was 'still able to take it seriously,' in other words, the one who 'believes in it' for us, in place of us." For this reason, nostalgia is "always divided, split between fascination and ironic distance" (*Looking* 112). The *Lay*'s frame, where we are actually presented the naïve spectator hearing the last minstrel sing, or the

Introductions to *Marmion*, where Scott acts out for us the proper response to his fictions, merely underlines the point. Scott's decision to set many of his medievalist fantasies in the *Renaissance* rather than the middle ages similarly illustrates his understanding, even on the level of his works' diegesis, that medievalism is always already in the process of being superseded.[22] We as readers are thus encouraged at once to avow and disavow our knowledge in the present.

The secret to Scott's success lay not only in his insistence on the fictionality of his work but also in his reconceptualization of romance as the preserver of barbaric virility within a market that normally served up only "cordial and luscious drafts." Scott thus made consumers feel good about their own consumption, facilitating the transition into a mass market in books. Indeed, the romance was, in the end, not only exemplary of mass cultural appeal but executive of it, for, as Peter J. Manning has pointed out, "it was paradoxically the phenomenal popularity of romance that made literature the trade of 'oeconomists, and calculators' and gave its name to the entire period." Chivalry at once "pleased the audience, whether noble or aspirant, and disguised the new conditions of authorship" ("Childe" 182).[23] It thus helped to effectuate, facilitate, and legitimate the entrance into both commodity culture and the modern nation-state.

THE LAST MINSTREL

Scott was particularly important for this transition, given the fact that he managed almost single-handedly to legitimize for the nineteenth century both the novel and the romance form. Numerous studies have explored this operation in Scott's novels;[24] what still needs some clarification is the role of Scott's metrical romances in this process of legitimation.[25] We can read in Scott's poetical romances the same maneuvers Scott would later employ in both his novels and George IV's pageant of state. Scott was attempting to deal with two traumas in these works: the political antagonisms and transitions of the Romantic period on the one hand and the technological changes affecting the very material of the literary text on the other. Both are addressed in Scott's metrical romances by way of a performative self-allegorizing that implements the fetish as the regulator of trauma. The vehicle that serves to deny and asseverate the fact of castration (here, the loss of aura) is none other than the book itself. As this chapter will go on to argue, both the market for literature and the technology of mechanical reproduction manifest themselves within the very fabric of Scott's first metrical romance, *The Lay of the Last Minstrel* (1805); indeed, it is precisely fabric or, rather, its scarcity in paper production due to the Napoleonic wars that in the Romantic period allowed for one last reign of poetry before a mass audience and mass production impelled the rise of the periodical review and the popular novel. Scott's book-fetish in his metrical romances was also designed to protect Britain against the threat of revolutionary violence; like the fetish of George IV's kilt, the fetish of Scott's book relied on French fabric, in other words, to protect it—and its hidden lack—from those nasty sansculottes.

The romance genre was especially suited to represent the various transitions and contradictions that troubled the Romantic period. As Fredric Jameson argues in *The Political Unconscious*, romance's "ultimate condition of figuration . . . is to be found in a transitional moment in which two distinct modes of production, or moments of socioeconomic development coexist" (148). What I wish to underline in this chapter is the ideological operation that allows "two distinct modes of production, or moments of socioeconomic development to coexist": that is, the fetish and its ability to hold mutually exclusive propositions in productive tension. It is this balanced tension as well as the ability at once to acknowledge and to deny the impossibility of the fantasy that, in turn, ensured the form's purported healthiness in Scott. The romance is adapted to figuring transitions because it invites the reader to participate in psychic projection, be it to some posited future Utopia or, more commonly, to an already-lost golden age (or both, as in the Arthurian romances of the mid-Victorian period that I will examine in the Coda, in which Arthur, "the once and future king," represents a lost past *and* a promised future). Scott's romances followed in this tradition by fantasizing a place *where* and, more importantly, a time *when* ideological contradictions and social antagonism were reconciled. Through the romance, Scott allowed his readers to invest themselves in a fantasy of wholeness against which they could then measure and perhaps even refashion the traumatic transitions and antagonisms of the present, even as Scott *encouraged* his readers to acknowledge the maneuver as artificial, fictional, and romanticized. Romance's fantasy of harmonizing antagonism is clear in Scott. As many critics have illustrated in terms of his novels, Scott's goal in his fiction was to indulge in the "barbarity" of the middle ages or of Highland culture only to effect a harmonizing with "modernity" and British culture. I would only add that that harmonizing was also understood as an invigoration—an effort to protect modernity from its own luxuriousness and resultant nervous disorders by way of nostalgia. Nostalgia, in other words, served as defense against neuralgia.

As in the novels, Scott's ideological strategy in his metrical romances is clearest on the elementary level of plot. In the *Lay of the Last Minstrel*, for example, a war between the English and the Scots is averted when the English forces agree to trial by combat in order to avoid unnecessary bloodshed. When the disguised English lord, Henry Cranstoun, fights in the place of the wounded Scottish knight and wins, the Scottish Lady Buccleuch allows Cranstoun to marry her daughter, a marriage she has vociferously opposed throughout the tale. By subscribing to a chivalric code that transcends even clan ties, the English and the Scots thus achieve a symbolic union in the story that transcends the violence of an earlier feudal order. In the 1810 *Lady of the Lake*, this operation is perhaps even clearer. In that story, all is forgiven after the exiled Scottish chief, Lord Douglas, quells a mob contesting his wrongful imprisonment at the hands of James V, King of Scots. Douglas's address to the crowd is an exemplary instance of Walter Scott's use of chivalrous action to defend a sense of nationhood that, as in the code of chivalry, transcends kinship:

> "Hear, gentle friends, ere yet for me
> Ye break the bands of fealty.
> My life, my honor, and my cause,
> I tender free to Scotland's laws.
> Are these so weak as must require
> The aid of your misguided ire?
> Or if I suffer causeless wrong,
> Is then my selfish rage so strong,
> My sense of public weal so low,
> That, for mean vengeance on a foe,
> Those cords of love I should unbind
> Which knit my country and my kind?" (5.772–83)

Even black Sir Roderick Dhu, a Scottish chieftain "wild as Bracklinn's thundering wave" (2.270), refuses to take advantage of the Saxon Fitzjames when he finds him exhausted and lost earlier in the tale. Instead, he feeds the knight, tends him, and even sleeps next to him, explaining "But not for clan nor kindred's cause/ Will I depart from honour's laws" (4.177–78).

When Scott does represent actual military conflict, as in *Marmion*'s Flodden Field, Scott's ultimate message is a call for forgiveness, which then gets translated to the political struggles of his own day. Regarding his evil protagonist, Scott not only has de Wilton spare Marmion's life rather than choose the path of vengeance, but Scott also warns the reader to do the same:

> If ever in temptation strong
> Thou left'st the right path for the wrong,
> If every devious step thus trod
> Still led thee further from the road,
> Dread thou to speak presumptuous doom
> On noble Marmion's lowly tomb;
> But say, "He died a gallant knight,
> With sword in hand, for England's right." (6.1139–46)

That warning to the reader brings full circle a text that begins with almost the very same rhetorical structure applied to the Whig politician, Charles James Fox, who supported many of the principles of the French Revolution and thus represented a common target for Tory attacks. Imagining himself before Fox's tomb, Scott in the introduction to the first canto exhorts his readers:

> *Here*, where the fretted aisles prolong
> The distant notes of holy song,
> As if some angel spoke again,
> "All peace on earth, good-will to men;"
> If ever from an English heart,
> Oh, *here* let prejudice depart,
> And, partial feeling cast aside,
> Record that Fox a Briton died! (146–53)

In the place of present struggles and enmities, Scott offers the "vision of enchantment's past" (219) offered by "the ancient minstrel's strain" (253), on which "Time lays his palsied hand in vain" (254). He offers to revive chivalry, though we may be "dwindled sons of little men" (285), and replaces the threat of revolution with

> Pure Love, who scarce his passion tells;
> Mystery, half veiled and half revealed;
> And Honor, with his spotless shield;
> Attention, with fixed eye; and Fear,
> That loves the tale she shrinks to hear;
> And gentle Courtesy; and Faith,
> Unchanged by sufferings, time, or death;
> And Valor, lion-mettled lord,
> Leaning upon his own good sword. (301–09).

Scott's message to his readers is clear in his metrical romances: modern Britain must escape the barbarity and superstitions of the past but must also inherit the medieval values of strength, fealty, and moral rectitude that will protect against the dangers of revolution and war. The best way to achieve this effect, apparently, is through the act of reading metrical fiction. Indeed, Scott's list metonymically aligns the strategies of romance fiction—"Mystery, half veiled and half revealed" or "Fear,/ That loves the tale she shrinks to hear"—with the values associated with an unsullied sense of chivalry—pure love, spotless honor, gentle courtesy, unchanging faith, and valor. Through the reading of fiction (in a sense that is, of course, not tied exclusively to the novel), one manages somehow to transcend the traumas of the present, thus accessing a pure and virgin truth. Indeed, chivalric codes serve in this way to ensure the cohesion of Scot and Saxon not only in these texts but in present-day Britain, protecting the "bands of fealty" and the "cords of love" that "knit" country and kind against the "changeling crowd" (5.819)—that "many-headed monster-thing" (5.834) that threatens to "rise against the law" (5.766) in *The Lady of the Lake*. In all three tales, Scott presents the medieval code of chivalry as a sort of cure for or regulation of the rather similar antagonisms that threaten a modern Britain in which allegiances and moral codes have become less certain.

Indeed, that regulative function is precisely how Scott understood the vestige of chivalry in modern culture. In his 1818 essays on chivalry and romance for the *Encyclopædia Britannica*, he created a narrative of devolution for both, illustrating how they suffered from the rise of civilization. Although chivalry "degenerated into brutal intolerance and superstition" (*Essays* 20–21), he explains, "nothing could be more beautiful and praiseworthy than the theory on which it was grounded" (*Essays* 21). The degeneration was aided by the entrance of the romance into a mass market. Whereas the first romances were addressed to "the tables of the great" (*Essays* 178), the "professional poet" (*Essays* 164) soon became "the companion and soother only of idle and convivial hours" (*Essays* 164). Eventually becoming "the companions and encouragers of revelling and excess," poets "became contemptible in the eyes, not only of the aged and the serious, but of the libertine himself, when his debauch palled on his recollection" (*Essays* 165). Scott makes the same argument in the metrical introduction to the first canto of *Marmion*; whereas the "mightiest chiefs of British song/ Scorned not such legends to prolong" (271–72), a "ribald king and court" in the eighteenth century "Demanded for their niggard pay,/ Fit for their souls, a looser lay,/ Licentious satire, song, and play" (277–81). As Scott explains in the *Britannica* article on the romance, the subsequent dependency on the market "accelerated the total downfall of [the minstrels'] order, and the general discredit and neglect into which they had fallen" (*Essays* 165), for the "composition of the Metrical Romance" was thus "gradually abandoned to persons of an inferior class" who "brought themselves and their occupation into still greater contempt and disregard" (*Essays* 177). Chivalry followed suit, becoming but the "worship of the *Vaga Venus*" (*Essays* 22). Nonetheless, the original pure principle of chivalry, which according to Scott is closely tied to romance, persists in modern society as a principle of restraint and regulation: "[I]ts effects are rather to be sought in the general feeling of respect to the female sex; in the rules of forbearance and decorum in society; in the duties of speaking truth and observing courtesy and in the general conviction and assurance, that, as no man can encroach upon the property of another without accounting to the laws, so none can infringe on his personal honour, be the difference of rank what it may, without subjecting himself to personal responsibility" (*Essays* 124–25). In a time of social transitions, Scott here offers medieval chivalry as the ethico-moral justification for one's subjection to both the nation's laws and the existing social order, even as he acknowledges that it belongs "to a system inapplicable to the modern state of the world" (*Essays* 123). Scott at once acknowledges chivalry as past and argues that it persists into the modern state as a principle of health, tending "on the whole to the improvement of society" (*Essays* 48). Scott knew very well that the traumatic changes effected by the rise of democracy, industrialism, and the market had spelled the end of both chivalry and the traditional romance but, *nonetheless*, Scott maintained his belief in the persistence of both as a principle of regulation in the present.

Scott's medievalism attempted also to resolve a related *cultural* transition: the transformation that occurred in print culture from artisanship to machinic mass production.[26] We can read in the narrator of the 1805 *Lay of the Last Minstrel* Scott's own liminal position at the turn of the century. *The Lay*'s minstrel finds himself caught between an aristocratic past (when poets were patronized for their work by an elite readership) and a commercial present (when minstrels are forced to play either to "a peasant's ear" or the "gentle ear" of "fair maids"). Scott's minstrel is the last of his kind. The image of the fragility of poetic production poignantly raised in the figure of the aging, nearly obsolete, and failing harper becomes the dominant motif of the poem's frame, a motif so crucial to Scott that each Canto ends with a stanza that worries over the minstrel's fading health, the fading of art in general, or the pleasures and delights of the last minstrel's audience.[27] Through this elaborate framing device and the various self-allegorizing maneuvers in the plot of the *Lay*, Scott establishes the anthropological fetish of the quasi-magical book by employing the ideological tensions of the psychoanalytical fetish in order to preserve his enterprise from the diseases associated with that third fetish: Marx's commodity form. Before I can proceed, however, I need to clarify the relationship of Scott's poetry to the Romantic market in books; after all, the diseases arising from market luxuries (including romances) were precisely what the period's medical tracts most feared, as we have seen. Despite the perceived dangers of unregulated dissemination, Scott managed to recast his incredible popularity and his poetry's unprecedented market dissemination into a principle of health. However, behind the rhetoric we can read the real material conditions that were already facilitating the end of poetry's dominance in the popular imaginary.

THE CULT OF THE BOOK

The last minstrel speaks differently than the unspecified new entertainers usurping his cultural dominance. He also *speaks*, literally (or, rather, orally), for what marks his difference is precisely the medium in which he presents his story—a human voice. I concur with Marlon Ross: Scott represents an earlier transition in medium (orality to literacy) in order to figure a transition within the medium of print culture itself at the turn of the nineteenth century.[28] Scott wrote his metrical romances in the midst of the technological and ideological transition from what I term the Cult of the Book to the Culture of the Text. That transition and Scott's response to it are precisely analogous to the transition from the cult of the king to the culture of a constitutional monarchy that I explored earlier in the chapter. By refashioning his own entrance into capitalist culture, Scott established the ideological maneuvers by which England would understand its own fiction of statehood.

Like the cult of the king, the Cult of the Book still sees the materiality of the printed and bound object as invested with a degree of what Walter

Benjamin terms "aura." The Book calls attention to itself; it maintains a certain distance from the reader, manifested in the very awkwardness of its weight, the ornamentation of its cover, the extravagant spacing of its margins, even in the bookcase one sometimes had to penetrate to reach the book itself. When Leigh Hunt recalled his childhood, he made it clear that even the cheap reprints were appreciated as much for their feel as for the feelings the texts provoked: "I doated on their size; I doated on their type, on their ornaments, on their wrappers containing lists of other poets, and on the engravings from Kirk" (Altick 54). Ideally, the Book as opposed to the "text" is an object to be reverenced irrationally until it achieves the full power of the fetish, in the anthropological sense: an inanimate object instilled with the power of magic or enchantment. Of course, the first editions of books were even more clearly objects to inspire fetishistic doting. They were published in such sumptuous quarto and octavo editions that the *Gentleman's Magazine* in 1794 was led to remark that learning "now seldom makes her appearance without the expensive foppery of gilding, lettering, and unnecessary engravings, hot pressing and an extent of margin as extravagant as a court lady's train. The inferior orders of society can scarce get a sight of her" (Altick 52).

Even the bookshops presented themselves as centers of fashionable culture, pretending at times to the literary salon, thus leading the "inferior orders of society" to approach them warily if at all. As the publisher, James Lackington, wrote in 1794, recalling his youth,

> As we could not tell what to enquire for, we were ashamed to go into the bookseller's shops; and I assure you, my friend, that there are thousands now in England in the very same situation; many, very many, have come to my shop, who have discovered an enquiring mind, but were totally at a loss what to ask for and who had no friend to direct them. (89)

Lackington knew what he was talking about given that he was the founder of the famous remainder bookstore that, as Alvin Kernan writes, "first put bookselling on a large-scale basis with a turnover of about 100,000 volumes in 1791" (220). Still, the aura of the Book clearly persisted for Lackington since, although he prominently displayed the banner CHEAPEST BOOKSELLERS IN THE WORLD on the store's façade, the name of his shop was, of all things, the Temple of the Muses.

The Culture of the Text, on the other hand, regards the literary work as endlessly reproducible and readily consumable. In this way, the Culture of the Text resembles and, arguably, makes possible the kitschy culture of kingship after George IV; in both cases, that which formerly remained inaccessible to the masses, maintaining power precisely through its exclusivity, was made to negotiate the fact of mass opinion and enter the street in the most literal of senses. In both cases, the transition can be read as the movement from a traditional anthropological sense of the fetish into a psychoanalytical sense. That which in fact drives the transition in both cases, however, is the increasing dominance of that third disavowed fetish: Marx's commodity form.

As Benjamin has argued, "[T]hat which withers in the age of mechanical reproduction is the aura of the work of art" (221). Although Benjamin is concerned in his essay with photographic and cinematic technologies, the effect of technological advancements on poetry is just as striking, for it was machinic mass production that in the nineteenth century finally turned the book as cult object into the text of pop culture. In this culture, publishers sought to break down separations between the mass-distributed text and its intended mass public. As a result, the text was brought out of the fashionable bookshops and onto the street. Robert Chambers, who established a second-hand bookshop in 1818, for example points out that "[h]undreds, I found, as Lackington had done before me, would buy books from a stall, who would not purchase them equally cheap in a shop" (A. S. Collins 188). As for the texts themselves, the weight of the paper or the feel of the cover mattered not; in fact, the heavy quarto and octavo editions that were common for poetry were impediments to easy consumption, both unnecessarily increasing the price of the work and making it *physically* more difficult to read in one sitting. Instead, pocketbook duodecimo editions allowed the mass-market text to come closer to the consumer in the most physical and literal of ways. The effect, according to Coleridge, is indeed a loss of aura. As he explains in the *Biographia*,

> In times of old, books were as religious oracles; as literature advanced, they next became venerable preceptors; they then descended to the rank of instructive friends; and as their numbers increased, they sunk still lower to that of entertaining companions; and at present they seem degraded into culprits to hold up their hands at the bar of every self-elected, yet not the less peremptory, judge, who chuses to write from humour or interest, from enmity or arrogance, and to abide the decision (in the words of Jeremy Taylor) "of him that reads in malice, or him that reads after dinner." (1.57–58)

Literature has been transformed, according to Coleridge, into nothing more than a morsel for easy consumption. In his turn to the idea of a "clerisy," Coleridge attempted to reclaim all the ceremony of religion in order to maintain the aura of a premodern estate system even as he was forced to acknowledge society's entrance into a modern system of production and consumption. Coleridge thus imposed the "culture" of the canon as a brake on the textual system, establishing the distinctions between high and low literature that would legitimate the rise of the professional intellectual class.

A mass-distributed "text," by contrast to both the canon and the Cult of the Book, is transmitted to the excited and voracious mind with as little ceremony as possible. For this reason, essays and fictional narratives naturally subscribe to the Culture of the Text insofar as one reads them to reach the end of, respectively, the argument or the story. A dense work of poetry, on the other hand, threatens to retard the easy and immediate consumption of the market product. Because essays and novels are designed to provide straightforward messages and narratives that enter directly into the reading mind, they resemble nothing less than a contagion; the material of the books themselves are merely the viral carriers. And, indeed, as many studies have explored, representations of the burgeoning number of readers at the end of the eighteenth century quickly gravitated to the language of pathology, with market dissemination exactly analogous to the contagions threatening a body politic.[29] The technological revolution in printing that was still to come allowed that contagion to reach truly epidemic proportions. One can begin to see, then, why—although the mechanical reproduction of print had existed since the Gutenberg revolution—it was not until the technological advancements of the nineteenth century that the "art" of printing truly passed from the artisan to the machine. It was the machine that turned the book as cult object into the text of pop culture.

Scott, like every other Romantic, was in a position to feel this transition especially strongly because, although all indications at the end of the eighteenth century pointed to the inexorable growth of a mass-market economy, a number of contingent conditions at the turn of the nineteenth century allowed the reading revolution to stall, allowed, that is, for one last reign of both poetry and the Cult of the Book, with the Romantic poet as totemic king.

Before Scott began writing, it was clear that a mass market was being formed. Thanks in part to its dissemination by "Jacobin" societies in sympathy with the ideals of the French Revolution, the second part of Thomas Paine's *The Rights of Man*, published at the price of only sixpence in 1792, was said to have sold one million and a half copies by 1809, when only a couple of decades earlier the most successful novels saturated the market at only nine thousand copies. Regardless of whether the figures for Paine's circulation are perfectly correct, people believed a radical publication had achieved the sort of dissemination that would have placed it in the hands of one in ten English citizens within a space of seventeen years.[30] It seemed, in fact, that the only way to fight pamphleteering fire was with fire. Hannah More's *Cheap Repository Tracts*, which imitated the look and feel of the cheap pamphlet, though designed to counter seditious and anti-Christian literature, sold possibly as many as 2,000,000 copies between 1795 and 1796 at prices ranging from a halfpenny to one-and-a-half pence.[31]

The technological revolution that was to fuel the rise of pulp fiction and that was to threaten the death of poetry was also well under way when Scott was writing his metrical romances. The plaster-of-Paris method of casting stereotypes, which allowed a printer both to distribute his type and to produce new impressions of a book whenever required, was perfected in 1802. In 1804

Andrew Wilson printed the first stereotyped book in Britain and in 1805 Oxford University Press, which had underwritten the development of the technology, employed Wilson to print Bibles and prayer books. By 1840, stereotyping had become the standard printing practice, helping to make the production of cheaper editions possible. Stanhope's iron press, which reduced the labor involved in printing, was patented in 1798 and its introduction in 1810 led to a 25 percent reduction in the prices for press work between 1810 and 1816.[32] The Fourdrinier continuous papermaking machine was in full operation by 1807, reducing the cost and improving the quality of paper. As a result, the price of paper dropped, Lee Erickson explains, "from thirty-two shillings a ream in 1810 to twenty shillings a ream in 1835, during a period in which both demand and production increased enormously" (27). Given that the cost of paper accounted for one-half to two-thirds the price of printing a book, printers saw a 40 percent reduction in the cost of printing. By 1825 more than half of all the paper in Britain was made by machine.

Despite clear indications of a ready mass market and the general implementation of the necessary technologies of mass production, however, the movement into a mass market was very much an uneven one over the course of the Romantic period. Because of the French Revolution and the Napoleonic Wars, the importation of rags (still the raw material for paper) was sharply curtailed in the period causing the price of paper "to rise," Erickson explains "from twenty shillings a ream in 1797 to thirty-two shillings a ream in 1810, an increase of over 50 percent" (20). Despite the implementation of new machines of mass production, the price of books therefore doubled in the first two decades of the nineteenth century, leading publishers to produce expensive-looking editions marketed to the aristocratic classes that could afford them.[33] And poetry was for the last time in particular demand given that its "cultural capital" recommended it to an elite readership and its concentrated language arguably provided more pleasure upon rereading at a time when even the rich could not afford to buy a new book a week.[34] Books were so dear at this time that Southey was led to state in 1805 that "they are becoming rather articles of fashionable furniture more than anything else; they who buy them do not read them, and they who read them do not buy them." Regarding the prospects for his own *Madoc* (1805), he goes on to state that "[i]f [it] obtain any celebrity, its size and cost will recommend it among these gentry—*libros consumeri nati*—born to buy quartos and help the revenue" (*Life* 2.329–30). Books were "conspicuous tokens of wealth," as Richard Altick puts it, "whose costliness was obvious to the most casual beholder" (261). They were, in fact, still the products of the artisan. Indeed, printing house compositors continued to be the best-paid skilled workers in London, earning thirty-three shillings a week in 1801 and thirty-six shillings a week from 1811 until 1832.[35] For largely contingent reasons, the Cult of the Book persisted despite the development of a mass market and the existence of machinic technologies.

In the midst of these technological transitions and mass-market interruptions, Scott wrote his metrical romances, publishing them in sumptuous quarto and octavo editions. In fact, he managed almost single-handedly to push the price of books even higher, for publishers realized that the gentry and the circulating libraries were willing to pay the price. *The Lay of the Last Minstrel* (1805), for example, sold 15,050 copies in three years, with the initial quarto edition selling at twenty-five shillings; *Marmion* (1808) sold 11,000 copies in its first year, with its initial quarto edition costing thirty-one shillings sixpence; and *The Lady of the Lake* (1810) managed to sell 20,300 copies in its first year, with the initial quarto edition selling at the previously unheard of price of two guineas or forty-two shillings.[36] To put these figures in perspective, consider that a pension for a surgeon with six years' service in 1816 was 42 shillings a week and for a commander in the Royal Navy 60–70 shillings a week.[37] Carpenters in 1831, on the other hand, earned only 14 shillings a week and handloom weavers only five shillings, sixpence a week.[38]

We can begin to see, then, why Scott's class ideology in his metrical romances and—later—his novels would be so popular. Regardless of his own efforts to join the gentry through the creation of his estate at Abbotsford, Scott had very good financial reasons for turning to a feudal social structure and morality that supported the gentry and the status quo—only the upper classes were initally able to buy his books. But this is too simple. Scott turned to the medieval past not only because of this readership but also because of changes in the very medium in which he wrote. Scott put his first metrical romance in the mouth of "the last minstrel" because he was quite conscious of the changes occurring in the market status of the poetic text; after all, Scott's own quarto editions were soon followed by octavo and, finally, pocketbook editions marketed to an ever-larger readership. The very reason for writing the *Lay* appears caught between opposing cultural systems. According to Scott's 1830 Introduction, which was written after the full implementation of a mass market and the distribution of Scott's own work in cheap reprints, the *Lay*'s genesis hearkened back to a time of aristocratic patronage. It was Harriet Duchess of Buccleuch who had, he contends, "enjoined on me as a task to compose a ballad on the subject [of Gilpin Horner]. Of course, to hear was to obey" (*Poetical* 44). The work was thus presented as an homage to "the intellectual character, . . . manners, . . . understanding, and . . . benevolence" of a patron (*Poetical* 44), the very Buccleuch seat, in fact, where Scott housed the king during George IV's visit to Scotland. Scott even chose to have an early ancestor of the duchess be the audience for the minstrel in the final work. And yet, as Scott makes clear in an 1812 letter to Crabbe, his ulterior motive for writing the *Lay* was very much a commercial one, if one that was supposed to defend Britain against insurrection: "I wrote The *Lay of the Last Minstrel* for the purpose of buying a new horse for the Volunteer Cavalry" (*Poetical* 40). As with the visit of the king, Scott here invokes a feudal past in which one still believed in both the aura of the book and the aura of the aristocracy (not to mention the aura of the king) while allowing that past to be lost, except, that is, as the nostalgic stuff of romance and mass-market fantasy. As always in Scott, the potential contagions of mass-market dissemination are, however, recast as cure, as that which would enable his defense of empire: his healthy *corps* (in both the English and the French sense of the term).

The minstrel of Scott's *Lay* similarly seeks a patron at a time when "Old times were changed, old manners gone" (Introduction 19). The story he chooses to recount to his new benefactor is presented as "an ancient strain/ . . . not framed for village churls,/ But for high dames and mighty earls" (Introduction 76–79), even though he has been forced, ever since "A stranger filled the Stuarts' throne" (Introduction 20), to beg "his bread from door to door" and tune "to please a peasant's ear,/ The harp a king had loved to hear" (Introduction 24–26). Once again, one cannot help but see a parallel in Scott's own cultural situation. After all, although the house of Stuart fell in 1688, it was the Hanoverian successors of the eighteenth century who truly spelled the end of the British monarchy's participation in art patronage, with mad King George's reign (1760–1820) coming under especial fire during Scott's day.[39] If in the minstrel's age it was the oral storyteller that was being replaced by the productions of the Gutenberg revolution, in Scott's period it was the collapse of the patronage system and the rise of a mass market that threatened the very genre of poetry. Scott of course *knew very well*—and all too personally—that "Old times were changed," but, *nonetheless*, he offered up the fantasy of a feudal patronage structure in order to salvage a certain degree of cultural capital for his own market productions, offering up aristocratic fantasy (as Scott did for the Hanoverian George IV) in order to obfuscate even as he acknowledged Great Britain's transition into the increasingly dominant ideologies of capitalism and the bourgeois subject. In so doing, Scott ensured for the romance a continuing political influence while safeguarding the form from the charge of disseminated disease by insisting that the form's very obsolescence was a marker of healthy robustness: barbarity as a superseded yet nonetheless necessary principle of health within a market of debilitating luxuries.

The *Lay*'s parallels with Scott's day do not end here, for a printed book appears in the very plot of the metrical romance, a fact that underlines the story's formal self-consciousness. The book is sought by the Lady Buccleuch, who, adding to that self-consciousness, is not only the addressee and supposed inspiration but also the very subject of the poem. When she hears the voices of the "River Spirit" and the "Mountain Spirit" warn her to allow the marriage of her daughter to Lord Cranstoun, she instructs her knight, Sir William of Deloraine, to proceed to Melrose where a monk will unearth for him "the treasure of the tomb" (1.240), but she warns him:

> "What he gives thee, see thou keep; . . .
> Be it scroll or be it book,
> Into it, knight, thou must not look;
> If thou readest, thou art lorn! (1.245–49)

William finally reaches Melrose at midnight, after which the monk informs him of the provenance of this dangerous book. It had belonged, he tells him, to

> the wondrous Michael Scott;
> A wizard of such dreaded fame
> That when, in Salamanca's cave,
> Him listed his magic wand to wave,
> The bells would ring in Notre Dame! (2.138–42)

William is then directed to unearth the "Mighty Book," buried with the wizard so "That never mortal might therein look" (2.161–62). When William does finally move "the massy stone" of Michael's tomb, they find that there "Before their eyes the wizard lay,/ As if he had not been dead a day" (2.210–11) and that in his left hand was held "the Mighty Book,/ With iron clasped and with iron bound" (2.217).

What we have here is an allegorical riddle, for one is tempted to ask: what other book is able to preserve an author "As if he had not been dead a day" and can, when invoked with the magic wave of a pen (if not a wand), be able to ring effects many leagues away? If not a magic book, then the mass-produced text of a transnational economy. The implied analogy does not end here. After William leaves Melrose, he encounters Lord Cranstoun and his "goblin page," Gilpin Horner, and immediately attacks the lord once he recognizes him for an Englishman. Because of his weariness from travel, he is defeated and Lord Cranstoun takes pity on him, instructing his page to tend his wounds; however, the page, who "was always for ill, and never for good" (3.148), stops when he finds the Mighty Book and attempts instead to discover its "secret":

> The iron band, the iron clasp,
> Resisted long the elfin grasp;
> For when the first he had undone,
> It closed as he the next begun.
> Those iron clasps, that iron band,
> Would not yield to unchristened hand
> Till he smeared the cover o'er
> With the Borderer's curdled gore;
> A moment then the volume spread,
> And one short spell therein he read.
> It had much of glamour might,
> Could make a ladye seem a knight,
> The cobwebs on a dungeon wall
> Seem tapestry in lordly hall,
> A nutshell seem a gilded barge,
> A sheeling seem a palace large,
> And youth seem age, and age seem youth—
> All was delusion, nought was truth. (3.93–110)

Of course, the spell of glamour is precisely the power of Sir *Walter* Scott's book, whose stories were desired particularly by the young and a largely female readership because they magically allowed such readers to live the life of a knight in large palaces and lordly halls. And, as with Michael Scott's magical art, Walter Scott's powerful spell is activated only through the act of reading.

That power is also quite dangerous, as we are reminded a number of times over the course of the *Lay*'s narrative. One can imagine the trouble such a spell could wreak if allowed to disseminate and be read indiscriminately by anyone who cracked open the book's weighty cover. I believe that Scott here represents not only his own storytelling might but the dangers inherent in the indiscriminate market dissemination of fiction's spell of glamour, at least when that glamour *is taken for the real*. Indeed, one cannot help but read the goblin "page" as the intrusion of a negative spirit of romance, for he appears completely out of place in what is otherwise a *heroic* not a *gothic* romance.[40] He is representative of the reader who breaks down the distinction between fantasy and reality, who actually and completely believes in the delusion, who falls for the spell of glamour. Indeed, given the extreme self-consciousness of the *Lay*, with its elaborate frame and embedded allegory of reading, it is hard not to read the "goblin page" as the very principle of the Culture of the Text threatening the premarket boundedness of the Book. For this reason, a certain distance between the book and the indiscriminate reading of the *textual* "page" must be maintained—the iron band, the iron clasp, a christened hand, even the fiction of an overseeing authorial presence, for Gilpin Horner is ultimately punished for his indiscriminate reading: a buffet strikes him down in the very next lines of the story and the *Lay* culminates with Gilpin's obliteration by a lightning bolt conjured by Michael (or should we read Walter?) Scott himself. In the end, the "elfin" Gilpin Horner—a diminutive and dangerous reader who might simultaneously point to the "lower" classes and the "weaker" sex—must literally be effaced from the storyline, thus preserving the generic purity of the rest of Scott's romance.[41] Scott does not deny that the romance is potentially dangerous. Instead, he defines a specific form of romance as perverse (the *pages* of the gothic) in order to ensure the good health of his own fetishized *book* of romance.

Scott's medieval works were a striking achievement; at a time of technological revolution, of war, of colonial expansion, of class unrest, Scott managed—through the figuring of another time of transitions and within the harmonizing magic of the romance form—to effect a retardation of not only a social but also a technological revolution and, through the power of only half-believed glamour, to figure a glorious Britain of colonial expansion in the very dissemination of both a commodified and an enchanted, even chanted text. Scott's medievalism, read here in his efforts to sustain the Cult of the Book, constituted an attempt to retard the withering of the aura of his art in an age of mechanical reproduction. Scott hearkened back to a time and place he could imagine as having been beyond market exchange, when the aura of the unique and quasi-magical book was unsullied by its reproduction, when a youthful and robust poet sang for high dames, mighty earls, and the king himself. The fact that Scott *at the same time* acknowledged that era as past and acknowledged the poet as both superseded and in failing health did not hinder but may, rather, have facilitated Scott's ideological maneuver. After all, in the end, Scott would adopt the role of the last minstrel in 1822 and, using this same strategy of nostalgic fetishization, would replay his maneuvers in his "romancing" of Britain and the king. Scott could accomplish this realization of his own fantasy only *because* it continued to be acknowledged as fantasy. Otherwise, Scott's literalization of his own fiction would have surely been received with ridicule rather than kitschy nostalgia. His maneuvers were all the more effective at regulating his readers for being acknowledged as but harmless fictions. Behind those fictions still lay the traumas of his own day, which were at once acknowledged and, nevertheless, denied.

Ultimately, the rhetorical strategies that secured for Scott his political influence also in the end ensured his obsolescence. On the one hand, the rhetoric persisted throughout the nineteenth century as one option for the poetic enterprise. This demand for an antidote that could counteract the enervating diseases of a prosaic age pervaded the poetry reviews of the Victorian age. Alba H. Warren in fact claims that "[t]he theory of poetry as one kind of panacea or another was almost universal in the period" (169). Poetry, according to such formulations, is "a kind of medicine divinely bestowed upon men: which gives healing relief to secret mental emotion."[42] It is, as even Prince Albert states, "somewhere between religion and Hygiene" (Starzyk 8). As will be explored more fully in the Coda, such formulations however tended to recast poetry as a pure, virgin, and therefore *ineffective* form, at one step removed from the concerns of the present. Although Scott's fetish-logic may have for a time allowed him to speak effectively to that present, allowing him even to have an influence on political ceremony in the period, the insistence on the fictional and superseded nature of his work may have ensured the eventual recharacterization of his romances as the stuff of adolescent reading. Indeed, when in 1811 Scott tried to address contemporary events in his "Vision of Don Roderick," he was quickly chastised by the *Edinburgh Review*:

> The great charm of poetry is, that it places before us the newest and most extraordinary objects;—and by its vivid colours, and artful combinations, makes us present, as it were, to the remote or fabulous transactions. When it chooses, therefore, to employ itself on transactions that are actually present and before us already, in all their detail and reality, it evidently has no scope for its deceptions. (380)

Poetry should only "make us present" to the fabulous through our suspension of disbelief, thus keeping us always at one step removed from the actual present, from "subjects of temporary interest . . . on which a bombastical pamphlet will always produce more present effect than the most exquisite poetry" (392). Unlike the realist novel, which borrowed some of Scott's fictional strategies, poetry entailed not only a suspension of disbelief but also a suspension of the present, keeping the poetic at one step removed from the "real." Poetry, thanks in part to Scott's medievalizing and fetishizing maneuvers, was thus already in the process of being rarified into complete inefficacy.

Even Scott's rhetoric of health would soon be turned against him. Although, as we have seen, Carlyle acknowledged a "general healthiness of mind" (*Critical* 74) in Scott's novels, and, by extension, his poetry, Carlyle's ultimate goal in that essay was to underline the fantastical and, therefore, ineffectual nature of Scott's temporal strategy. In the end, Carlyle characterizes the poetry of *both* Scott and Byron as productive of "feelings which arise from *passion incapable of being converted into action*, which belong to an age as indolent, cultivated and unbelieving as our own" (*Critical* 59), except that, whereas Scott offered the "languid age" the promise of a "cure for its miserable paralysis and languor," Byron offered "an indignant Ernulphus' curse" (*Critical* 59): "Half-regretful lookings into the Past gave place, in many quarters, to Ernulphus' cursings of the Present" (*Critical* 59). Thanks to Scott, "[t]he reader was carried back to rough strong times, wherein those maladies of ours had not yet arisen" (*Critical* 56); however, the effect, according to Carlyle, was completely artificial and only "*half*-regretful." The formula of *je sais bien mais quand-même* is thus turned back on Scott, for Carlyle argues that such reading practices ultimately contribute to the listlessness of the recumbent reader precisely because the actions depicted are fictional: "What the Turkish bathkeeper is said to aim at with his frictions, and shampooing, and fomentings, more or less effectually, that the patient in total idleness may have the delights of activity,—was here to a considerable extent realised" (*Critical* 57). The frictions of the Turkish bathkeeper are thus aligned with the fictions of a Scottish bookkeeper who writes "impromptu novels to buy farms with" (*Critical* 83). Carlyle here resuscitates the vaguely sexual connotations of the romance formerly associated with female readers, except that Carlyle now has in mind "indolent languid men" (*Critical* 73) as those most endangered by such purportedly healthy fictions. As Ferris has argued with regard to this passage and to the rise and fall of Scott's celebrity as a novelist,

> The scene of reading is now exclusively male, pointing to the hardening of gender boundaries even as its homoerotic undertones testify to the anxiety over gender generated by that very hardening. In Carlyle the battle is over male reading and writing. And here the Waverley Novels—as both writing and reading—stand for the shallowness, effeminacy, and mechanization that have overtaken men in these sorry times. (*Achievement* 250)

As we will see in the chapters that follow, a similar trajectory can be traced in representations of male writers and readers of *poetry*. Although Scott provided the nineteenth century with a positive, healthy model for the male poet of genius, it may be, as I will argue in the Coda, that the rhetoric of health ultimately contributed to poetry's marginalization as much as did the rhetoric of perversity that was applied to Byronic poetry. In either case, be it that of cure or curse, poetry's influence on a mass market and on the politics of the Romantic period was, respectively, either sublimed or abjected into obscurity.

THREE

BYRON'S SPECTROPOETICS AND REVOLUTION

> Why must one begin with a poem when one speaks of the gift? And why does the gift always appear to be the *gift of the poem*?
>
> —Jacques Derrida, *Given Time*

> No one ever made a bargain in verse.
>
> —Adam Smith, *Lectures on Rhetoric*

UNLIKE SCOTT, BYRON COMPLICATED THE HARMONIZING FUNCTION of the romance by "unromantically" discussing the present. This chapter will argue that Byron countered Scott's efforts both to familiarize the past and to harmonize antagonism by instead defamiliarizing the present and inciting revolution, thus completely recasting the ideological effect of the romance form. Byron's ideas held the potential for disruptive effects because he fused the temporal dynamics of the romance form to an all-encompassing satire of the present, thus countering Scott's fetishistic nostalgia with an insistent melancholia that sought to "disjoint" a reader's relationship to the status quo. Byron's contemporizing of the medieval also drew attention to the textuality of his medium, thus opposing the Cult of the Book explored in the previous chapter. Byron however sought to escape the threatened commodification of his poetry by offering the reader an alternate way of understanding one's relation to the market and to the dominant ideologies of the day. It was the specter of this alternate vision that haunted the critical reviewers of the rest of the century, impelling various apotropaic maneuvers against this threatening spirit of poetry.

Poetry's influence in the Romantic period is all too easily forgotten after poetry's utter marginalization in the twentieth century. This chapter argues that this eventual marginalization is due not only to the rise of the novel and the mass market, and not only to the tendency, encouraged by Scott, to view poetry as a rarefied form outside the concerns of the present, but also to nineteenth-century society's active response to a perceived threat in poetry's critique of the emergent social order. As chapter 4 illustrates, the sort of poetry associated with Byron's Satanic school was actively exorcized to obscurity by nineteenth-century periodical reviews, psychological tracts, and even medical treatises that feared the effects of reading such poetry and therefore aligned hyper-Romantic, idealist poetry and its attendant "temperament," the nervous disposition, with the worst sorts of physical effects: masturbation, pathology, degeneration, madness, and death. For now, however, this chapter will set aside the nineteenth-century reception of Byron's corpus as perverse in order to explore what precisely is most threatening in Byron's work. Does the sexualization of Romantic poetry after Byron perhaps hide what is truly disruptive in such poetic texts? We must ask, after all: Why all this concern about poetry, a concern that, at first blush, appears to make little sense to us today? As I argue here, one reason for this phenomenon is that poetry after Byron was felt to offer the reader a truly *radical* critique of capitalist exchange and of the various ideological maneuvers that sustained political economy and the status quo.[1] The sexualizing rhetoric discussed in chapter 4 was designed, in part, to counteract by emasculating this more serious threat.

BYRON'S REVOLUTIONARY ROMANCE

Identified as secretly aristocratic, attacked as amoral, diagnosed as pathological, dismissed as lacking any consistent system of thought, Byron has been laughed out of the house of literary criticism through most of the last two centuries. Reading earlier critical work on Byron, one is put in mind of Stephen Dedalus, who in James Joyce's *Portrait of the Artist as a Young Man* asserts that he thinks Byron is the greatest poet. The response from his friends is first ridicule—" 'He's only a poet for uneducated people' "—then moral outrage—" 'In any case Byron was a heretic and immoral too' "—and finally violence:

> —Behave yourself! cried Heron, cutting at Stephen's legs with his cane.
>
> It was the signal for their onset. Nash pinioned his arms behind while Boland seized a long cabbage stump which was lying in the gutter. Struggling and kicking under the cuts of the cane and the blows of the knotty stump Stephen was borne back against a barbed wire fence.
>
> —Admit that Byron was no good.
>
> —No.
>
> —Admit.
>
> —No.
>
> —Admit.
>
> —No. No. (81–82)

The goal of this chapter is not to defend Byron from attacks directed against his person or his actions. What I wish to do is to take what Byron had to *say* seriously and to make a case for a systematic philosophy in Byron's poetry, one that includes the potential for an effective critique of his time period's dominant ideologies and thus helps to explain the virulence of attacks against Byron throughout the nineteenth century.

Of course, one could, if one wished, point directly to Byron's life for evidence of his revolutionary proclivities. One might mention his three speeches to the House of Lords, which were all designed to stand on the side of personal liberty: he spoke in support of poor mechanics; he defended the right of Catholics to freedom of belief; and he presented the petition of the reformer Major John Cartwright, a document that sought to defend the people's right to petition the government for reform. One might mention the fact that Byron continued to write and publish what he knew would be received as radical and dangerous and that he did so despite the fact that so many of his friends had been imprisoned for making similar statements; despite censorship from his friends, his publisher, and the state; despite his fear that a libel suit would lead to the loss of legal rights to his daughter Ada.[2] One might finally mention that Byron spent his life questioning the sovereignty of foreign states, supporting first the Italian and then the Greek struggles for independence, or the fact that, in the end, he lost his life trying to join the Greek cause.[3]

One could make this argument; however, such an approach is open to the obvious critique, for we know that Byron died before he fought for the Greeks, that he never came under fire in support of the Carbonari, that his speeches in a Tory-controlled Parliament led to no immediate changes. Indeed, such facts have led Malcolm Kelsall to claim that "[t]he life of Byron is of no political significance" (2). Kelsall offers Henry Brougham as a fitter symbol of heroism and of ideological critique:

> Advocates of Byron as the "iron revolutionary" may indicate the substantial galvanic outbursts elsewhere in his writing, and life. But to what end? Compare the hard slog of step-by-step redress of a successful humanitarian liberal like Brougham (whom Byron hated). The poet conceives of no such hero, and poets achieve no practical objective. (116)

This chapter contends, on the contrary, that Byron's writings did, indeed, have a political effect on his age and that they did so because Byron sought, throughout his verse, to establish a consistent philosophy of justice, one that resembles what Jacques Derrida has theorized in his most recent publications as the "undeconstructibility of a certain idea of justice" (*Specters* 90), what he terms in the *Specters of Marx* a "desert-like messianism (without content and without identifiable messiah)" (28). Through such a philosophy, Byron achieved a *more than practical* objective precisely because he managed to question the tendency to violence in any system, monarchical, capitalist, and revolutionary alike. Kelsall may cite such skepticism as an example of Byron's disenchantment, but it is precisely as a counter to Scott's attempted *re*-enchantment that

Byron's position assumed political force.[4] I wonder also to what extent Kelsall is himself subscribing to what we might term, countering McGann, the *Victorian* ideology, an ideology that sought to recast Romantic poetry and the romance form as but adolescent pursuits achieving "no practical objective." The alignment of romance with harmless entertainment was, of course, facilitated by the very logic of the fetish employed by Scott to reinvigorate the form. If the romance was so successful in King George IV's and Queen Victoria's romances of state, it was only because it recast itself as at once vigorous and unthreatening—nothing but a vestige, half forgotten, of barbaric violence. This strategy did have important material effects; however, as we saw in the previous chapter, the strategy could only work by disavowing its own seriousness, thus "skirting" the violent traumas that, in fact, impelled the maneuver in the first place.

Byron, by contrast, insistently returned to those traumas, refusing to see them dead and buried and it was this insistence that for a time threatened to disrupt Scott's carefully stage-managed romance of state. This chapter is interested, then, in determining what it is in Byron's romances that did, in fact, inspire a number of activists of quite different stripes, from the Luddites of his own time period; to the Decembrist revolutionaries of the 1825 Russian uprising (the poet, Kondratii Ryleev, one of the leaders of the Decembrists, taking a copy of Byron to his execution); to the Corn-Law agitators and Chartists of the early Victorian period; to the Italian revolutionaries of the *Risorgimento*; to the most recent example, the Lord Byron Foundation for Balkan Studies, founded in October 1994 in response to the breakup of and ethnic violence in the former Yugoslavia.[5] Are these examples irrational responses to Byron's histrionic grandstanding or can one make an argument for a consistent philosophy of justice in Byron that has the potential for revolutionary effects?

Perhaps a good place to begin is to distinguish Byron from his contemporary, Scott. After all, on the face of it, Byron has much in common with Scott given his privileged social position, his incredible popularity in the period, and his turn to the romance form in *Childe Harold* (not to mention their shared lameness).[6] What is it, then, that distinguishes Byron's use of the romance form from Scott's? What precisely makes Byron's romance available to the appropriations of disparate revolutionaries over the next century? What is it precisely that gives Byron's poetry its radical force?[7]

If Scott's method is to familiarize the past and harmonize the present, Byron's method can be said to be the defamiliarizing and antagonizing of the present. As I have suggested, the romance form is ideally suited to articulate fantasies of wholeness because it invites the reader to participate in a program of psychic projection, either to a place *where* or a time *when* social antagonisms may be reconciled and national crises overcome. Medievalism, in Scott's romances, serves an apotropaic fantasy: medieval temporal "otherness" wards off the geographic and socioeconomic infractions and infections represented by the presence of colonies *outside* the nation-space, the infraction of bellicose foreign states *against* the nation-space, even the alienating urban landscapes spreading *within* the nation-space. The manly romance is thus reconceived as *sovereign* remedy.

Byron's *Childe Harold* subscribes to a program of psychic projection as well; indeed, he asks us to imagine both a *time* other than our own (the past that haunts the present) and a *space* other than our own (the foreign climes of the travel narrative); however, rather than use these fantasy-frames to idealize the present, Byron uncovers the logic behind romance's strategy of apotropaic projection—the fetish in the psychoanalytical sense I explored in the previous chapter: something that maintains connection to the lost object (the aura-filled work of art, an idealized medievalist past) while also allowing the object to be lost (which is to say exchanged, turned into a commodity on the mass market). When Byron prefaces his poem with the bold assertion that the medieval past was as profligate as his own day ("I fear that a little investigation will teach us not to regret these monstrous mummeries of the middle ages" [*Byron* 21]), he collapses the temporal fantasy that drives Scott's ideological project and his romance narrative. As Manning puts it, "Byron emptied out the romaunt, writing within the form while depriving it of its sustaining ideology" ("Childe" 170). Byron points out that the medieval past Scott portrays must almost by definition already be lost (hence the "ism"). How else, except as the always-already lost object of nostalgia, can medievalism function as a cohesive force for a modern Britain of capitalist and imperialist expansion?

In fact, Byron allowed the romance fetish to backfire; he employed it to imagine the present as itself always already lost, thus creating a space from which to question the values of a capitalist and imperialist status quo. Byron's romance medievalism contributed not to a nostalgia for the past but a nostalgia for the present—an anticipation of decay that would inevitably fuel the "condition of England" paranoia of the rest of the century.

The examples are many. It is almost as if Byron's examination of the ruins of past empires forced him also to anthropologize England's present. Anthropology, paleontology, and archaeology as disciplines were, of course, in the process of being established in nineteenth-century England and could be said to foster a new chronotopic relation to the present, a new sense of space that is filled to bursting with historical time. Byron shared with Goethe what Mikhail Bakhtin defines as "the ability to read in everything *signs that show time in its course*, beginning with nature and ending with human customs and ideas (all the way to abstract concepts)" (*Speech* 25).[8] Through such a historicization of the present, Byron helped to prepare the way for the nineteenth-century fascination with history and for what Gerald Bruns calls a "pure historicality" that is "completely outside the ideality of meaning, an open, unstructured, unstable space of colliding or intersecting surfaces that cannot be mapped by any external geometer (cannot be thought)" (129). Byron gained this sense of historicity, one could argue, from Gibbon's *Rise and Fall of the Roman Empire*, which he owned and cherished, and from the work of the founder of paleontology, Georges Cuvier, whom Byron mentions in both *Don Juan* and the Preface to *Cain*.[9] As Byron explains in that Preface, Cuvier argued

> that the world had been destroyed several times before the creation of man. This speculation, derived from the different strata and the bones of enormous and unknown animals found in them, is not contrary to the Mosaic account, but rather confirms it; as no human bones have yet been discovered in those strata, although those of many known animals are found near the remains of the unknown. (*Byron* 882)

The result of this new sense of temporality and of a spatiality stratified by time—what one might term a geo-historical rather than merely personal "spot of time"—is the feeling that the present is itself no longer present *to* itself, that " 'The time is out of joint' " (9.322), as Byron states after referring to Cuvier again in *Don Juan*:

> But let it go:—[my lost advice] will one day be found
> With other relics of "a former World,"
> When this World shall be *former*, underground,
> Thrown topsy-turvy, twisted, crisped, and curled,
> Baked, fried, or burnt, turned inside-out, or drowned,
> Like all the worlds before, which have been hurled
> First out of, and then back again to chaos—
> The superstratum which will overlay us.
>
> So Cuvier says. (9.289–297)

Once one sees "Men" as "but maggots of some huge Earth's burial" (9.312), suddenly the "great relics" of civilization begin to "Look like the monsters of a new Museum!" (9.319–20). The present can be imagined as already past, in ruin, and thus irreducible to a simple teleology of historical progress or a simple tropology of healthy constitution. We are presented instead with revolution (in the temporal sense of the term); in this way, even tyrants are stripped of their presence (in every sense of the term): "Think if then George the Fourth should be dug up!" (9.305).

The goal of such an archaeology for Byron is the disjointing of the present—" 'The time is out of joint' " (9.322), as he puts it, echoing *Hamlet* (1.5.188). Byron refuses, for example, to accept any existing form of "authority" as inherently and permanently self-present, which is to say transcendently signified rather than historically contingent. Instead, he presents his reader with history in order to historicize the present. Byron's evocation of the *ubi sunt* tradition thus transforms into an *ubi sunt* of the *hic et nunc*, a call to arms directed to the present, with an eye to the future and not the past. When he asks "august Athena" (*Childe Harold* 2.10), for example, "Where are thy men of might? thy grand in soul?" (2.11), the response is not merely rhetorical nor nostalgic as the next line suggests ("Gone—glimmering through the dream of things that were"). As we come to realize, the question is also a literal one:

> Who now shall lead thy scatter'd children forth,
> And long accustom'd bondage uncreate?
> Not such thy sons who whilome did await,
> The hopeless warriors of a willing doom,
> In bleak Thermopylae's sepulchral strait—
> Oh! who that gallant spirit shall resume,
> Leap from Eurotas' banks, and call thee from the tomb? (2.695–701)

The past is used in Byron not as a psychological strategy for projecting and resolving antagonism elsewhere (Scott's move), but as a call to arms in the present: "Who would be free themselves must strike the blow" (*Childe Harold* 2.721). When Byron does represent the past as heroic rather than merely profligate, as in his depiction of ancient Greece, he does so only as a goad to the present, as a way to "shame [Greece's] now degenerate horde" into action (*Childe Harold* 2.791).[10]

By the fourth canto of *Childe Harold's Pilgrimage*, while looking over the buildings of Venice's now eclipsed empire, Byron is also careful to bring his moral home:

> Albion! to thee: the Ocean queen should not
> Abandon Ocean's children; in the fall
> Of Venice think of thine, despite thy watery wall. (4.151–53)

Rather than offer Britain's own glorious past as a legitimization for empire, Byron's romance strategy is to look elsewhere, in addition to elsewhen, in order to enlist England in the revolutionary overthrow of an imperial overseer and thus also to question England's own imperial status as "Ocean queen." Byron expects of England as a nation no less than he does of the European monarchy restored upon Napolean's defeat: Why must we "Pay the Wolf homage? proffering lowly gaze/ And servile knees to thrones? No; *prove* before ye praise!" (3.170–71). Whereas in Scott chivalric codes provide the ethico-moral justification for one's subjection to law and order, in Byron the ethics of freedom and liberty take precedence over nation precisely because no one state has ever proven eternal: "A thousand years scarce serve to form a state;/ An hour may lay it in the dust" (2.797–98). Whereas in Scott chivalry maintains the status quo ("do not encroach upon the property of another"), in Byron "Chivalry, [Spain's] ancient goddess, . . . speaks in thunder through yon engine's roar:/ In every peal she calls—'Awake! Arise!" (1.406–11) until "Red Battle stamps his foot, and nations feel the shock" (1.422).[11]

One way that Byron achieved his disjointing of the romance is by rethinking the object of his satires, melding the temporal disjunctions of his romance form with an all-encompassing satirical critique of the present. In this way, Byron transformed both the romance form and the traditional temporal structure of carnivalesque laughter. It is not enough, that is, to say that Byron made his contemporary reader question the legitimacy of the status quo through carnivalesque laughter at a time when almost all efforts at Whig-led opposition and reform were being met with opprobrium and even oppression, for carnival suffers from similar temporal, spatial, and psychoanalytical limitations as traditional romance: "Carnivalization . . . is acceptable," Umberto Eco points out, "when performed within the limits of a laboratory situation (literature, stage, screen . . .)" (6–7). One can think of numerous proscribed carnivalesque times and spaces in our own culture that, even as they set the stage for carnivalesque inversions, are in no way threatening to existing laws and conventions (Hallowe'en, New Year's Eve, Spring Break; New Orlean's French District, football stands, the mosh pit). And, of course, Byron in his own age was quite familiar with the temporal and spatial parameters of the Venetian Carnival. The logic of these carnival spaces resembles that of the fetish, albeit with a twist: I know very well that these carnivalesque acts do not threaten the law but, nonetheless (and *for that very reason*), I will pretend that they do. Because of carnival's ability to exist alongside the status quo, a number of critics have questioned Bakhtin's overly optimistic belief that the carnivalesque can successfully overturn dominant ideologies.[12] As Eco explains,

> Carnival, in order to be enjoyed, requires that rules and rituals be parodied, and that these rules and rituals already be recognized and respected. One must know to what degree certain behaviors are forbidden, and must feel the majesty of the forbidding norm, to appreciate their transgression. Without a valid law to break, carnival is impossible . . . .
>
> In this sense, comedy and carnival are not instances of real transgression: on the contrary, they represent paramount examples of law reinforcement. They remind us of the existence of the rule. (6)

Byron offers up instead something that approaches Eco's term "cold carnival," an acknowledgment of the limitations of all laws and political frames, a position that is connected to Byron's historicization of the present. Kelsall has argued that even Byron's most incendiary writings are pathologically designed to "provoke situations in which action within the system is impossible and, therefore, not required" (77–78). I would counter that it is Byron's recognition of the limitations of all systems of convention, of law and of government that undergirds his positing of a justice *beyond law*. As a result, Byron does not so much promise global liberation, as he "warns us about the impossibility of global liberation, reminding us of the presence of a law that we no longer have reason to obey" (Eco 8).[13]

Eco counters Bakhtin's utopic theories about carnival by pointing out that, if they were true, "it would be impossible to explain why power (any social and political power throughout the centuries) has used *circenses* to keep the crowds quiet; why the most repressive dictatorships have always censured parodies and satires but not clowneries; why humor is suspect but circus is innocent" (3). It is this very distinction between carnivalesque laughter and a politically more dangerous form of humor that Francis Jeffrey himself pointed to when he decided in 1822 that Byron was, in fact, subversive and, therefore, a dangerous influence on his age. Although Jeffrey at first applauded the "plain manliness" and "nervous simplicity" of *Childe Harold* I and II (*RR* 2.837), which, he claimed, "is infinitely refreshing after the sickly affectations of so many modern writers" (*RR* 2.837), by 1822—the year Scott staged his George IV extravaganza—Jeffrey was writing that Byron's poetry in *Childe Harold* harbors a "fatal power of corruption" (*RR* 2.936). As he explains,

> When a rash and gay voluptuary descants, somewhat too freely, on the intoxications of love and wine, we ascribe his excesses to the effervescence of youthful spirits, and do not consider him as seriously impeaching either the value or *the reality of the severer virtues*. . . . The reveller may pursue his orgies, and the wanton display her enchantments with comparative safety to those around them, *while they know or believe that there are purer and higher enjoyments, and teachers and followers of a happier way*. (*RR* 2.936; my italics)

Jeffrey is quite conscious of the fact that in traditional carnival the "majesty of the forbidding norm" remains intact, inviolate. Byron is much more dangerous, according to Jeffrey, because "he has exerted all the powers of his powerful mind to convince his readers, both directly and indirectly, that all ennobling pursuits, and disinterested virtues, are mere deceits or illusions—hollow and despicable mockeries for the most part, and, at best, but laborious follies" (*RR* 2.936). Jeffrey makes it clear that he is not attacking the "indecencies and indelicacies, seductive descriptions and profligate representations" of the poetry; his charge against Byron, rather, is "that his writings have a tendency to destroy all belief in the *reality of virtue*—and to make all enthusiasm and constancy of affection ridiculous" (*RR* 2.936; my italics). When critics try to reduce Byron to nothing but the indecencies and indelicacies of his poetry—a phenomenon we will witness in the next chapter—they undercut what is, in fact, most disruptive about his poetry. Byron's brand of humor, like that described by Eco, "undermines the law" because "[i]t makes us feel the uneasiness of living under a law—any law" (Eco 8). John Stacy in 1820 similarly makes a distinction between the "genuine satirist" who "selects appropriate subjects," marking "them with discriminating severity" (20), and Byron's poetry, where "love is illusion—nature a name—religion a farce—and futurity a jest" (11). As Jeffrey puts it, "Love, patriotism, valour, devotion, constancy, ambition—all are to be laughed at, disbelieved in, and despised!" (*RR* 2.936).[14] Jeffrey also explains, "How opposite to this is the system, *or the temper*, of the great author of Waverley—the only living individual to whom Lord Byron must submit to be ranked as inferior in genius—and still more deplorably inferior in all that makes genius either amiable in itself, or useful to society!" (*RR* 2.937; my italics).[15]

Whereas Scott offers medieval chivalry as the ethico-moral justification for one's subjection to the nation's "bands of fealty," Byron's satirical archaeology uncovers those bands of fealty as mere fictions of power, subject to change and eventual subversion.[16] It was precisely this unveiling of various ontologies and theologies—Patriotism, Statehood, Church, Monarchy, Law—as ideological, which is to say *per*formed on the social stage rather than *pre*formed in some imagined and transcendental *logos*, that critics such as Jeffrey found most disturbing in Byron's poetry. George Ellis in an 1812 review of *Childe Harold* in the *Quarterly*, for example, decries in similar terms the antiwar sentiment of the poetry, particularly the lines attacking the ideology of honor and military fame (*Childe Harold* 1.450–55). As Ellis cannily retorts, "These joys of triumph, it may be said, are mere illusions; but *for the sake of such illusions is life chiefly worth having*" (*RR* 5.1992; my italics). The remark anticipated one of the most common attacks of the criticism directed at Byron between 1816 and 1824. As a reviewer in the *Gentleman's Magazine* asked in December 1822, "Has not Lord Byron, oftentimes, employed pleasantry and sarcasm to the confusion of what is just, honourable, and virtuous, and to incalcate [*sic*], in its tendency, open and unblushing vice, and the neutralization of those compacts which materially form the basis of universal society?" (Lohmar 56).

By forcing the reader to question "the reality of virtue," Byron provided a position from which people from different classes could question the values propagated by a state hegemony that tried to define virtue for "*universal* society." I do not mean to deny that Byron was in a conflicted position and that he found himself in such a position largely due to his class allegiances; on the contrary, that is precisely my point: Byron was guided by a larger principle of justice, one that often led him to act against the best interests of his class and against the prejudices of his own well-documented class snobbery.[17] My interest here, however, is not to reconstruct Byron's "actual" radical tendencies. Regardless of Byron's personal beliefs, which are notoriously difficult to pin down, his poetry, through its dissemination to increasingly diversified levels of the population, contained the potential for revolutionary effects. His major tool for achieving such effects was a defamiliarization of the present that broke down the temporal and spatial proscriptions of traditional comedy and romance. Through such disjunctions, Byron uncovered the performative, and therefore contingent, nature of all ideologies, the "monstrous mummeries" of convention, thus countering the ideological fetishism of Scott.

Figure 3.1.

THE SATANIC HERO

One indication of the potential threat in Byron's reworking of both comedy and romance is the very rhetoric used by critics to characterize Byron's relationship to the society around him. Of particular interest is the notion of the melancholic man of genius that was often applied to Byron in the period. As we have seen in the two previous chapters, the category of genius was a fraught one in the Romantic period, one that was both lauded and feared. Like Jeffrey, critics commonly contrasted Scott's healthy form of genius to Byron's in an effort to argue that the man of genius could still be domesticated, healthy, and useful to society under the right conditions and the right bodily constitution. Byron's version of genius and melancholia, by contrast, were often associated with Milton's heroic Satan. Such a characterization represented Byron as awe-inspiring but also dangerous and, ultimately, immoral. Jeffrey, in his review of *Childe Harold* III, for example, comments on the fact that Byron "delights too exclusively in the delineation of a certain morbid exaltation of character and of feeling," characterizing Byron, in the same sentence, as "a sort of demoniacal sublimity" with "traits of the ruined Archangel" (*RR* 2.865). Jeffrey thus re-uses the Satanic label that he conferred on Byron back in his 1812 review of *Childe Harold* I–II: "[T]he mind of the noble author has been so far tinged by his strong conception of this Satanic personage [Milton's Satan], that the sentiments and reflections which he delivers in his own name, have all received a shade of the same gloomy and misanthropic colouring which invests those of his imaginary hero" (*RR* 2.837). In his review of *Childe Harold* III, Jeffrey picks up the label once again, this time in preparation for a discussion of the long tradition of the melancholic great man, which Jeffrey thus expressly connects to the Satanic hero. Jeffrey in fact questions that tradition in the article but, at the same time, acknowledges that it is perhaps most applicable to the poet, "confessedly the most irritable and fantastic of all men of genius" (*RR* 2.876). Through such rhetorical maneuvers, Jeffrey aligned the melancholia of genius with both Byron and the position of the Satanic rebel.

In the Victorian period, this alignment would become stereotype, as in Doré's well-known representation of Milton's Lucifer, where Satan is made to appear in the traditional pose of the melancholic: solitary, brooding, and perversely separated from the properly heterosexual domestic scene in the background. The figure of Satan was so intimately connected with Byron's melancholia after the Romantic period that, when he turned to this illustration, Doré was in fact borrowing the engraving he had earlier done for Byron's *Deformed Transformed* (Fig. 3.1).[18] The scene has Arnold, the deformed character through which Byron figured his own lameness, addressing Satan, who has just appeared out of a cloud: "I said not/ You *were* the demon, but that your approach/ Was like one" (1.1.93–95). By rewriting the lines in the image's caption as if they were spoken by Satan himself to the deformed analog for Byron ("I did not say that you are the demon but that your *aspect* resembles his"), Doré was in 1853 merely commenting upon a common nineteenth-century reading of Byron's deformity as proof of his Satanic nature. The scene, like the illustration, was thus made over as mirror reflection. (We should remember that in the *Deformed Transformed* the mirror relationship is underlined by the fact that Satan takes over Arnold's discarded body after Byron's analog agrees to transfer his identity into the body of Achilles.) With *Paradise Lost*, when Doré returned to this representation, the gaze is instead directed outward to the reader as a challenge posed in language that raises the question of justice: "O Earth, how like to Heaven, if not preferred/ More justly" (9.99–100). The danger represented in this later image is that the reader will follow Byron's lead and identify himself with Satan against the Law of the Father, thus in subversion of the "normal" process of subjectification. The image and Satanic gaze in the *Paradise Lost* engraving ask us to choose between two naked male figures: do we identify with Adam, in the process of instructing Eve how to be a proper female subject, or do we identify with Satan's perverse rejection of such subjectification (and subjection)?

This Victorian representation of the Satanic grew out of the Romantic reinterpretation of Milton's Satan as the true hero of the tale. And that Satanic hero was for the age most fully embodied in not only Byron's characters but also Byron's very self. The Satanic label at once acknowledged Byron's position as a revolutionary and condemned his ideals as both unwholesome and hopeless. Although we can already look ahead to the next chapter and see how easy it would be for critics to pathologize this characterization of the melancholic revolutionary, much of the criticism of Byron during the teens and twenties worried about Byron's subversive potential rather than his bodily deformities or sexual perversities. The fear, in other words, was that Byron could effectuate a real revolution through his unveiling of the performative, ideological nature of social conventions. The Satanic label is a telling one because it underlined the seriousness of the threat Byron was seen to pose to contemporary society (i.e., Cromwell-inspired revolutionary hero) even as it prepared the way for the successful dismissal of Byron as "a heretic and immoral too," as Stephen Dedalus's friends so aptly put it.

Between the English years of radical foment, 1816–20, and continuing through to Byron's death in 1824, a number of critics picked up the Satanic label to characterize Byron's melancholic position as a particularly dangerous one.[19] For a time, that is, Byron was represented not as the sickly and perverse melancholic but, rather, as the subversive and potent rebel directing mobs of radicals against the status quo. What was underlined in these attacks was precisely the power of Byron's genius, which, as Jeffrey puts it, is able to "oppress the spirits of ordinary mortals with too deep an impression of awe and repulsion" (*RR* 2.865). A good example of this tendency to align Byron and his satires with the Satanic rebel is a pamphlet from 1820 entitled *The Radical Triumvirate, or, Infidel Paine, Lord Byron, and Surgeon Lawrence, Colleaguing with the Patriotic Radicals to Emancipate Mankind from All Laws Human and Divine*. Under the pseudonym, Oxonian, the author aligns Byron with the demonic on a number of occasions, arguing that "[h]is verse, like the serpent's eye, allures virtue only to destroy it" (43). Writing of *Don Juan*, he goes so far as to characterize the baleful passions and misanthropy of both Byron's melancholia and his satire as "demoniacal dispositions" (37). The pamphlet concludes by putting Byron at the head of a whole troop of subversive characters in the England of the time, including not only radical booksellers such as William Hone and radical authors such as Paine, but also the very scientists (such as William Lawrence) who would give new fodder for attacks against Byron in the 1820s and '30s:[20]

> [T]he titled Poet takes command of the whole, and with the gems of genius bestudding his sword and glittering on his helm attracts myriads of our youth to his splendid standard, and soothes them into voluptuous security, or rouses them to violence by the voice of the Muses who follow in his train.
>
> What though the mart of Reason, *alias* Treason, in Fleet-Street, be closed, there are other marts, almost as pestiferous whence, [*sic*] issue publications fearlessly derisive of the Government and the Priesthood; formed to bring religion and rule, law and order, into contempt. A shilling pamphlet, fraught with rhymes to excite a sneer and provoke a laugh, with prints to hold up the authorities of the land

> to public ridicule; may wonderfully though silently undermine the principles of the subject, and effect as much as the combined efforts of the more noisy Revolutionists, who collect assemblies and enflame them to insurrection. (47)

And if there is any question about the biblical overtones of the passage, the author goes on to imagine the final conflict as akin to apocalypse: "The weapons of this great battle of God are already forging—the crisis is hastening when, perhaps, the most enlightened nations of the earth shall divide on this great question, and come to the predicted battle of God at Armageddon" (48).

Expressly "colleaguing" Byron with the French Revolutionists, the author also aligns Byron's poetry specifically with the dissemination of his ideas to the lower classes and with such radical publishers as Hone, whose poetic satire, *The House That Jack Built* (1819), caused such an uproar—and real fear—among the politicians of the age. Indeed, by placing Byron at the command of the train of revolutionaries threatening to "burst forth, like a flame and consume us when too late to be quenched, in one blaze of ruinous rebellion" (49), Oxonian makes the same rhetorical maneuver of the counterrevolutionary pamphlet that—also in 1820—came out precisely to counter Hone's publication. Entitled *The Dorchester Guide, or, the House That Jack Built*, the work concludes by placing Byron not at the head but the rear, in this case, of a "reprobate pack/ Who Religion, morality, Probity, lack" (7). These include Orator Hunt, Major Cartwright, Hone and, finally, Byron himself:

> And this is the devil, to bring up the rear,
> By mischief disguised in the dress of a Peer.—
> Pursue the old method, you'll find out the cheat,
> And the Imp stand confessed, if you look at his feet.
> Distortion of Nature's the taste of the age.—
> Make a Story obscene,—'twill be read ev'ry page.
> His verses so sweet and harmonious appear,
> The mind is corrupted while tickling the ear. (31)[21]

While focusing attention on Byron's *bodily* distortion of nature and his corrupting influence on his readers' sanity, the author at the same time underlines the revolutionary force of Byron's poetry by putting him in the company of the most radical figures of the age. In fact, Oxonian was merely repeating Hone's own 1819 *Don Juan, Canto the Third*, in which Hone imagines Don Juan setting up a radical print shop in England to publish "a paper called **The Devilled Biscuit**" (13).

John Stacy, in *A Critique on the Genius and Writings of Lord Byron*, yet again in 1820 made the connection between the radical power of Byron's poetics and his Satanic as well as melancholic genius. Accusing Byron of a "misanthropy run mad," of trying "to make the world believe he is miserable, and to persuade it to be as miserable as himself" (30), the author writes: "I grant him genius . . . , an eloquence of poetry that might draw after it the third part of heaven's host were they yet untempted—an imperial command of the whole region of poetry" (12). Characterizing Byron's many generic forms as a "Satanic host" (12), he imagines Byron presiding "as the master demon—the god of hell—in all the dazzling glory of omnipotent depravity" (11), threatening to "shake the world from its place" through "the dissolution of the moral universe" (12).

When in 1821 Southey attacked Byron and his "Satanic school" in a *Vision of Judgement*, then, he was following a common rhetorical maneuver of the previous year, one that we can trace back to Jeffrey's review of 1812. What is interesting about Southey's take on the Satanic trope is that he counters the revolutionary overtones of the rhetoric by turning Satanic hero into patient zero. Southey writes that the "Satanic school" is made up of "[m]en of diseased hearts and depraved imaginations" who are driven by "a Satanic spirit of pride and audacious impiety, which still betrays the wretched feeling of hopelessness wherewith it is allied" (7). Although he does warn of "the destruction of governments" caused "by poisoning the waters of literature," Southey in 1821 is already moving toward the sort of medicalization of Satanic and melancholic genius (those "diseased hearts") explored in the next chapter. As he goes on,

> Let rulers of the state look to this, in time! But, to use the words of South, if "our physicians think the best way of *curing* a disease is to *pamper* it, . . . the Lord in mercy prepare the kingdom to suffer, what He by miracle only can prevent!" (7)

Even while he sounds the alarm for "rulers of the state," Southey is already superimposing a medical terminology onto the theological rhetoric, accusing the Satanic school of laboring "to make others as miserable as themselves, by infecting them with a moral virus that eats into the soul!" (7). As we will see, such a rhetorical maneuver would become an ever more common one, particularly after the premature death of Byron in 1824.[22]

Even in the teens and twenties, one can find the rhetoric of Satanic power and rebellion competing with a rhetoric of perversity, pathology, and emasculation in the characterization of Byron. Scott himself is a good example of this rhetorical dialectic. On the one hand, he borrowed the trope of quasi-demoniacal sublimity when describing Byron's genius in the eulogy for the poet that he published in the *Edinburgh Weekly Journal*. Scott there describes his "rival . . . in the art of attracting popularity" (*Poetical* 230) as "[t]hat mighty genius, which walked among men as something superior to ordinary mortality, and whose powers we beheld with wonder and something approaching to terror" (P. H. Scott 62). Scott betrays here, despite the documented admiration he had for Byron, the fears about the dangers of reading represented in his own early works.[23] Though he admired the wonder of Byron, he ultimately felt the need to pathologize the character of "genius" represented by Byron, even denying himself the label of genius, as we saw in chapter 2, in order to escape the terror increasingly instilled by the figure of genius in the medical tracts of the period.

At other times, however, Scott sought to deny the frightening elements in Byron's poetry by aligning Byron with dandifying pusillanimity rather than terrifying sublimity. Indeed, one could argue that Scott thus consistently refused to read the radical potential of Byron's works, arguing instead that Byron's liberalism had no real conviction due to his aristocratic upbringing.[24] As he states in his 1816 unsigned review of *Childe Harold* III, "We would willingly avoid mention of the political opinions hinted at by Childe Harold, and more distinctly expressed in other poems of Lord Byron—; the more willingly, as we strongly suspect that these effusions are rather the sport of whim and singularity, or at best the suggestion of sudden starts of feeling and passion, than the expressions of any serious or fixed opinion" (*RR* 5.2039). In such statements, the subversive elements of Byron's poetry are recast as but the momentary transports of an ephemeral passion, a critical move that would become increasingly common over the course of the nineteenth century. When Scott reviewed *Childe Harold* IV in 1818, he tried to relegate politics to Hobhouse's politicized endnotes to Byron and, even then, could not help but voice his disbelief:

> [T]he frenzy which makes individuals of birth and education hold a language as if they could be willing to risk the destruction of their native country, and all the horrors of a civil war, is not so easily accounted for. To believe that these persons would accelerate a desolation in which they themselves directly, or through their nearest and dearest connections, must widely share, merely to remove an obnoxious minister, would be to form a hasty and perhaps a false judgment of them. The truth seems to be, that the English, even those from whom better things might be expected, are born to be the dupes of jugglers and mountebanks in all professions. (*RR* 5.2056)

In this way, Scott was able to rationalize a friendship with a man whose works seemed to run counter to his most cherished beliefs, painting Byron as but a dupe, led astray, indeed, by the sorts of characters ("jugglers and mountebanks") that one would more likely find in the ideologically unthreatening space of a carnival or local fair. The desire, in short, was to align Byron precisely with those rash and gay voluptuaries that Jeffrey identified as far *less* dangerous to society and the status quo.

And yet, through the height of radical unrest, from about 1816 to the Peterloo massacre of August 1819 and its immediate aftermath in 1819 and 1820, such efforts to dismiss Byron competed with a real fear about his radical force. John Wilson Croker, for example, even as he sought to read Byron's apparent radicalism as but whim or dupery, could not help but hear rumors of a potential connection to real insurrection at home. As he wrote on March 26, 1820, in a letter to John Murray,

> In politics, he cannot be what he appears, or rather what Messrs Hobhouse and Leigh Hunt wish to make him appear. A man of his birth, a man of his taste, a man of his talents, a man of his habits, can have nothing in common with such miserable creatures as we now call *Radicals*. . . . And yet it was only yesterday at dinner that somebody said that he had read or seen a letter of Lord Byron's to somebody, saying that if the Radicals only made a little progress and showed some real force, he would hasten over to get on horseback to head them. This is evidently either a gross lie altogether, or a grosser misconstruction of some epistolary pleasantry. . . . Yet see how a bad name is given. We were twelve at dinner, all (except myself) people of note, and yet (except Walter Scott and myself again) every human being will repeat the story to twelve others—and so on. (*BC* 194)

Even while acknowledging the radical potential of Byron ("he cannot be what he *appears*"), Croker thus insists on a misprision in reading to exculpate Byron from the charge of misprision of treason, and yet the charge of treason was one that Croker and Scott himself could not help but hear whispered around them throughout the year of 1820.[25]

BYRON AND THE CULTURE OF THE TEXT

To pin Byron down to his class ideology or to characterize his poetry as nothing but entertaining whimsy were two ways for critics to dismiss the threatening aspects of his poetry and thus to proscribe Byron's rampant satire of contemporary laws and conventions. Of particular interest to this study are not Byron's actual class allegiances, which are difficult to determine definitively, but, rather, the ways readers from different classes imposed a particular, ideological vision onto Byron's romances, sometimes through an acknowledgment of their radical potential, sometimes through a conscious refutation of disturbing aspects in the poetry.

The problem with much of the criticism directed at Byron both in the nineteenth and twentieth centuries, it seems to me, is the desire to pin him down to a particular class. Indeed, I would question the very idea of class that predominates in these critical renderings. As more and more scholars have done, I wish to counter the tendency to view, for example, the rise of the middle classes as a smooth ascendance to the throne of nineteenth-century hegemony. The differences between Scott and Byron help point to the problems inherent in reducing social antagonisms to class allegiances. Scott's desire to establish himself within the aristocracy is exemplary less of an upper-class ethos than of a continuing desire on the part of the nineteenth-century middle class to achieve the legitimation and cachet of the higher orders. Indeed, as Martin Wiener has argued, it is the persistence of this nostalgic affirmation of the aristocracy that both allowed the upper classes to continue to wield power over the course of the nineteenth century and arguably led to the decline of industrial expansion in Britain by the end of that period. It is also the case that, though Scott and Byron ostensibly spoke from a position of "class," they spoke at cross-purposes because of an antagonism within the very class of the aristocracy: *Sir* Walter Scott wished to join the gentry, a desire that was exemplified by the construction of his estate at Abbotsford, whereas *Lord* Byron belonged to the peerage, a fact exemplified by his willingness to *sell* his estates in order to maintain a decidedly unbourgeois lifestyle of excess. A similar antagonism existed within the working classes between artisans and the proletariat.[26] What we begin to see, then, following Ernesto Laclau and Chantal Mouffe is a plurality of political and social spaces or "nodal points" that do not refer to any ultimate unitarian basis such as class but that employ the "articulatory discourse" of medievalism in antagonistic ways. The radical power of Byron's work is its ability to bring together individuals from disparate social groups in a shared opposition to relations of oppression.

We cannot, however, begin to determine the ideological effect of Byron's idiosyncratic version of the romance without considering such issues as reception history, publication history, even market accessibility. We must, for example, ask whether Byron's work was even available to a radical readership, given the market dynamics explored in chapter 2. After all, Byron's romances, like Scott's, were at first offered up as expensive commodities in the Romantic period and marketed to the upper classes, thus putting them out of the reach of most any other class *but* the aristocracy. Indeed, his poetry contributed to the inflation in the price of books that I outlined in the previous chapter. As William St. Clair explains, this meant that "[w]hen the Duchess of Devonshire wrote that *Childe Harold* was 'on every table', she meant on about twelve and a half per cent of the tables of the few thousand families who could afford thirty shillings or fifty shillings from their weekly budget" (6). We should remember that the first edition of *Childe Harold* that made Byron so famous sold out at only five hundred copies and cost 30s, a price that would jump to 50s if we account for the subsequent binding, which was considered *de rigueur*.[27] Even the poems' advertisement, which appeared five days before the actual appearance of the poem, underscored the luxury of the edition: "Lord Byron's new Poem.—In a few days will be published, handsomely printed in Quarto."[28]

Reviewers commonly mentioned this poetry inflation in the years that followed. As one review of Byron's pseudonymously published *Waltz* exclaimed in April 1813, "A decently exorbitant price for a Poem of about 240 lines! But, thank Heaven! Poetry is becoming a lucrative trade, and by and by we may all thrive and live genteelly" (*RR* 5.2123). The *Satirist* made a similar comment about the *Giaour* only a few months later in July:

> The noble lord appears to have an aristocratic solicitude to be read only by the opulent. Four shillings and sixpence for forty-one octavo pages of poetry! and those pages very happily answering to Mr. Sheridan's image of a rivulet of text flowing through a meadow of margin. My good Lord Byron, while you are revelling in all the sensual and intellectual luxury which the successful sale of Newstead Abbey has procured for you, you little think of the privations to which you have subjected us, unfortunate Reviewers; compelled as we have been to subsist for a week and a half on our usual allowance of "broth and bullock's liver," in order to enable us to purchase your lordship's expensive publication.
>
> "How little do you landsmen know
> Of what we sailors feel!" (*RR* 5.2134)

Aligning the new expense of poetry with the "genteel class of landsmen," which is to say the aristocracy, the magazine also revealed the contradictions of this situation since literature was, after all, now a "trade." By making mention of the sale of Newstead Abbey (also mentioned in an earlier review of *Childe Harold's Pilgrimage* [*RR* 5.2122]), the magazine at once underlined Byron's class and the fact that he was, in actuality, no longer an English landsman but both functionally and literally a tradesman.[29]

Byron was himself quite conscious and even resentful of the high price Murray was demanding for his works and also of the luxury market that drove the demand for beautiful editions of poetry during his time period. As he wrote to Hobhouse in 1810, with tongue firmly in cheek,

> Odious! In boards, twould any Bard provoke,
> (Were the last words that dying Byron spoke)
> No let some charming cuts and frontispiece
> Adorn my volume, and the sale increase,
> One would not be unpublished when one's dead
> And, Hobhouse, let my works be found in *Red*. (*Letters* 2.15)

Byron played both sides of the argument at this point, making fun of the poetry market while allowing Murray to benefit from the inflation, since he virtually gave away control over both the printing and copyright of his writing early in his career. However, Byron became increasingly hostile about the implications of the Romantic poetry boom. As he remarks in an anonymously published periodical review from 1812,

> The "mob of gentlemen who write with ease" has indeed of late years (like other mobs) become so importunate, as to threaten an alarming rivalry to the regular body of writers who are not fortunate enough to be either easy or genteel. Hence the jaundiced eye with

> which the real author regards the red Morocco binding of the presumptuous "*Littérateur*;" we say, *the binding*, for into the book itself he cannot condescend to look, at least not beyond the frontispiece. (*Prose* 10)

On July 1, 1813, Byron in fact responded to the review in the *Satirist* quoted earlier, in which the reviewer attacked the extravagant price of the *Giaour*. Byron writes to John Murray:

> There is a critique in the *Satirist*, which I have read,—fairly written, and, though *vituperative*, very fair in judgment. One part belongs to you, viz., the 4s. and 6d. charge; it is unconscionable, but you have no conscience. (*Letters* 11.228)

In 1815, Byron went so far as to acknowledge a certain advantage in the many piracies of his work. It was in that year that George Ticknor, an American visitor, presented him with an American pirated edition of his poetry. As Ticknor later wrote, Byron "expressed his satisfaction at seeing [his work] in a small form because in that way, he said, nobody would be prevented from purchasing it" (St. Clair 15).[30] Indeed, Byron even tried to convince Murray to imitate the pirated editions and, thus, to out-pirate the pirates.[31]

By the time Byron published *Don Juan*, England saw in that text's successive editions, and in part due to Byron's instigations, a drop in price from twelve shillings to five shillings and then, after Byron's switch from John Murray to John Hunt, to one shilling.[32] This so-called common edition and the many pirated editions of his other works were what would establish Byron's reputation as a radical among a new group of readers, for, as St. Clair explains, "After 1822 *Don Juan* was sold in a different class of bookshops, not the elegant premises at 50 Albemarle Street but centres of the radical culture which were regularly raided and their owners fined and imprisoned" (18). Another important date one might mention is 1816, which is the year that saw not only the shift in public opinion about Byron because of his separation from his wife but also the publication of William Hone's one-shilling volume of *Poems on his Domestic Circumstances by Lord Byron*, which, despite the title, was composed of poems that "are not domestic but political," marking "Byron's sympathy with Napoleon against the reactionary monarchies that had defeated him," as Manning explains (*Reading* 217). This edition was followed the next year by Hone's *Lord Byron's Corsair*. As Manning points out, "Hone's proud advertisement of his address" in this edition "attests the co-opting of Byron . . . by the radical cause: an adaptation of *The Corsair* emanating from the *Reformists' Register* office stands in quite another light than did the original, issued by the Tory John Murray from Albemarle Street" (*Reading* 223). The four-pence price, less than a sixteenth the cost of Murray's 5s.6*d*. edition of the time, also "brought Byron, or at least [Hone's] version of Byron, to this working-class but literate public" (*Reading* 223).

It was only with the mass circulation of Byron's texts that the revolutionary fervor of his work could be said to catch up with the radical sectors of the population, which explains why *The Radical Triumvirate*, *The Dorchester Guide*, and *A Critique on the Genius and Writings of Lord Byron* identified Byron's association with radical publishers as particularly distressing. Indeed, in the next couple of decades, leaders of both the Reform and the Chartist movements could be found reading Byron's works and "even [wearing] open-necked shirts *à la Byron*" (St. Clair 23).[33] Pirated duodecimo editions of Byron's works, distributed by working-class publishers, were so successful in disseminating Byron's poetry in the teens and twenties that Lockhart as "John Bull" characterized the dissemination of Byron's *Don Juan* as a struggle between what the previous chapter termed the Culture of the Text and the Cult of the Book: "pirated duodecimo competing it all over the island with furtive quarto" (*BC* 184).[34] Because of such rampant dissemination, even Friedrich Engels was led famously to remark in 1845 that "it is the workers who are most familiar with the poetry of Shelley and Byron" (273).[35]

One might stop here and argue, as, for example, Peter Manning has expertly done, that "the shadow double of the splendid Byronic hero is the alienated reader of the mass market" ("Childe" 186) or that Byron thus subscribed to a general commodification of reality.[36] After all, the commodity form appears to resemble the Culture of the Text described in chapter 2.[37] It abstracts itself from the materiality of the object to be exchanged in order to set up a system of equivalences that then makes possible easy circulation within an economy. The actual labor of the worker that produces the object and any exploitative inequalities in the system of production are forgotten in the abstracting process, which also reduces the worker to his now-exchangeable labor-power. The commodity also resembles writing, for it can be exchanged (and thus exist) because of notations on pieces of paper—money. The culture of the text similarly seeks to abstract itself from the materiality of the book in order to lubricate the exchange of textual goods. In so doing, the work of the author—not to mention that of the printing-house compositor—is devalued and reduced to the exchangeable abstraction of labor-power. Writers thus become subservient to the fetishizing tendencies of the market or, as Marx puts it, the very movement of laborers "within society has for them the form of a movement made by things, and these things, far from being under their control, in fact control them" (167–68).

I believe, however, that the power of Byron's text does not stop at the level of the commodity exchange, for it represents a critique of both sides of the Romantic divide, aristocratic and capitalist alike. In the end, I question the tendency of critics to dismiss Byron, or, for that matter, nineteenth-century poets generally, as ineffectual in their critique of the market, even as I seek to illustrate by what strategies readers undercut the potential radicalism of Byron's romance form.[38] Kurt Heinzelman, in a superb reading of Byron's poetry, for example, concludes that Byron "has shown himself able to understand the amassing irony of such vulnerability [to the commoditization of his labor] but without being able to do anything about it" ("Byron's Poetry" 385); to reach such a conclusion, however, Heinzelman seems to accept that a poem can do nothing more than be reduced to a commodity the moment it exits the private act of composition and enters into a system of production and exchange. To an extent, that is, it is Heinzelman and not Byron who becomes vulnerable to commodification's colonization of all human endeavor by not acknowledging that an alternative might exist in the very act of dissemination.[39] Heinzelman argues, for example, that Byron's "irony" in *Don Juan* is merely "deflationary and that poems on paper are not likely to be worth any more than deflated paper money" ("Byron's Poetry" 384). I would argue, on the contrary, that one must distinguish between the sort of satire that seeks only to entertain (and thus subscribes to a form of simple consumption) and what I have termed, following Eco, a cold carnival that unveils for the reader the inconsistencies of the economic system, that unveils for us a law we no longer have reason to obey. Byron seeks to inspire not only a *reaction* but also some just *action* on the part of the reader—and such an action need not be interpreted as merely a *transaction*. Once Byron's work participated in the disseminations of a mass market and was able to access a new category of reader, the radical elements of his new vision for the romance suddenly opened up the potential for subversive effects.

THE GIFT OF THE POEM

One can, in fact, find in Byron's poetry a critique of economy's fantasy of perfect circulation and colonization, one that is connected to Byron's superposition of romance temporality onto his satirical archaeology of the present. Byron achieves this effect in large part because of his idiosyncratic reworking of the romance form in *Childe Harold* and *Don Juan*. Rather than have his protagonists believe in the "monstrous mummeries of the middle ages," Byron instead offers up to the public the figure of the *flâneur ennuyé*, who must then walk through a world that still believes—in chastity, pure love, glory, honor, chivalry, empire, and the legitimation of the king, in short all the ideals formerly applied to the romance form. *Don Juan*, in this sense, is but an extension of *Childe Harold*. After all, in *Don Juan* we are still within the general parameters of the romance—from pastoral (Haidee) to oriental (Gulbeyaz) to heroic (the siege of Ismael) to courtly (Catherine) to gothic (Fitz-Fulke!) romance. In short, Byron chose to work in the same romance tradition explored by Cervantes through his own Don, Quixote. The difference is that, whereas Quixote is a figure that continues to believe in his impossible ideals before a world of skeptics, Don Juan quickly loses his idealism after the Haidee episode and then allows us to see that it is the rest of world that is, in fact, made up of Quixotes. By thus overturning the very structure of romance in both *Childe Harold* and *Don Juan*, Byron opens up the form to a radical deconstruction of his period's most cherished laws and beliefs, now uncovered as but illusions and mummeries. Not only the fetish of the Cult of the Book but also the religion of God's very Book of the World are thus reduced to nothing but the performative fictions of a general textuality: "The universe is a kind of book of which you have read but one page when you have seen only your own country. I have leafed through a sufficient number to have found them equally bad" (*Byron* 17; McGann's translation).

And yet, even as Byron embraced the leveling of a proto-deconstructive textualization of reality (*il n'y a pas de hors-texte*), which is intimately connected to his rejection of medievalist aura and the Cult of the Book, Byron resisted the reduction of his text into either bourgeois commodity or the hopelessness of extreme skepticism.[40] Byron attempted, that is, to move away from "Byron" as toothless commodity and devote himself to his text's bite rather than its easy consumption. From the beginning, Byron resisted the "calculation" of the market, seeking to benefit from mass dissemination not in terms of economic gain alone but in terms of political effect.

One might recall, for example, that Byron gave away his copyright early in his career, even offering up copyrights to others as gifts.[41] His turn to John Hunt for the publication of *Don Juan* Canto 6 represented a similar giving (up) of his text as something beyond mere exchange, for he refused Hunt's offer of money for the copyright of *Don Juan*.[42] As with the examples of Byron's commitment to radicalism in his life, one could choose such a biographical course in a discussion of the gift; however, we must be conscious of the obvious critique. We must recognize that such generosity was a way for Byron to perform his *noblesse oblige*, that Byron was capable of such magnanimous gestures precisely because of his independent wealth. As Derrida has illustrated in his reading of Marcel Mauss's *The Gift*, it is, on some level, impossible to offer a pure gift without some form of economic or symbolic calculation.[43] Nonetheless, Byron does appear to seek, in his poetry if not his life, an understanding of gift giving that is intimately connected with, on the one hand, a proto-deconstructive textualization of reality that questions all law and, on the other, an undeconstructible sense of justice *beyond* economic calculation and the ontology of presence. As to the former, consider one of the most famous stanza's of Byron's *Childe Harold*:

> Could I embody and unbosom now
> That which is most within me,—could I wreak
> My thoughts upon expression, and thus throw
> Soul, heart, mind, passion, feelings, strong or weak,
> All that I would have sought, and all I seek,
> Bear, know, feel, and yet breathe—into *one* word,
> And that one word were Lightning, I would speak;
> But as it is, I live and die unheard,
> With a most voiceless thought, sheathing it as a sword. (3.905–13)

Denied the very power of speech, denied even the breath of one word, Byron must die unheard, for he must die into his text. After all, what is that voiceless thought if not the written word, which speaks not? And though the thought may be sheathed in the sheets of the printed text, the s/word still threatens. By the fourth canto, Byron does, indeed, imagine himself dying into his text. Remembering England, "The inviolate isle of the sage and free" (4.71), he writes:

> should I lay
> My ashes in soil which is not mine,
> My spirit shall resume it—if we may
> Unbodied choose a sanctuary. I twine
> My hopes of being remembered in my line
> With my land's language. (4.73–78)

Like the "spell of glamour" cast by the wizard Michael Scott, Byron here recasts himself as commodity in a transnational economy that will determine his afterlife and ensure his return to England as spirit. Unlike Walter Scott, however, Byron resists the allegorization of exchange as enchantment or as encryption (either in tome *or* tomb). Instead, he pins his hopes precisely on dissemination and reception:

> If my fame should be, as my fortunes are,
> Of hasty growth and blight, and dull Oblivion bar
> My name from out the temple where the dead
> Are honoured by the nations—let it be. (4.80–83)

The "voiceless thought" of the text, unlike the "glamour might" of the enchanted book, holds no magic except in the exchange.

But this is not to say that the commodified text can carry with it no material effects beyond the materiality of the book itself or beyond the abstraction of the commodity-form. Indeed, by the time Byron switched publishers from the conservative John Murray to the radical John Hunt, he began to underline the radical potential of precisely his voiceless thought—that print could function not as the sheath but the sword itself.[44] As Byron, for example, writes to Thomas Moore (July 1822), discussing the description in *Don Juan* of the bloody siege of Ismael,

> With these things and these fellows, it is necessary, in the present clash of philosophy and tyranny, to throw away the scabbard. I know it is against fearful odds; but the battle must be fought; and it will be eventually for the good of mankind, whatever it may be for the individual who risks himself. (*Letters* 9.191)

Jerome Christensen has argued in relation to *Don Juan* that "[t]he realization of an ethics of strength is a textual phenomenon: a benchmark for Lord Byron was . . . his final break with the covering cherub of his bookseller and his virtuous commitment to continue publication of *Juan* 'though it were to destroy fame and profit at once' ([*Letters*] 10.126)" (215).[45] I agree with Christensen that the realization of an ethics of strength is a textual phenomenon in Byron but I disagree that one must wait until *Don Juan* to see this ethics realized. *Childe Harold* already anticipates and prefigures the radical effects of *Don Juan* through an analogous textualization of culture that underscores the performative nature of all ideologies, of all claims to truth.

Childe Harold, like *Don Juan*, also attempts to go beyond a deconstruction of existing ideologies and posits, like Derrida in his most recent work, an undeconstructible idea of justice that is inextricably tied to the "textual phenomenon" and that escapes economy's fantasy of a perfect circulation without loss and without excess. Just as we must question any gift as potentially reinscribed in a circulation of exchange, so too must we question the inviolability of exchange-value, according to Derrida: "[I]t is likewise inscribed and exceeded by a promise of gift *beyond exchange*" (*Specters* 160; my italics). As Derrida asks, "[I]s not the gift, if there is any, also that which interrupts economy? That which, in suspending economic calculation, no longer gives rise to exchange?" (*Given Time* 7). This idea of the gift, however, must exist outside of time—the "present" (in every sense) that can remember and anticipate (calculate) some return—and outside the subject who calculates (even if only symbolically: for example, "I congratulate myself for having given"). The gift must remain impossible, unknowable, for, "[t]he moment the gift, however generous it be, is infected with the slightest hint of calculation, the moment it takes account of knowledge [*connaissance*] or recognition [*reconnaissance*], it falls within the ambit of an economy" (*Gift of Death* 112). Derrida aligns this idea of the impossible gift with a dissemination that exceeds any economic circulation, any calculated return. He aligns it, that is, with the idea of "dissemination as 'that which doesn't come back to the father' " (*Gift of Death* 96):

> [T]he structure of trace and legacy of this text—as of anything that can be in general—surpasses the phantasm of return and marks the death of the signatory or the non-return of the legacy, the non-benefit, therefore a certain condition of the gift—in the writing itself.
>
> That is why there is a problematic of the gift only on the basis of a consistent problematic of the trace and the text. (*Given Time* 100)

The gift of death, the writing of the voiceless thought, the textuality of the trace: we are seeing the very trajectory that Byron outlines as his own gift of death, not only the giving of his life in a cause (a good) outside the economy of his own home, but also a dying into his text that can return to his home only as the endless surplus of a dissemination outside the calculation of a simple exchange of goods, outside a calculated return (of fame or profit) to Byron.

MELANCHOLIC ROMANCE AND SPECTRAL POETICS

There is one more issue that needs to be addressed before this chapter can complete its argument about Byron's theory of justice in his romance form. I have stated that Byron responded to Scott's romances by uncovering the psychoanalytical logic of the fetish: something that maintains connection to the lost object (the aura-filled totem, the medieval past) while also allowing the object to be lost (which is to say exchanged, in the present). I must be clearer on this point, however; it is in fact not sufficiently disruptive merely to uncover this logic, for, as we saw in the previous chapter, the fetishist knows what he is doing but he does it nonetheless; he knows that the fetish is nothing more than a stand-in for the lost object.[46] Scott too was quite conscious about what he was doing, as we have seen, a fact underlined by the formal self-consciousness of the *Lay*. He knew that the "spell of glamour" that manages to transform the world through the power of writing is nothing more than a fantasy—"All was delusion, nought was truth" (*Lay* 3.110). Indeed, it is not even clear if Scott is putting it over on the reader, for the reader also knows that market exchange does not conform to any magical circulation; the reader knows that the book includes no magic, knows too perhaps that the idea of chivalric virtue is nothing but a fiction—"These joys of triumph, it may be said, are mere illusions; *but for the sake of such illusions is life chiefly worth having*," as George Ellis so aptly put it. The reader knows what s/he is doing, but s/he does it nonetheless.

How, then, do we distinguish this nostalgic fetishism from the structural position of the reader in *Childe Harold* and *Don Juan*, a reader who, as this chapter has argued, is put in the position to acknowledge that the entire social world suffers from quixotic illusions? Perhaps the more helpful distinction is the one that can be made between the nostalgia of mourning and the more insistent memory of the melancholic, a distinction that helps explain the rhetorical alignment of Satanic hero and melancholic genius in the antiradical pamphlets of the period. Scott's romances are clearly working through a process of mourning—for a lost aristocratic, feudal order; for the dissipating aura of the artisan's book; for the now-silenced voice of the last minstrel.[47] Indeed, if there is one thing that ties together the three versions of the fetish explored so far, it is precisely the figure of loss. In each case, a substitute is made to stand in for the lost object of desire: God in the anthropological fetish, the mother's phallus in the psychoanalytical fetish, unalienated labor in the commodity fetish. Responding to the traumas of his own time period—the American, French, and Industrial Revolutions—Scott could be said, then, to be performing a kind of mourning work. Byron responded by refusing to follow through in that work, by refusing to give up the lost object, by insisting on the dead object's endlessly recurring, spectral return, by refusing even work itself, turning instead to indolence and ennui as his principles of justice and morality. The languorous passing of "the sauntering hours" in nature may appear idleness, he writes ("though to the eye/ Idleness it seem"); however, the truth is that it "hath its morality":

> If from society we learn to live,
> 'Tis solitude should teach us how to die;
> It hath no flatterers, vanity can give
> No hollow aid; alone—man with his God must strive:
>
> Or, it may be, with demons, who impair
> The strength of better thoughts, and seek their prey
> In melancholy bosoms, such as were
> Of moody texture from their earliest day,
> And loved to dwell in darkness and dismay,
> Deeming themselves predestin'd to a doom
> Which is not of the pangs that pass away;
> Making the sun like blood, the earth a tomb,
> The tomb a hell, and hell itself a murkier gloom. (4.291–306)

Byron adopts, that is, the very position of the melancholic that, as we have seen, was being increasingly pathologized in his time period. He does so, however, with a strong understanding of that melancholic position's moral imperative—it "hath its morality."[48] To what extent, this book asks, is the pathology of melancholia, like the pathology or panacea of romance, a simple abstraction *created* by the nineteenth century in order to hide or counter melancholia's alternative and altercative political instantiations?

That pathologization continues into the twentieth century, of course. Kay Redfield Jamison goes so far as to diagnose Byron as manic-depressive, even offering the image of Byron facing off a DNA strand on the title page of her book, *Touched with Fire.* Although she does wonder whether "in our rush to diagnose, to heal, and perhaps even to alter [the] genes" of such artists" we do not "compromise the respect we should feel for their differentness, independence, strength of mind, and individuality," she ultimately decides that medication is the best course since to deny the effects of melancholia "risks unnecessary suffering" (259). Following this same ideological maneuver, which is, of course, a legacy of the *nineteenth-century* pathologization of melancholia, E. L. McCallum suggests in her book, *Object Lessons*, that the fetishist has a much better relationship to loss than does the melancholic: "Certainly the fetishist seems to tolerate the loss better by replacing it with a satisfying substitute rather than disconsolately clinging to the lost object by trying to become it" (114). It seems to me, however, that McCallum's conception of fetishism remains disconcertingly aligned with capitalism, a fact underlined by her continual turn to commodified objects, for example: "If a subject invests in a red sports car at midlife, this sports car may become a fetish object that both guarantees the subject's youth and vivacity and acknowledges her aging" (159). "As a fetish object," she explains, "the car could produce, through iteration, a subject with confidence and a stronger sense of self in the face of the threat of loss—of death, obsolescence, or waning prestige" (150). The problem with this formulation is that fetishism also determines the strategies of advertising and marketing, which are all too capable of self-consciousness, including the transgressions, ironies, ambivalences, and contradictions that McCallum associates with fetishism (161). At the end of the book, McCallum argues, by contrast, that fetishism escapes commodification: "We do not impute enough personal, private value to our objects, and instead we cave in to the pressures of capitalist rationality that insists on the impersonality—the exchangeability, the lack of specialness—of the object" (168); capitalism does, however, work through mechanisms of desire, particularly the overvaluation of individual items that, in the exchange, then leads to satisfaction (one of McCallum's privileged terms). McCallum's strategy ultimately resembles Solomon's *Guide to Health* except that, in this formulation, luxury saves rather than kills. In the logic of capitalism as in that of fetishism, subjectivity is determined by the objects one invests (oneself) in. The problem with this model is that one risks imposing as healthy a happy normality that refuses suffering of any sort; one risks positing as normal precisely the happy consumer that McCallum, in her critique of melancholia, offers as the better model for healthy desire.

Instead of corroborating the Victorian pathologization of the melancholic position, I wish here to take seriously Byron's idiosyncratic understanding of the melancholic position and thus to tease out an alternative reading of it. It is, as the above quotation suggests, a position caught between spirits and specters, between Gods and demons. Contemplating the ruins of Venice and imagining the present repeopled with the past, Byron in *Childe Harold,* for example, writes:

> For us repeopled were the solitary shore.
>
> The beings of the mind are not of clay;
> Essentially immortal, they create
> And multiply in us a brighter ray
> And more beloved existence: that which Fate
> Prohibits to dull life, in this our state
> Of mortal bondage, by these spirits supplied
> First exiles, then replaces what we hate;
> Watering the heart whose early flowers have died,
> And with a fresher growth replenishing the void. (4.37–45)

These spirits of the past tell us that our present is, perhaps by fated necessity, "out of joint." The spirits offer the possibility of something better: "they create/ And multiply in us a brighter ray/ And more beloved existence." Despite our perhaps inescapable "state/ Of mortal bondage," such spirits refuse and "[replenish] the void" even though they cannot properly exist in the present as self-presence: "I saw or dreamed of such,—but let them go—/ They came like truth, and disappeared like dreams" (4.55–56), "for waking Reason deems/ Such over-weening phantasies unsound" (4.61–62). Pointing at once to the past and the future, the spirits thus disjoint the present, robbing it of any sense of unquestioned self-presence in the capitalist narrative of progress, in *telos*. We are back to Byron's peculiar inversion of the romance form—an anthropologization of the present that collapses Scott's romance nostalgia by allowing the reader to see the present as itself always already out of joint, filled in fact with the spirits that continually disturb our present "state/ Of mortal bondage."

Such renewing *spirits* in Byron are also intimately connected with those *specters* that disturb the present and haunt the melancholic sensibility:

> But ever and anon of griefs subdued
> There comes a token like a scorpion's sting,
> Scarce seen, but with fresh bitterness imbued;
> And slight withal may be the things which bring
> Back on the heart the weight which it would fling
> Aside for ever: it may be a sound—
> A tone of music,—summer's eve—or spring,
> A flower—the wind—the ocean—which shall wound,
> Striking the electric chain wherewith we are darkly bound;
> And how and why we know not, nor can trace
> Home to its cloud this lightning of the mind,
> But feel the shock renew'd, nor can efface
> The blight and blackening which it leaves behind,
> Which out of things familiar, undesign'd,
> When least we deem of such, calls up to view
> The spectres whom no exorcism can bind,
> The cold—the changed—perchance the dead—anew,
> The mourn'd, the loved, the lost—too many!—yet how few! (4.199–216)

The specters perceived by the melancholic sensibility—those "demons, who . . . / seek their prey/ In melancholy bosoms"—ensure that Spirit never gets reified as the singular manifestation of the ideal in the world—"Nor worth nor beauty dwells from out the mind's/ Ideal shape of such." The specters resist any hierarchized systematization of the spirit in the present, for such a reification can only function by exorcising "The spectres whom no exorcism can bind."

Much in the same way that he reworked Scott's metrical romance, Byron thus reworked the gothic romance, recasting the gothic specter not as that which must be exorcized by the return of law (let us not forget Gilpin Horner) but as that which makes us question the very *presence* of law. As Byron makes clear in his letters and his religious poetry, he believed in a sense of justice that impels action in the present but he found the institutionalization of the idea of justice (in law, for example) as inevitably dangerous. As he states in a letter of 1811, "I am no Platonist, I am nothing at all; but I would sooner be a Paulician, Manichean, Spinozist, Gentile, Pyrrhonian, Zoroastrian, than one of the seventy-two villainous sects who are tearing each other to pieces for the love of the Lord and hatred of each other" (*Letters* 2.89). If we are presented with a messianism in Byron's poetry, it is, indeed, without messiah. "Even gods must yield," Byron states in *Childe Harold*, "religions take their turn" (2.21-23). We are not even offered an ontology, but what Derrida terms a hauntology. As Derrida explains, "Ontology opposes [hauntology] only in a movement of exorcism. Ontology is a conjuration" (*Specters* 161). Such a hauntology is precisely how Byron himself came to understand ontology proper:

> But, *onward!*—it is now the time to act, and what signifies *self*, if a single spark of that which would be worthy of the past can be bequeathed unquenchably to the future? It is not one man, nor a million, but the *spirit* of liberty which must be spread. . . . [W]hatever the sacrifice of individuals, the great cause will gather strength, sweep down what is rugged, and fertilise . . . what is cultivable. And so, the mere selfish calculation ought never to be made on such occasions; and, at present, it shall not be computed by me. I was never a good arithmetician of chances, and shall not commence now. (*Letters* 8.20)

We are again presented with the idea of a gift of death beyond calculation, understood now as that which can be bequeathed from the past to the future, understood, that is, as the "*spirit* of liberty," as a hauntology of the self. One must exercise one's specters not exorcise them, according to Byron, and one must seek never to calculate one's returns, for chance is such that the event—any act, any sacrifice, any gift—must always be uncertain, undecidable. The very desire to realize such an impossible exorcism or such an impossible calculation can only lead to those documents of barbarism that Byron decries as the "one page" of historical tyranny, a tyranny that seems to follow, as if by ineluctable necessity, from the reification in the present of the Spirit of Freedom (*Childe Harold* 4.964–76).[49]

Instead Byron turns to the past and to the future in his critique of the present, and thus approaches Derrida's theorization of justice and of our responsibility to others. Derrida points out that, just as any evocation of spirit (in whatever form—ontology, theology, teleology, etc.) is inevitably haunted by its spectral supplements, so too is any deconstruction overwhelmed and also impelled by a certain undeconstructible idea of justice, by a certain "messianic without messianism" that opens us up to the singular other and that ensures our responsibility to all others, particularly those that are no longer or are not yet here, now in the present. Like Byron, Derrida turns, in this way, to a spectralization that disjoints the present:

> No justice—let us not say no law and once again we are not speaking here of laws—seems possible or thinkable without the principle of some responsibility, beyond all living present, within that which disjoins the living present, before the ghosts of those who are not yet born or who are already dead, be they victims of wars, political or other kinds of violence, nationalist, racist, colonialist, sexist, or other kinds of exterminations, victims of the oppressions of capitalist imperialism or any of the forms of totalitarianism. (*Specters* xix)

Byron too finds himself confronted by "the ghosts of those who are not yet born or who are already dead" and this position impels his own sense of justice. As he states in *Don Juan*, looking forward, in fact, all the way to our own new millennium,

> For I will teach, if possible, the stones
> To rise against Earth's tyrants. Never let it
> Be said that we still truckle unto thrones;—
> But ye—our children's children! Think how we
> Showed *what things were* before the World was free!
> That hour is not for us, but 'tis for you:
> And as, in the great joy of your Millennium,
> You hardly will believe such things were true
> As now occur, I thought that I would pen you'em;
> But may their very memory perish too!—(8.135–36)

Immediately following this proleptic scene, Byron looks backward to those that are already dead; he has Don Juan weep for a Moslem orphan who "was homeless, houseless, helpless," for "Her very place of birth was but a spectre/ Of what it had been," following Alexandr Vasilievitch Suvaroff's attack on Ismael in 1790. Confronted with this specter, which, like the specter of "our children's children," calls to the individual to defend against injustice, Don Juan makes "a vow to shield her, which he kept" (8.141).

Byron invokes the dead in an effort to forge a revolutionary spectropoetics through a refusal to exorcise one's debt to the suffering of others, particularly the suffering of those that have come before and those that are yet to be born.[50] As he puts it in a fragment from the journal he kept at Cephalonia, "The dead have been awakened—shall I sleep?/The World's at war with tyrants—shall I crouch?" (*Letters* 11.29). Byron wakes the dead not to bury them once and for all but to have them speak their injunctions again and again to the present. Between the specter of those who are still to be born and those who have passed, Byron assumes a sense of "responsibility, beyond all living present." This haunted position is also how he comes to understand the very spirit of poetry: "What is Poetry?—The feeling of a Former world and Future" (*Letters* 8.37), or, as he characterizes the purpose of his return to *Childe Harold* in the third canto, "to feel/ We are not what we have been, and to deem/ We are not what we should be" (3.1032–34).

According to Byron, "the palace of the present hour/ Must yield its pomp" to a different kind of "power/ And magic" than the one that Scott keeps entombed/entomed in his metrical romances, for this power asks us not to see the apparitions of "glamour" but see that the "reality of virtue" is itself, in fact, but an apparition, a "false nature" (*Childe Harold* 4.1126):

> Who loves, raves—'tis youth's frenzy—but the cure
> Is bitterer still; as charm by charm unwinds
> Which robed our idols, and we see too sure
> Nor worth nor beauty dwells from out the mind's
> Ideal shape of such; yet still it binds
> The fatal spell, and still it draws us on,
> Reaping the whirlwind from the oft-sown winds;
> The stubborn heart, its alchemy begun,
> Seems ever near the prize,—wealthiest when most undone.
>
> We wither from our youth, we grasp away—
> Sick—sick; unfound the boon—unslaked the thirst,
> Though to the last, in verge of our decay,
> Some phantom lures, such as we sought at first—
> But all too late,—so are we doubly curst.
> Love, fame, ambition, avarice—'tis the same,
> Each idle—and all ill—and none the worst—
> For all are meteors with a different name,
> And Death the sable smoke where vanishes the flame.
> (*Childe Harold* 4.1099–1116)

We are caught, it seems, between a "spirit's feeling" (*Childe Harold* 4.1157) that drives our desire to improve the world and the fact that this spirit can never fully "be" in the present, an inescapable fact that then "phantomizes" all our beliefs as mere fetish objects—"as charm by charm unwinds/ Which robed our idols." Or is it that this "phantom" unveils our desires as a mourning work that seeks to hide from our eyes "the sable smoke where vanishes the flame," i.e., death itself? As Byron puts it when he bids farewell to his Childe Harold, through the "universal pall" of "Destruction's mass" "all things grow phantoms"

(4.1476–80). Rather than seek a magic cure for the ills of the body and the body politic—the fetishizing maneuver we witnessed in Scott—Byron acknowledges that "the cure/ Is bitterer still" and instead accepts the decay of the human condition as the necessary shadow-side of any just relation: "Sick—sick; unfound the boon—unslaked the thirst,/ Though to the last, in verge of our decay,/ Some phantom lures."

Byron would thus have us uncover the performative nature of all identities, personal as well as political ("Nor worth nor beauty dwells from out the mind's/ Ideal shape of such"), even as he performs the Byronism his readers sought in his biography and his self. Numerous critics have made fun of Byron's histrionic gestures in his poetry and his life.[51] I believe, however, that there is, in fact, much method to Byron's supposed madness and melancholia, including a recognition of the performative nature of all convention, a general textualization of culture, an anthropologization of the present, and a general cold-carnival sensibility that questions all law. As Byron puts it, upon his return from an actual Carnival in Venice, "Life becomes for the moment a drama without the fiction" (*Prose* 192–93). Resisting at once the commodification of reality and the fetish-logic of ideological contradiction, not to mention the temporal and spatial parameters of the carnivalesque, Byron underlines instead a performative force of words irreducible to any one class position or to the *déclassé* commodity form. He also resists describing constatively the utopic future that directs him, for the moment this desired future is systematized in the present it is immediately open to abuse, it threatens to become yet another document of barbarism. For this reason, Byron argues that he is "made for opposition," for he recognizes how quickly even revolutionary fervor can abuse and be abused:

> I was born for opposition.
>
> But then 'tis mostly on the weaker side:
> So that I verily believe if they
> Who now are basking in their full-blown pride,
> Were shaken down, and 'dogs had had their day',
> Though at the first I might perchance deride
> Their tumble, I should turn the other way,
> And wax an Ultra-royalist in loyalty,
> Because I hate even democratic royalty. (*Don Juan* 15.22–23)

And yet the hope that the world could be better cannot be eliminated; it must remain as the essence of Byron's oppositional philosophy of justice. It must remain, that is, as a promise, a performative. It must remain as a never-realized specter that obligates, that comes both from the past and the future, from all those who have been and who are yet to be, an undeconstructible emancipatory promise, an idea of justice that must be distinguished from any law.

FOUR

POETRY AND PATHOLOGY

> Would you thank a man for fitting up your study, and adorning it with much that is beautiful; and if, at the same time, he filled it with images and ghosts of the most disgusting and awful description, which were to abide there, and be continually dancing around you all your life? Is he a benefactor to his species, who, here and there, throws out a beautiful thought, or a poetic image, but, as you stoop to pick it up, chains upon you a putrid carcass which you can never throw off? I believe a single page may be selected from Lord Byron's works, which has done more hurt to the mind and the heart of the young than all his writings have ever done good; but he will quickly pass from notice, and is doomed to be exiled from the libraries of all virtuous men. It is a blessing to the world, that what is putrid must soon pass away. The carcass hung in chains will be gazed at for a short time in horror; but men will soon turn their eyes away, and remove even the gallows on which it swung.
>
> —Reverend John Todd, *The Student's Manual*

BYRON USES WHAT POWERS OF ENCHANTMENT HE COMMANDS IN his poetry not to bury the past in the past (the mourning work that in Scott reburies the wizard in his tomb even as it rebinds the wizard's tome against the endless return that is the reading act), but instead uses his enchanter's wand to cast the present as past, thus completely *re*casting the ideological effect of the romance form. As I argued in the previous chapter, Byron wakes the dead not to bury them once and for all through the work of nostalgic mourning but to have them speak their melancholy-producing injunctions again and again to the present. His *Childe Harold* in particular is peopled by those ghosts that haunt the present, peopled, as the Reverend John Todd puts it in his extremely popular *Student's Manual* (1835), by "ghosts of the most disgusting and awful description" that threaten to be "continually dancing around you all your life."[1] Byron offers the reader a "putrid carcass which you can never throw off." He refuses to let the dead lie and thus opens up a crack in the present—the *ubi sunt* of the *hic et nunc*. Is it so surprising that, perhaps as a result, one of the images associated with Byron over the course of the nineteenth century was the undead Vampyre of Polidori's tale, a story first attributed to Byron himself?[2] One might say, in fact, that the nineteenth century responded to the revolutionary potential in Byron's texts by attempting to exorcise Byron's undead spirit—to doom him to exile "from the libraries of all virtuous men"—and to bury once and for all the figure of the revolutionary melancholic he inspired.

To do so, the nineteenth-century critic had to neutralize the radical *potential* of Byron's poetics by reducing the poet, as we will see, to no more than an adolescent sexual perversity. The strategy of subsequent reviewers was double-edged: they acknowledged the radical power of Byron's position but they also undercut that position through the disciplining of the body—hanging the rebel's carcass in chains on the gallows, if necessary. Their response took the form of three interrelated strategies: 1) diagnosing the body of Byron as perverse (effeminate, ill, mad, corrupt, or, as Lady Caroline Lamb put it, "mad, bad, and dangerous to know"); 2) diagnosing the bodily act of writing poetry, particularly Byronic, Romantic poetry, as inherently pathological; 3) diagnosing the body politic as a cohesive social entity that requires the administration of specialists. Through such power of embodiment, reviewers sought to counter the resistance to normative frames in Byron's idiosyncratic reworking of the romance form in *Childe Harold* and his other works. The romance, along with Romantic ideology, was thus also successfully stereotyped for posterity as but an adolescent pursuit that one must grow out of in order to reach healthy and productive adulthood, a characterization that eventually also swallowed up Scott's own romance forms despite his rhetoric of health and archaic purity. Byron represented for nineteenth-century critics the curse to Scott's cure, as I suggested in chapter 2, and as Carlyle facetiously put it before dismissing Scott along with Byron in his "Sir Walter Scott." Romantic subversion was thus recast as somatic perversion.

Of course, to a large extent it was Byron himself who was responsible for his own overthrow, or as he puts it: "I have been cunning in mine overthrow/ The careful pilot of my proper woe" ("Epistle to Augusta" 23–24). As this chapter illustrates, Byron was not only the most popular and visible manifestation of the "perversity of poetry" but he was also one of the main contributors to the myth of the sexualized and pathologized male genius. He thus himself undercut the radicalism in his poetry and set the stage for the Victorian's reception of Romantic poetry as "mental masturbation," to quote Byron's own characterization of the poetry of Keats.

Critics followed not only Byron but also certain aspects of Romantic ideology, especially the valuation of extreme emotion, the poet's self-imposed isolation, and the all-consuming search for an inaccessible sublimity. Aided also by the early deaths of the second-generation Romantics, many critics began to reduce such Romantic commonplaces into an increasingly disseminated cliché: the wasting away of the overwrought lyric poet. Isolated, hyperemotional, unbalanced, this figure appeared to be the opposite of everything the high Victorian novel valued: social stability, bourgeois domesticity, and political economy. Worse, the figure evinced the sorts of symptoms that any physician of the time would consider more commonly indicative of that other solitary fantasizer—the masturbator.[3]

What we witness in the movement from the Romantic into the Victorian period, in other words, is an important turning point in the fate of the nineteenth-century poet: whereas the novel had previously been singled out as dangerous and perverse (a phenomenon that has been much discussed), by 1826, thanks to the growing critical acceptance of historical and domestic novels after Scott and Austen, the rhetoric of pathology became increasingly disentangled from the novel and applied instead to poetry, so that, as Edward Bulwer-Lytton puts it in 1833, "the more than natural distaste for poetry that succeeded the death of Byron . . . increased the appetite for prose fictions" (*England* 2.107), leading directly, according to Bulwer-Lytton, to the fall of poetry and the rise of the novel (*England* 2.107–112). To be more precise, the high domestic and realist novel defined itself against those forms that it figured as its nonetheless constitutive opposites: romance, sensation fiction, the French novel, popular theater, and the Romantic poet.[4] What has still to be properly explored is the role of the lattermost figure in the rise and self-legitimization of not only the novel, but also the middle-class Victorian subject. As I will argue here, there is what we might term a certain patho-*logic* in Victorian culture's pathologizing sexualization of Byron, a logic that speaks to the very formation of bourgeois, capitalist ideology in the period. I wish to understand the relation of the masturbatory to the social much as Eve Sedgwick explores the link between homophobia and society's actual homosocial organization. In fact, as Sedgwick herself has noted in "Jane Austen and the Masturbating Girl," the anti-onanism rhetoric of the nineteenth-century not only predated but also made possible the later patho-logic of homophobia at the turn of the twentieth century.

My argument therefore functions as a complement to Andrew Elfenbein's book, *Romantic Genius: The Prehistory of a Homosexual Role*. Elfenbein examines how the rhetoric applied to the Romantic poet of genius closely resembles the rhetoric also directed at the emergent homosexual in the period. As I will illustrate, the major figure that needs to be more fully examined is that of the masturbator, who was, in fact, much more closely aligned with the figure of the perverse poet. As Elfenbein himself admits, "[M]edical writers from this period were far more worried about masturbation than homosexuality as a danger to masculinity" (65). I would go farther and argue that it was the rhetoric directed at the masturbator that yet more clearly set up the "prehistory of the homosexual role" by establishing a rhethoric of pathology that would, after the Oscar Wilde trials, be redirected to the homosexual. Throughout the period, it was the anti-onanism rhetoric of various medical tracts that helped to establish the figure of the wasting Romantic poet of genius as dangerous, deranged, delinquent, and diseased.

The goal of this chapter is to determine the role Byron had in these developments. The previous chapter purposively concentrated on the philosophy of justice that can be gleaned from Byron's romance form so as to disentangle his revolutionary ideals from a critical tradition that has tended to concentrate not on Byron's corpus but his body—his actual and imagined sexual relationships, travels, mental instability, even eating habits.[5] The fact is, however, that one cannot properly examine the ideological effects of generic change in isolation from a work's reception history. I here turn to that critical tradition in order to make sense of why we now tend to disavow Byron's radicalism and to help explain how it was that the nineteenth century took what were examined in the previous chapter as the radical elements in Byron's poetry—the melancholia, the idiosyncratic reworking of the romance, the critique of capitalist circulation—and successfully characterized those elements as but impotent adolescent perversities. As with Byron's dialectical twin—the healthy romancer, Scott—poetic politics in Byron were met with a medicalizing rhetoric that not only diagnosed the poet's own body (and body of works) but also explained to the nation's social body what kind of poetry (and politics) would do that body good.

PATHOLOGIZING THE MELANCHOLIC GENIUS

For better or worse, and as Marilyn Butler correctly states, "Byron played a larger part than any other single artist in shaping the stereotype soon recognized throughout Europe, the passionate, rebellious Romantic Poet" (2–3). He did so not only through his own work and life but also through the incredibly successful cottage industry he inspired, what Annabella Milbanke—soon to be Lady Byron—dubbed Byromania in 1812.[6] As Bulwer-Lytton put it in 1833, Byron "became the Type, the Ideal of the state of mind he represented," which Bulwer-Lytton calls "this very satiety—this very discontent—this profound and melancholy temperament" (*England* 2.71). In the same year, R. R. Madden characterized Byron as "the very epitome of melancholy" (150). Given the previous chapter's concern with the morality of Byron's melancholia, perhaps we should begin precisely with that melancholy temperament. Indeed, Byron's melancholia underscores just how inextricably intertwined are the two sides of Byron's perceived genius: the hero and the radical on the one hand, the pervert and the madman on the other.[7]

Byron himself had a continuing fascination with the figure of the melancholic, one that he cultivated from a series of sources. He not only admired Tasso but published his own *Lament of Tasso* in 1817. He was a great admirer of Robert Burton's *Anatomy of Melancholy* (*Prose* 6–7); and he also owned John Haslam's 1809 *Observations on Madness and Melancholy* (*Prose* 249), which I discussed in chapter 1. Perhaps his greatest influence, however, was Isaac D'Israeli, whose *Literary Character* did much to disseminate the figure of the perverse poet.[8] Indeed, the interactions between D'Israeli and Byron point to a collaborative formulation of the emergent notion of the melancholic "man of genius" (as distinct from the earlier sense of genius as "characteristic disposition"). We can see the increasing importance of this emergent concept even in D'Israeli's change of title from the earlier *An Essay on the Manners and Genius of the*

Literary Character (1795) to *The Literary Character, Illustrated by the History of Men of Genius* (1818). In between, the phenomenon of Byron had occurred to corroborate D'Israeli's feeling that "[t]he Literary Character has, in the present day, singularly degenerated in the public mind" (*Essay* 34). That statement from the 1795 *Essay* would prove prescient, for, whereas in the early work D'Israeli meant only that literary characters were no longer praised and lauded as they had been in former times, largely due to the proliferation of books in an emergent mass market, over the next two decades D'Israeli would explore the ways that men of genius must pay for their creations due to the physical and mental effects of what he calls "enthusiasm": "Yet what less than enthusiasm is the purchase price of high passion and invention?" (*Literary* 426); without it, "genius will produce nothing but uninteresting works of art" (*Literary* 427).[9] Unfortunately, as he explains, "[g]enius is a dangerous gift of nature," which can lead either to "glory or infamy" (*Literary* 430), for "[t]he imagination of genius is the breath of its life, which breeds its own disease" (*Literary* 430).

D'Israeli's new model for the "man of genius" became Byron himself. Indeed, in his new preface, D'Israeli expressly highlighted the direct influence of Byron on his revisions (in the process underscoring his own influence on Byron):

> During the long interval which has elapsed since the first publication, the little volume was often recalled to my recollection, by several, and by some who have since obtained celebrity; they imagined that their attachment to literary pursuits had been strengthened even by so weak an effort. An extraordinary circumstance has occurred with these opinions;—a copy which has accidentally fallen into my hands, formerly belonged to the great poetical genius of our times; and the singular fact that it was twice read by him in two subsequent years, at Athens, in 1810 and 1811, instantly convinced me that the volume deserved my attention. (*Literary* 405)

He goes on to state that Byron's marginal notes in that copy conveyed "no flattery—but amidst their pungency and sometimes their truth, the circumstance that a man of genius could, and did read, this slight effusion at two different periods of his life, was a sufficient authority, at least for an author, to return it once more to the anvil" (*Literary* 405). What is more, after D'Israeli published—and presented to Byron—his 1822 edition of the *Literary Character*, Byron in a letter to D'Israeli actually offered himself up for analysis as a characteristic example of diseased genius, a fact that D'Israeli made note of in his yet further expanded edition of 1828, where he included Byron's letter in the new preface. As Byron states in that letter of June 10, 1822, "I really cannot know whether I am or am not the Genius you are pleased to call me, but I am very willing to put up with the mistake, if it be one. It is a title dearly enough bought by most men" (*Letters* 9.172). He goes on to offer D'Israeli a perusal of his *Memoir*, which he suggests would add to D'Israeli's "Philosophy of the literary Mind (*if* mine be a literary mind)" (*Letters* 9.172): "I do not know whether you have seen those M.S.S.; but as you are curious in such things as relate to the human mind, I should feel gratified if you had" (*Letters* 9.172). Byron also offers to answer any questions D'Israeli might like to pose him regarding his "literary mind," although his departure for Greece a year later put an end to any further correspondence. By placing this letter in the preface of his 1828 edition of the *Literary Character*, D'Israeli further cemented the link between his own description of literary genius and the character of Byron. Given the remarkable popularity and influence of both this work and D'Israeli's *Curiosities of Literature*, which supports the arguments of *The Literary Character* and with which *The Literary Character* was often bound after 1847, we can here begin to trace the influence of an increasingly visible figure in the nineteenth century, one that was now expressly bound with the figure of Byron: the melancholic poet of genius.[10]

Of course, as I explained in chapter 1, the stereotype of the diseased genius grew out of a long tradition of melancholia, a tradition that aligned greatness in various fields with the melancholic disposition. What happened in the nineteenth century was that melancholia was increasingly associated particularly with the poet, along with other artists, and was also, in contradistinction to the previously *venerated* tradition of the melancholic, fully pathologized. We saw in chapter 1, for example, how Haslam in 1809 tried to separate the scholarly work of the medic from a melancholic temperament that he nonetheless attributed to anyone indulging "in those reveries which keep the imagination on the wing, and imprison the understanding" (220). Although he tried to safeguard his own genius from the charge of disease, Haslam thus fell short of excluding *literary genius* from the melancholic diagnosis, a fact that was quickly picked up by D'Israeli in his own 1812 exploration of the "calamities of authorship":

> There is a case in Mr. Haslam's "Observations on Insanity," who assures us that the patient he describes was insane, which will appear strange to those who have watched more poets than lunatics!
>
> "This patient, when admitted, was very noisy, and importunately talkative—reciting passages from the Greek or Roman poets, or talking of his own literary importance. He became so troublesome to the other madmen, who were sufficiently occupied with their own speculations, that they avoided and excluded him from the common room; so that he was at last reduced to the mortifying situation of being the sole auditor of his own compositions. He conceived himself very nearly related to Anacreon, and possessed of the peculiar vein of that poet."
>
> Such is the very accurate case drawn up by a medical writer. I can conceive nothing in it to warrant the charge of insanity; Mr.

> Haslam, not being a poet, seems to have mistaken the common orgasm of poetry for insanity itself. (*Calamities* 333)

We are thus presented in D'Israeli with a specific equation being suggested between the poet and the madman, one that would become increasingly common over the course of the nineteenth century. Unlike the long-standing tradition claiming "The lunatic, the lover and the poet/ Are of imagination all compact" (Shakespeare, *Midsummer Night's Dream* 5.1.7–8), what we see in the nineteenth-century association of poetry with madness is a move from florid conceit to full-blown concern.[11] Notwithstanding his backhanded defense of the poet here, D'Israeli states that one of the goals of his book is, in fact, to "bring forward an evidence that the immoderate pursuit of poetry, with a very moderate genius, creates a perpetual state of illusion; and pursues grey-headed folly even to the verge of the grave" (*Calamities* 329).

Like Haslam, D'Israeli also separates his own critical work from this new pathologization. He distinguishes the man of letters from both those writers that publish *as a profession* and those authors he deems men of genius and thus beyond the ken of the market.[12] This is a distinction D'Israeli felt obliged to make over the course of revising his *Essay*. In 1795, he still sometimes conflated the man of genius and the man of letters so as to claim for himself the veneration traditionally commanded by the melancholic great man. By 1818, however, D'Israeli made it clear that the man of letters alone tends to be healthy and well balanced. In this way, D'Israeli responded to medical work such as that of Tissot's *An Essay on Diseases Incidental to Literary and Sedentary Persons* (1768), which D'Israeli cites.

D'Israeli, by contrast to Tissot, sought to disassociate the man of letters altogether from both genius and melancholy, thus safeguarding his own critical study from the charge of disease. What is more, he counteracted the pathologization of the scholar by aligning the work of the man of letters with that of the physician, arguing that it was the man of letters' task to diagnose the health of the body politic and of culture at large. Already in the 1795 *Essay*, D'Israeli compares his method to that of the "judicious physician" and states that he will trace "the progress of actual cases, in the operation of actual remedies" (vi–vii). In the 1818 Preface to the *Literary Character*, after mentioning Byron's marginalia, he goes yet farther, while now denying the possibility of "actual remedies" for the diseases of genius:

> It may be thought that men of genius only should write on men of genius; as if it were necessary that the physician should be infected with the disease of his patient. He is only an observer, like Sydenham who confined himself to vigilant observation, and the continued experience of tracing the progress of actual cases (*and in his department, but not in mine*) in the operation of actual remedies. (*Literary* 405; my italics)

D'Israeli presents himself as a man of letters, which he takes pains to distinguish now from the man and, by implication, the disease of genius. Men of letters "are ingenious men, not men of genius" (*Essay* 21), he states, although they serve as guides ("like guides over the Alps, though no travelers themselves" [*Essay* 13]) and, of course, as *physicians* of troubled genius, albeit without any cures: "Were we to erect an asylum for venerable genius, as we do for the brave and the helpless part of our citizens, it might be inscribed a Hospital for Incurables" (*Curiosities* 10). The man of letters is now conceived as the physician of culture, diagnosing two diseased conditions: men of the literary profession and men of literary genius, both of whom suffer equally from all sorts of mental and physical problems, according to D'Israeli. Indeed, the worst possible situation occurs when a man of genius becomes an author by profession, seeking recognition, either monetary or otherwise, on the public stage and the literary market.

Having safeguarded himself from the charge of disease, D'Israeli, in the revisions he effectuated between 1795 and 1818, proceeded to pathologize the literary character ever more fully. Whereas in 1795 D'Israeli mentioned only that enthusiasm "has sometimes arisen into a delirium" (*Essay* 84), by 1818 he greatly expanded this section to suggest that "[i]t is but a step which carries us from the wanderings of fancy into the aberrations of delirium," arguing that "barren will be his imagination, and luckless his fortune, who, claiming the honours of genius, has never been touched by such a temporary delirium" (*Literary* 426). Quoting Byron's *English Bards* in this expanded section (" 'Twas thine own genius gave the fatal blow,/ And helped to plant the wound that laid thee low") and referring to Tissot's work on the diseases of men of letters (*Literary* 426), D'Israeli characterizes men of genius as having "sealed their works with their blood: they have silently borne the pangs of disease; they have barred themselves from the pursuits of fortune; they have torn themselves away from all they loved in life, patiently suffering these self-denials, to escape from those interruptions and impediments to their studies" (*Literary* 427).[13] The symptoms are various—"now an intermittent fever, now a silent delirium, an hysterical affection, and now a horrid hypochondriasm" (*Literary* 430)—although the cure, "Plato's reason" (*Literary* 430), is clear. The problem is that "men of genius . . . rarely pass through this slow curative method" and instead "remain with all their tortured and torturing passions about them, often self-disgusted, self-humiliated" (*Literary* 430).

And the poet by this point was already beginning to be seen as a principal example of the man of genius affected adversely by laboring for profit and recognition in a mass market that refused to acknowledge him. As D'Israeli states in his *Calamities of Authorship* (1812), "*None but a poet* can conceive, for *none but a poet* can experience, the secret wounds inflicted on a mind of romantic fancy and tenderness of emotion, which has staked its happiness on its imagination; for such[,] neglect is felt as ordinary men would feel the sensation of being let down into a sepulchre, and buried alive"

(*Calamities* 276–77; my italics). D'Israeli concludes that, for this reason, "[t]here is no greater enemy to domestic quiet than a confirmed versifier" (*Calamities* 324). By associating Byron with melancholic genius in the various prefaces to the *Literary Character*, D'Israeli helped to instantiate an association of Byron, in particular, with perverted poetic genius, an association that would persist for two centuries, from Madden's 1833 *The Infirmities of Genius*, which devotes a full one-sixth of its two volumes to Byron (105–202), diagnosing him as an epileptic, to Kay Redfield Jamison's 1993 *Touched with Fire*, which diagnoses Byron as manic-depressive (chapter 5).

BYRON AND THE MEDICALIZATION OF THE POETIC ACT

What is so fascinating about the case of Byron is that he not only himself subscribed to and helped disseminate this image of himself (and of the Romantic poet) as unstable genius, but he had an active role in reworking a common belief that poets were, in fact, *immune* from insanity, which suggests that we can trace in the Romantic period a cultural transformation in the figuration of the poet, thus countering medical critics from R. R. Madden to Kay Redfield Jamison who argue for a transhistorical malformation in the figure of the poet. As Lionel Trilling correctly points out,

> The eighteenth century did not find the poet to be less than other men, and certainly the Renaissance did not. . . . At any rate, no one was likely to identify the poet with the weakling. Indeed, the Renaissance ideal held poetry to be, like arms or music, one of the signs of manly competence. (162–63)[14]

One physician espousing this positive opinion of poetry even into the Romantic period was Beddoes, who concludes his 1803 essay on nervous disorders by suggesting that poetry can even serve as a preservative against illness, since it has the ability, as he puts it, to "restore [the mind's] equipoise":

> The doctrine that the knowledge of the excesses (les ecarts) of the imagination, is a preservative against them, might receive illustration from an enquiry into the reason *why so few great poets have run mad*? None perhaps have derived their insanity from their poetical vein. Is it not because those, that deserve the name of poets, must have a practical knowledge at least of the way, in which imagination is affected? They are therefore in the secret. They stand in the situation, in which we would wish to place those, who seem in most danger. They are not merely worked up by passion; but however much they may work themselves up, they have a goal in view, which hinders their thoughts from going astray past recal [*sic*]. (3.10.85–86)

In such statements, we can identify the view that poetry and poetry writing are healthy, even a sort of panacea, a characterization that Scott helped to disseminate, as we saw in chapter 2. Beddoes identifies novels, rather, as the "most injurious" to "young females" because "they increase indolence, the imaginary world indisposing those, who inhabit it in thought, to go abroad into the real" (1.3.77). The difference, according to Beddoes, is that novel readers come to believe in the reality or superiority of the imaginary world represented in fiction and thus turn away from the real, whereas poets remain "in the secret"; they remain conscious of the difference between the excesses of the imagination and the "practical" way that the imagination is affected in the real world or affects one's real-world body. As in Scott's rhetoric about romance reading, the safeguard against disease is precisely poetry's acknowledgment of its own fictionality.

At first, Byron appeared to agree with Beddoes's estimation of the poet, albeit with reservations. As he wrote to his then-fiancée, Annabella Milbanke, in 1813,

> I by no means rank poetry or poets high in the scale of intellect—this may look like Affectation—but it is my real opinion—it is the lava of the imagination whose eruption prevents an earth-quake—they say Poets never or rarely go *mad*—Cowper & Collins are instances to the contrary—(but Cowper was no poet)—it is however to be remarked that they rarely do—but are generally so near it—that I cannot help thinking rhyme is so far useful in anticipating & preventing the disorder. (*Letters* 3.179)

At this point, Byron at once formulated his famous characterization of poetry as "the lava of the imagination" and claimed that rhyme perhaps helps to contain the worst effects of the eruption. However, it was not long before Byron associated this implied volatility and instability of the poetic act with actual, full-blown madness and disease.

One article that led Byron to change his mind about poetry writing's healthful sanity was William Hazlitt's "On the Causes of Methodism," first published anonymously in the *Examiner* of October 15, 1815. As Hazlitt writes,

> [T]he same reason makes a man a religious enthusiast that makes a man an enthusiast in any other way, an uncomfortable mind in an uncomfortable body. Poets, authors, and artists in general, have been ridiculed for a pining, puritanical, poverty-struck appearance, which has been attributed to their real poverty. But it would perhaps be nearer the truth to say, that their being poets, artists, etc. has been owing to their original poverty of spirit and weakness of constitution. As a general rule, those who are dissatisfied with themselves, will seek

> to go out of themselves into an ideal world. Persons in strong health and spirits, who take plenty of air and exercise, who are "in favour with their stars," and have a thorough relish of the good things of this life, seldom devote themselves in despair to religion or the Muses. Sedentary, nervous, hypochondriachal people, on the contrary, are forced, for want of an appetite for the real and substantial, to look out for a more airy food and speculative comforts. (4.58)[15]

Byron not only wholeheartedly agreed with this judgment of the poet, a judgment that aligns the constitutionally weak creative artist with the sorts of ideal worlds and speculative comforts associated in the popular imaginary with philosophy and the romance; he explicitly rejected a later defense of poetry writing by Leigh Hunt in the next issue of the *Examiner*, as Byron informed Hunt in a letter that Leslie Marchand guesses to be from November 4–6, 1815. What is more, Hunt later included that letter as the last item in his portrait of Byron, one of many examples of what we might call pathographies of the poet, in which Hunt claims faithfully to "have drawn . . . the *infirmities* of Lord Byron" (vi; my italics). As Byron states in that letter,

> The paper on the Methodists was sure to raise the bristles of the godly. I *redde* it, and agree with the writer on one point, in which you and he perhaps differ; that an addiction to poetry is very generally the result of "an uneasy mind in an uneasy body;" disease or deformity have been the attendants of many of our best. Collins mad—Chatterton, *I* think, mad—Cowper mad—Pope crooked—Milton blind—Gray—(I have heard the last was afflicted by an incurable & very grievous distemper, though not generally known) and others——. I have somewhere redde, however, that poets *rarely* go mad. I suppose the writer means that their insanity effervesces & evaporates in verse—may be so. (Hunt 164; Byron, *Letters* 4.332, where punctuation differs)

By virtue of being the final lines in Hunt's portrait, Byron is thus put in a position not only to cement the alignment of poetry writing and madness but also to diagnose for posterity his own condition as "the result of 'an uneasy mind in an uneasy body.' " Byron is yet once again put in the position of offering *himself* up as the preeminent example of the mad poet of genius, the very opposite maneuver from the one we saw Lockhart use in opening his work with Scott's autobiographical fragment.

Because of D'Israeli's influence, Byron also soon dropped any suggestion that "poets rarely go mad" and instead finally argued the very opposite. As he wrote to Richard Hoppner on November 25, 1818, only a day after writing to John Murray about his admiration for D'Israeli's newly revised *Literary Character* of 1818,

> [W]e are all heirs to misfortune and disappointments—but *poets* especially seem to be a marked race—who has not heard of the blindness of *Milton*—the wretched life, and still more unhappy death of *Otway*—the long sufferings & unrequited services of *Cowley* and of *Butler*—the struggles against poverty & malice which occupied the life of *Dryden*—the constitutional infirmities which embittered the existence of *Pope*—the lamentable idiocy & madness of *Swift*—the almost unparalleled miseries and unhappy end of *Savage*—the frenzy of *Collins*—the indigence of *Goldsmith*—the morbid melancholy and sullen discontent of *Johnson*—the hypochondrianism of *Gray* and of *Beattie*—the tragical catastrophe of *Chatterton*—the disappointed hopes and premature death of *Burns*—and the sickness, despondency, and madness of *Cowper*? To this deplorable list many additions might be made." (*Letters* 6.85)

Not only did Byron recognize that his own fame was closely bound up with "this Melancholy which hath made me a bye-word" (*Letters* 9.38), but, through the publication of such letters following his death, Byron also put himself in the position of diagnosing his own pathology. As he states in his "Detached Thoughts" of 1821–22, after referring specifically to Aristotle's association of all great men with melancholia,

> Whether I am a Genius or not—I have been called such by my friends as well as enemies—and in more countries and languages—than one—and also within a no very long period of existence.—Of my Genius—I can say nothing—but of my melancholy that it is "increasing—& ought to be diminished" but how?" (*Letters* 9.47).[16]

Byron's own biography—and the plethora of pathographies that followed his death—served only further to instantiate this diagnosis.

Of particular note is the oft-cited fact that, before finally seeking an official separation, Lady Byron even consulted physicians to determine whether Byron was completely off his rocker. Although the doctors ultimately convinced Annabella that Byron was, indeed, sane, for a time in early 1816 she even had a particular condition in mind: hydrocephalus acutus, a disease that one doctor, Caleb Hillier Parry, associates in his 1815 *Elements of Pathology and Therapeutics* with "the Sick Headach [*sic*] of authors" (352), particularly when the condition is discovered in adults. What's more, Dr. Matthew Baillie, who according to Hobhouse, "did come to Lord Byron's own house, and in Lord Byron's own parlour did examine these medical charges preferred [*sic*] against Lord Byron by Lord Byron's own wife" (Marchand 2.560), had published his own highly regarded *Morbid Anatomy* (1793), which included a description of hydrocephalus (274–75, 282), although in the end Baillie "declined giving a decided opinion" about Lord Byron (Marchand 2.560). In any case, such pathologization helps to make sense of Lady Byron's otherwise mysterious warning to Byron in January 1816:

> I hope you are *good* and remember my medical prayers and injunctions. Don't give yourself up to the abominable trade of versifying—nor to brandy—nor to anything or anybody that is not *lawful* and *right*. (Marchand 563)[17]

This statement by Lady Byron has mystified scholars in the past, but it becomes clear in light of poetry's connection to pathology. Indeed, Lady Byron could be said to encapsulate in her caveat the major strategy of future critics of Byron: the willful misreading of Byron's *subversion*—his tendency to associate himself with activities *such as poetry-writing* that are no longer considered lawful or right—as *perversion* (in the medico-scientific sense), hence the command that Byron remember his wife's "medical prayers" and injunctions. In those *medical prayers*, theology becomes inscribed on the body as nosology; proscription becomes prescription. Byron's historicizing of the present was thus countered by a hystericizing of Byron. The endless series of biographies analyzing the Byron separation, by a similar strategy, quickly devolved over the course of the nineteenth century from either hagiography or demonography to pathography and eventually, as we will see, to pornography.

DIAGNOSING THE POETICAL TEMPERAMENT

The response to Byron in the periodical reviews and newspapers of the period helped to fix the image of the mad poet of genius in the minds of the general public. Indeed, the reviews often employed the same medical language formerly applied to the novel. As William Roberts, for example, states in the *British Review* of August 1817, soon after the publication of *Manfred*,

> As we have long considered Lord Byron as our patient, every resource of our medical skill has been exerted upon his morbid intellect: every thing has been tried from a soothing syrup, to a blistering plaster; but since this poem of "Manfred" has appeared, we doubt whether any thing less potent than hellebore will prove efficacious. Sometimes, indeed, we are induced to doubt whether a cure might be altogether desirable, since, if the complaint is habitual, and constitutional, the removal of it might give room to some worse disease, or let in a general languor upon the system. Perhaps, after all, Dr. Spurzheim could show that some incurable tendency resides in the organs, to which the creation of such a monotonous series of whimsical hypochondriacs is scientifically to be ascribed. (*RR* 1.451)

Calling for the traditional, ancient cure for melancholy, hellebore, Roberts—like Hazlitt—identifies the disease of poetry writing in the very constitution of the author, even inviting one of the most influential of the new phrenologists, Spurzheim, to corroborate the case. The critic, like the medic, thus transforms the man of genius from "a sort of demoniacal sublimity," as Jeffrey had characterized him in the previous chapter, into a sort of hypochondriacal infirmity. Rather than cast genius' melancholic temperament as heroic rebel—the sort of Satanic hero we saw represented in Doré's Lucifer—Roberts here casts the melancholic as the chronically enfeebled figure of a "whimsical" hypochondriac. Indeed, by August of the following year, after reading *Childe Harold* IV, Roberts gave up on his patient altogether and called instead for poetic euthanasia as the only cure, all the while betraying his fear that Byron's poetry was, in fact, successful in disturbing the status quo: "Perish poetry, live the moral principle—the virtuous constitution of the soul! May genius rather be dumb than endanger the hopes of an hereafter, or even disturb the righteous dispositions of our present existence!" (*RR* 1.460).[18]

Roberts also followed Spurzheim's insistence that we pathologize rather than venerate anyone exhibiting the delineations of the melancholic temperament. Just before mentioning hellebore as the ancient cure for insanity (156), Spurzheim warns in his *Observations on the Deranged Manifestations of the Mind, or Insanity* (1817), which appeared in the same year as Roberts's review, that "[i]t is . . . a great fault on the part of the friends, and even of physicians, not to consider the deranged imagination as the effect of a bodily cause" (148–49). As we saw in chapter 1, Spurzheim and the other pathologists of his day were also careful to associate such temperaments specifically with certain creative endeavors and occupations, thus safeguarding medicine itself from the charge of disease.[19]

What occurred thanks to Byron was that critical reviewers increasingly pinpointed the poet as the preeminent figure in the sequence of occupations that were represented as exciting one's feelings, disturbing one's nervous system, and thus predisposing one to insanity. For this reason, I think, Jeffrey in his review of *Childe Harold* III took exception to the lines in Byron's poem associating all great men ("Conquerers and Kings,/ Founders of sects and systems, to whom add/ Sophists, Bards, Statesmen" [380–82]) with melancholia ("What stings/ Are theirs! One breast laid open were a school/ Which would unteach mankind the lust to shine or rule" [385–87]). Whereas Byron attempts in these lines to conform to the older Aristotelian tradition of the melancholic great man, Jeffrey tries to distinguish true from counterfeit genius in his review. And yet, although Jeffrey does offer a list of English poets who have escaped the melancholic disposition, he seeks, ultimately, to exculpate everyone *but* poets from the charge of "misanthropy or gloom in their genius" (*RR* 2.876). Although he makes it clear that philosophers, scientists, and leaders from all ages "have always escaped the unhappiness which is here supposed to be the inevitable lot of extraordinary talents" (*RR* 2.875), Jeffrey acknowledges that poets are "confessedly the most irritable and fantastic of all men of genius" (*RR* 2.876), as the case of Byron appears to prove. Although Byron was "perfectly pleased" (*Letters* 5.185) with Jeffrey's review, given that most everyone else found absolutely nothing to praise in the third canto, he also made a point of telling Moore in a letter that "I was not, and, indeed, am not even *now*, the misanthropical and gloomy gentleman he takes me for" (*Letters* 5.186), recognizing sadly that "now I shall never be able to shake off my sables in public imagination" (*Letters* 5.186).

Scott too came to realize that he was seeing a watershed in the public's estimation of the poet, that Byron was effectuating a complete transformation in the public's perception of the mental health of the "poetical temperament." As he states in his own review of *Childe Harold* III in the *Quarterly Review* (October 1816):

> [I]t is certain, that for many years past, though the number of our successful poets may be as great as at any period of our literary history, we have heard little comparatively of their eccentricities, their adventures, or their distresses . . . . It has been, however, reserved for our own time to produce one distinguished example of the Muse having descended upon a bard of a wounded spirit, and lent her lyre to tell, and we trust to soothe, afflictions of no ordinary description, afflictions originating probably in that singular combination of feeling which has been called the poetical temperament, and which has so often saddened the days of those on whom it has been conferred. If ever a man could lay claim to that character in all its strength and all its weakness, with its unbounded range of enjoyment, and its exquisite sensibility of pleasure and of pain, it must certainly be granted to Lord Byron. Nor does it require much time or a deep acquaintance with human nature to discover why these extraordinary powers should in many cases have contributed more to the wretchedness than to the happiness of their possessor.
>
> The "imagination all compact," which the greatest poet who ever lived has assigned as the distinguishing badge of his brethren, is in every case a dangerous gift. (*RR* 5.2029)

Even while he recognizes this shift as cultural, however, Scott is quick to corroborate the public's new estimation of the poet, concluding that

> [a] powerful and unbridled imagination is, we have already said, the author and architect of its own disappointments. Its fascination, its exaggerated pictures of good and evil, and the mental distress to which they give rise, are the natural and necessary evils attending on that quick susceptibility of feeling and fancy incident to the poetical temperament. (*RR* 5.2046)

Indeed, Scott goes so far as to suggest to Byron in the review a list of "the most obvious and certain means of keeping or regaining mental tranquility" (*RR* 5.2046). Like William Roberts in the *British Review*, Scott in the *Quarterly* thus recasts Byron: no longer revolutionary but valetudinary, the figure that would forever after change the constitution (in both senses) of the poet. Scott, that most healthful of writers, even imagines himself in the position of treating Byron, following the same theological nosology suggested by Lady Byron: "Let the patient submit to the discipline of the soul enjoined by religion, and recommended by philosophy" (*RR* 5. 2047).[20] As William Roberts puts it in yet another review of *Childe Harold* III from February 1817, "It never was meant that the head of that man should lie easy on his pillow who has first infected the healthy state of society, and then endeavoured to cut off the resort to the great Physician of the soul" (*RR* 1.442).[21] Once again, theology and nosology come together in the diagnosis of the poet's moral, mental, and bodily constitution. Even Satanic rebellion is thus reworked and reduced into the relationship between a patient and his doctor.

Largely, I think, because of the phenomenon of Byron and because of such responses to his poetry, by 1825, the year after Byron's death, Macaulay is in a position completely to overturn the earlier notion that poetry is a safeguard against insanity. As Macaulay states in his essay on Milton, a hugely influential work that I here quote from an 1849 issue of the *American Journal of Insanity*, "[N]o person can be a poet, or can even enjoy poetry, without a certain unsoundness of mind" (377).[22] As Macaulay goes on to explain, "Truth indeed is essential to poetry; but it is the truth of madness" (377–78). Cited in other alienist journals of the Victorian period, Macaulay's statement would influence a sequence of articles exploring the link between insanity and poetry writing.

Madden in his *Infirmities of Genius* of 1833 begins his eight-chapter section on Byron by commenting on the trend: "That tax of censure which is laid on the eminence of genius, has been pretty rigidly enforced in all ages, and in all countries; but of late years it has fallen more heavily than usual on literary men" (105). Like Scott, Madden eventually professes the universal *truth* of what appears at first to be a *cultural* transition in the characterization of the literary character. He concludes by arguing that this particular disease, arising "from a disturbance of the nervous functions of the brain" (269) and the eventual "exhaustion of mind and body" (270) is "a malady, which literary men are more subject to than persons of any other avocation" (266). What is more, every diseased writer he discusses in detail is either exclusively or in large part a poet (specifically, Pope, Johnson, Burns, Cowper, and Byron). The one exception with regard to the malady of poetry writing, as we saw in chapter 2, is Scott. Even defenders of Byron repeated this now-standard wisdom about poets; as Sir Cosmo Gordon, for example, states in his 1824 *Life and Genius of Lord Byron*, "*[A]ccording to the common standards*, poets have both [vices and follies], great usually in proportion to their own greatness" (14; my italics).

Following this "common standard," the Hon. Ezekiel Bacon, responding to an earlier article, "The Poetry of Insanity" (January 1845), exclaims in the April 1845 issue of the *American Journal of Insanity* (in an article entitled "The Poetical Temperament, and Faculty"):

> What . . . is the fancy, the fire, and the imagination, of the most highly gifted bard, minstrel, or poet, but a species of mental intoxication, and the regular and convulsive throes of a disturbed and unequally balanced system. . . . And if so, is it not one of the last faculties to be coveted or envied; or which one could rationally wish either himself or his dearest friend to be possessed of, or rather *possessed with*? (363)

So pervasive was this sentiment in the 1840s that it even trickled down to general practitioners, leading Elizabeth Barrett's doctor to echo such statements in the treatment of his own patients. As Barrett writes to Robert Browning on August 11, 1845,

> And talking of what may "hurt" you & me, you would smile, as I have often done in the midst of my vexation, if you knew the persecution I have been subjected to by the people who call themselves (lucus a non lucendo) "the faculty," & set themselves against the exercise of other people's faculties, as a sure way to death & destruction . . . . I had a doctor once who thought he had done everything because he had carried the inkstand out of the room—"Now," he said, "you will not have such a pulse to-morrow." He gravely thought poetry a sort of disease . . . a sort of fungus of the brain—& held as a serious opinion, that nobody could be properly well who exercised it as an art—which was true (he maintained) even of men—he had studied the physiology of poets, "quotha"—but that for women, it was a mortal malady & incompatible with any common show of health under any circumstances. And then came the damnatory clause in his experience . . . that he had never known "a system" approaching mine in "excitability" . . . except Miss Garrow's . . . a young lady who wrote verses for Lady Blessington's annuals . . . & who was the only other female rhymer he had had the misfortune of attending. And she was to die in two years . . . & *I*, of course, much sooner, if I did not ponder these things, & amend my ways, & take to reading "a course of history"—!! Indeed I do not exaggerate. (Browning 151–52)

Having separated itself from the earlier association of *all* scholars with incipient disease, a newly established medical *profession* ("the faculty") thus turned against those undisciplined "faculties" associated with creative thinking and feeling.

Indeed, a hierarchy of generic forms is suggested in Barrett's letter, with history the cure for the fungus of the metrical foot. The physiology of the lyrist is now represented as "incompatible with any common show of health" because of poetry's effect on a nervous system's "excitability." In the space of a few decades, poetry was in such ways transformed from a sign of mental health to "the regular and convulsive throes of a disturbed and unequally balanced system." The ancient association of poetry with the delirium of inspiration had in such instances clearly been transformed from tropology into pathology.[23]

As late as 1878 we find Frederick Treves, in the *Journal of Mental Science*, explaining that "such minds as are imaginative or poetic in a marked degree must be regarded as abnormal" (65). Indeed, he goes on to write,

> It may safely be stated that no body of men, eminent in the intellectual world, present so much eccentricity, and so much irregularity in actions, mental, social and moral, as is disclosed by the lives of those eminent in poetry. . . . Without lengthening the present paper by examples, it may be only necessary to mention the following characters, which will be found repeated over and over again, although in varying degree, in the histories of the poet's lives. The grossest immorality and wildness of living in the one case, and a hermit-like love of the most unsocial seclusion in the other; marked capriciousness of temper, subtle and uncertain, aroused by trivial acts into disproportionate fury on the one hand, and capable of displaying a more than womanly gentleness on the other. . . . [A]nd lastly, in how many cases with the details of which we are familiar have the domestic lives of these men been abnormal and marked by peculiarity and strangeness of conduct? (241–42)

The poet is clearly fingered here as the man of genius most likely to become a social deviant, with an abnormal domestic life, a tendency to "the most unsocial seclusion," and even "the grossest immorality and wildness of living." Treves also employs one of the commonplaces for the proper functioning of the healthy body and mind. He argues that what Bacon called an "unequally balanced system" can be at once overexcitable and listless; poetic temperament manifests itself both as "wildness of living" and "unsocial seclusion," as "disproportionate fury" and "womanly gentleness." As we saw in chapter 1, the two extremes are, in fact, intimately related, according to the science journals of the time period: overwrought intensity serves but to mask imminent, deathly exhaustion. Following this medical principle, Roberts, in the review of *Childe Harold* III quoted earlier, is able to write of "Lord Byron's muse" that "the morbid taint inly consumes the core of life, and produces a feverish action of the system, sometimes mistaken for energy, but the real forerunner of exhaustion and death" (*RR* 1.446).

Because of this figurative economy, a number of "nervous" activities could now be posited as equally dangerous to the constitution. At first, one of the greatest dangers was seen to arise from the reading of novels and romances, particularly among women and the young. However, as we have seen, a number of male figures soon became associated with such nervous complaints: the man of genius, the melancholic, the man of letters, and the masturbator. The character that needs now to be added to the list is the poet. We have already seen how genius, melancholia, and even the man of letters were brought together in the figure of Byron, who arguably redefined the character of the poet for the nineteenth century. We have yet to see to what extent the fifth nervous figure, the masturbator, could be said to enter into the mix.

According to the science journals of the time period, the stereotypical images of the Romantic poet—melancholic, poverty-stricken, distraught, sedentary, at once overexcitable and listless—suggested an individual who was, quite simply, abnormal and, hence almost by necessity, either mad, perverse, or diseased. As Leslie Stephen puts it in 1876, "[T]he keen sensibility which makes a man a poet, undoubtedly exposes him to certain types of disease" (208). Indeed, when poetic expression was attacked, it was often characterized as an abuse of the body, the soul and the mind, a self-depletion of the writer's "vital power" that resembled nothing more than the rhetoric directed in the Victorian period at what medical tracts identified as that greatest threat to the conservation of one's vital powers—masturbation. What was seen as particularly dangerous was the poet's "nervous temperament." As explained in the Appendix to the American edition of Spurzheim's *Education, Founded on the Nature of Man*, where the phrenologist George Combe is quoted,

> "The Nervous Temperament is recognized by fine thin hair, thin skin, small thin muscles, quickness in muscular motion, paleness of countenance, and often delicate health. The whole nervous system, including the brain, is predominantly active, and the mental manifestations are proportionally vivacious." (320)[24]

The appendix also goes on to explain that "[d]ifferent occupations . . . require and produce a predominance of one or more of the Temperaments over the other, as, also, of the Phrenological organs, each of which are capable of great change, even in a short space of time, as, for example, those engaged in literary pursuits, such as Writers, Teachers, and Clergymen, require a predominance of the Nervous or Mental Temperaments" (320).

The association of the poet with the nervous temperament was, indeed, an exceptionally common one throughout the nineteenth century. In an essay on Tennyson (1835), Mill, for example, claims that a "peculiar kind of nervous susceptibility seems to be the distinctive character of the poetic temperment" (67).[25] Although Mill is offering a positive assessment of poetry in this essay, it was precisely this "poetic temperment," so lauded by the Romantics, that made the Victorians uneasy. R. R. Madden explains, when discussing Byron, that "the 'poetic temperament' means nothing more than a peculiar constitutional state, arising from a predominant passion for poetry, and implying certain evils peculiar to the cultivation of that particular art" (112). Like study too long continued, he explains, "the result is a state of morbid sensibility, arising from bodily disease" (113). As Matthew Arnold writes of the "mysterious malady" suffered by such poets as John Keats, David Gray, and Maurice de Guérin, "The temperament is devouring; it uses the vital power too hard and too fast, paying the penalty in long hours of unutterable exhaustion and in premature death" (*Lectures* 32). Something like this seems also to be on Alfred Austin's mind when he warns that men of the "poetical nature and temperment" may "squander their lives in trying to attain the impossible [and] exhaust themselves in poetical spasms" ("Poetry" 192). The nervous temperament of the poet in such statements begins sounding very much like the nervous excitability of the masturbator. Indeed, the two figures share a number of particular characteristics, not only the nervous temperament but the pathologies associated with nervous susceptibility: melancholy, perversity, passion, effeminacy, and early death.

As with the rhetoric of pathology being applied to the melancholic poet of genius, Byron even anticipated the association through the hapless figure of Keats. Not only did Byron famously call Keats's poetry "the *Onanism* of Poetry," "the *outstretched* poesy of this miserable Self-polluter of the human Mind"(*Letters* 7.217; November 4, 1820), a "sort of mental masturbation" in which "he is always f——gg——g his Imagination" (*Letters* 7.225; November 9, 1820); Byron also made it clear in a subsequent letter, a couple of weeks after the previous pronouncements to Murray, that he had in mind the very tract I analyzed in chapter 1. As he wrote to Murray again on November 18, 1820, "Why don't they review & praise 'Solomon's Guide to Health' it is better sense—and as much poetry as Johnny Keates" (*Letters* 7.229).

When Steven Marcus comments in *The Other Victorians* on the affinity between the withdrawn, solitary, Romantic poet and the "overwrought intensity" of the onanist, he could therefore be said to be following Byron's own lead. Marcus begins by quoting extensively a passage from Acton's popular work, *The Functions and Disorders of the Reproductive Organs* (1857), in which Acton describes the inmates of an asylum for the insane:

> Engaged in no social diversion, the patients of this group [of masturbators] live alone in the midst of many. In their exercise they choose the quietest and most unfrequented parts of the airing-grounds. They join in no social conversation, nor enter with others into any amusement. They walk alone, or they sit alone. If engaged in reading, they talk not to others of what they may have read; their desire apparently is, in the midst of numbers, to be in solitude. They seek no social joys, nor is the wish for fellowship evinced. (Acton 111; Marcus 20)

Following the same strategy as D'Israeli, Roberts, and Byron himself—who, as we have seen, use tracts by Haslam, Spurzheim, and Solomon, respectively, to characterize the Romantic poet—Marcus does not fail to point out one perhaps odd yet strangely fitting parallel for such a description:

> It might be difficult to find a more apt or prettier description of the romantic artist: the Ancient Mariner, the poet of "Alastor," Endymion, any one of Byron's early heroes fit this bill of particulars. (20–21)

Marcus is quick to add that "[t]his hardly indicates that these characters masturbated themselves into insanity; it does serve to show, however, how in a single culture one set of descriptive terms is forced into the service of representing a variety of states, in this case extreme states of mental alienation" (21). Marcus is interested in how the language of sensibility was translated into works of pornography throughout the nineteenth century rather than in suggesting that poetry itself was perceived as masturbatory. I believe, however, that—particularly when pathology or melancholia was aligned with sexual perversity in the poet—the tropes associated with the onanist did, at times, get applied implicitly (and sometimes even explicitly) to the writing and reading of poetry, perceived now as a depletion of the body's vital power and a preamble to self-imposed isolation, moral perversity, mental imbalance, disease, and, ultimately, premature death. At the very least, we see "one set of descriptive terms," those associated with the "nervous temperament," forced "into the service of representing a variety of states," all of which were, indeed, aligned in the period with not only mental alienation but also bodily debility.

Indeed, if we follow Byron's dismissal of Keats and compare sample descriptions of the masturbator and the poet, the similarities are striking. First, here are two excerpts from nineteenth-century medical tracts that outline the symptoms that were believed to result from the loss of semen, either because of onanism or what was seen as the related medical condition, spermatorrhœa: "The pale complexion, the emaciated form, the slouching gait, the clammy palm, the glassy or leaden eye, and the averted gaze, indicate the lunatic victim to this vice" (Acton 111); "It usually exhibits itself in the form of melancholia . . . a desire for solitude, and irritability of temper; such are the principle mental signs leading to the inference that spermatorhoea lies at the foundation of the mental disturbance. . . . The pallid, wan countenance is the external indication of the gloom and shyness of the patient" (*Journal of Mental Science* 583). Now, here is an 1833 satiric representation of the poet by Bulwer-Lytton:

> Of all melancholy and disappointed persons, a young poet in this day is perhaps the most. Observe that pale and discontented countenance, that air at once shy and proud . . . he is consumed with the desire of fame; the loud celebrity of Byron yet rings in his ears: he asketh himself, why he should not be equally famous: he has no pleasure in

> the social world . . . he is awkward and gloomy; for he lives not in the present: he plunges into an imaginary future never to be realized . . . . He has no sympathy in other men's amusements. (*England* 2.237)

Aligned yet again with the figure of Byron, the melancholy, Romantic poet begins displaying the same sorts of symptoms that any doctor of the period would be more likely to diagnose as the result of an overwrought imagination bordering on self-abuse.

The cure for both the problems associated with the poetic temperament and for those resulting from masturbation was, perhaps not surprisingly, the same. Indeed, a number of medical sources began to align the acts of poetry writing and onanism. According to an 1855 issue of the *New Orleans Medical and Surgical Journal*, the best cure for masturbation is "hard labor, or abundance of exercise in the open air, simplicity of diet, rural life, restricted sleep, [and] the avoidance of books of an imaginative character," all characteristics understood as the opposite of writing poetry; indeed, the author goes on to write: "Many years ago, a young man of fine physical development, *who wrote good verses and practiced masturbation to excess*, asked for medical advice—begged to be emasculated—attempted suicide—but was persuaded to try severe manual labor; he cleared six acres of heavy timbered beech and sugar tree bottom—was cured, and rose to distinction in civil life" (704; my italics). The open question, of course, is whether the patient was also cured of writing poetry. The most explicit association occurs in Claude François Lallemand's *A Practical Treatise on the Causes, Symptoms and Treatment of Spermatorrhea*, the work that in the nineteenth century took over from Tissot the status as most-cited scholarly French source in anti-onanist tracts.[26] As Lallemand states in that work,

> When desires are only excited by spermatic plethora, they are appeased as soon as the want is satisfied, and only return when the loss is repaired. There could, therefore, never be a real excess in such a case, if other causes did not determine the more frequent repetition of the act. Grave excesses, however, are almost inevitable, when the desires are found in great disproportion to the real wants of the system. A brilliant and active imagination, an exquisite sensibility, and great brilliancy of ideas are often joined to this predominance of the sexual instinct. Individuals imbued with the spirit of poetry, whom we call nervous, frequently attach the most seductive colors to their recollections, and embellish them with imaginary charms; but their devouring passions are badly supported by their weak and irritable organs. (189)

Not only does Lallemand make a perhaps inevitable connection between the nervous sensibility of the masturbator and the nervous sensibility of the poet, but he makes it clear that the "real excess" derives not from any physical source but from the disproportion between poetic desires and "the real wants of the system," thus repeating the common formulation explored in chapter 1. It is precisely the search for a poet's "imaginary charms" that is now diagnosed as but "the regular and convulsive throes of a disturbed and unequally balanced system."

By aligning the poet with the search for seductive colors and imaginary charms that embellish the real—both the "real wants of the system" and the recollection of reality—Lallemand thus echoes and supports those literary critics who worried over the brooding melancholy of the poetical temperament, for example Hazlitt's concern that those people suffering an "original poverty of spirit and weakness of constitution" naturally "seek to go out of themselves into an ideal world," hence their inability to deal with "the real and substantial." The same rhetoric formerly applied to the novel reader, who, as Beddoes states, becomes indisposed to "go abroad into the real" (1.3.77), is now redirected to the writer of poetry, whose "desires are found in great disproportion to the real wants of the system."

Hypersensitivity, self-involvement, nervous irritability, morbidness, a desire for solitude, a search for unrealizable ideals—these are conditions that were applied to both the poet and the onanist in the nineteenth century. And, though the equation was rarely made so explicitly, I believe it functioned as an unspoken suspicion—if not an open secret—behind much of the pathologizing rhetoric, a rhetoric that was applied particularly to the activity of poetry writing itself, although it could at times be directed at the *reading* of Romantic poetry as well.

Perhaps the best example of this latter move, an example that also makes the link to Byron clear, is the *Student's Manual* by the Reverend John Todd (1835), with which I began this chapter. An early self-help book for students, this work by Todd sold extremely well in both North America and Britain throughout the century, running through numerous editions and selling more than one hundred thousand copies in Europe by 1854.[27] The work is notable because the Reverend discusses for some seven pages the dangers of reading what he calls "Bad Books." The results include lassitude, irritability, the inability to study, effeminacy, and even damnation. As he writes of these bad books,

> I do entreat my young readers never to look at one—never to open one. They will leave a stain upon the soul which can never be removed. . . .
>
> In connection with these books, allow me to lift up a loud voice against those rovings of the imagination by which the mind is at once enfeebled, and the heart and feelings debased and polluted. It is almost inseparable from the habit of reverie: but, in this life, a heavier curse can hardly hang upon a young man than that of possessing a polluted imagination. The leprosy fills the whole soul. (146–47)

Since the Reverend Todd does not specify what books he may be referring to here, one expects the worst at this point. Indeed, one would be forgiven to assume that the Reverend must surely be referring to pornography in this chapter. Todd then goes on to state the most deleterious effects of such writing:

> While I thus briefly allude to these wanderings of the imagination, by which the mind is debilitated, the soul polluted by a stain which tears cannot wash out, nor the deepest repentance fully do away, I cannot satisfy my conscience without going a step further, and saying *what others have, to my certain knowledge, wished to say, and ought to say, but which no one has yet had the courage to say, in tones loud and distinct.* May I entreat the young man who reads these pages not to pass the following paragraph without reading and pondering it. (147; my italics)

Now, the Reverend himself at this point loses courage and, so, switches to Latin for two pages to state the worst effects of such reading practices. "*Veneri servit—manus!*"; the hand is a slave to Venus. And I translate further: "No light except that of the last Day could bring to revelation the habit of constantly pouring forth **** by the hand (that is, the crime of Onan)" (147–48).[28] Having still not designated what books he might in fact be talking about, it is at this point that the Reverend Todd switches back to English: "What shall be said of such works as those of Byron?" (149–50).[29]

THE PERVERSION OF SUBVERSION

Todd's turn to the rhetoric of masturbation here marks a significant turn away from his earlier association of Byron with the Satanic rebel. His pamphlet, *A Remonstrance Addressed to John Murray, Respecting a Recent Publication* (1822), which was written under the pseudonym Oxoniensis, for example, offers as his frontispiece's epigraph the following lines from *Paradise Lost*: "Whence,/ But from the author of all ill, could spring/ So deep a malice? (*Paradise Lost* 2.380–82). Demanding that John Murray take responsibility for the ill effects of Byron's publications, especially *Cain*, Todd in his pamphlet accuses Byron of declaring "war with all the institutions of civilized humanity" (6) and aligns him, in conclusion as on the frontispiece, with Satan himself:

> [N]ow at last he quarrels with the very conditions of humanity, rebels against that Providence which guides and governs all things, and dares to adopt the language which had never before been attributed to any being but one, "Evil be thou my good." Such as far as we can judge is Lord Byron. (19)

Such a characterization of Byron has quite a different effect than the representation of Byron's poetry in Todd's 1835 *Student's Manual*, since Todd must thus also acknowledge the power of Byron's writings to affect—and potentially destroy—the institutions of society. Indeed, anticipating his later rhetorical shift to medical discourse, Todd makes a distinction in this earlier work between the political impact of immorality on society and the pathological effects of immorality on the body, all the while associating Byron with the revolutionary dangers represented by radical publisher, Richard Carlile. As Todd writes, addressing Murray,

> It is not to be supposed that the author of Cain will stop there; he already resembles the wretched Carlile in so many points, that we reasonably expect he will imitate him in his pertinacity also: will he find in you a willing instrument, a publisher ready to disseminate all the moral poisons he may think fit to prepare? Deliberate, Sir, before you decide this question in the affirmative, for be assured, that you challenge a heavy responsibility: I speak not of the responsibility to which the actions of every one of us shall be liable; on the deeds done in the body, whether they be good or bad, let no mortal be so presumptuous as to pronounce a judgment, or so deceived as to hope to escape one. But you are responsible to that society whose institutions you contribute to destroy; and to those individuals whose dearest hopes you insult, and would annihilate. (19–20)

In other words, Todd decides in 1822 to underline not the toxic impact of Byron's writings on the physical body but, rather, the adverse effects of Byron's works on the nineteenth-century social body, calling on "those institutions by which morality and religion are most effectually supported,—the Constitution in Church and State" (20) to defend against what is represented as the real political danger of Byron's work. What happens in the 1835 *Student's Manual* is that Todd transfers his attack from the register of law and politics to that of medicine and psychology, thus returning precisely to those "deeds done in the body."

Whereas in the earlier work Todd threatens Murray with the same imprisonment suffered by Carlile in 1822 (20), in the *Student's Manual* the turn to the rhetoric of pathology allows Todd, after Byron's death, to undercut the implicit political threat of Byron. He does so by dismissing those readers influenced by Byron as under threat of dispatch from God himself and by way of either the physical or mental degradation attendant upon masturbation. Referring to Benjamin Rush's *Medical Inquiries and Observations upon the Diseases of the Mind*, Todd, for example, states in a footnote to *The Student Manual*'s Latin section on onanism: "Physicians testify, that probably this is a greater source of derangement than all other causes" (148n).[30] In a second footnote to this section, he borrows the same rhetorical move we have already seen used by Lady Byron and Scott, proposing a theological nosology that is now applied to the effects of reading Byron: "The apoplexy waits hard by, as God's executioner, upon this sin" (149n). By turning to the mental and physical health of the individual reader, Todd is able to move away from the political threat of the radical mob and instead treats the physical threats to the pubescent student. Todd is therefore able finally to dismiss the threat of Byron altogether: "[H]e will quickly pass from notice, and is doomed to be exiled from the libraries of all virtuous men." Indeed, he goes on, "[i]t is a blessing to the world, that what is putrid must soon pass away" (151).

In this way, Todd follows a general tendency in the rhetoric applied to Byron and to "romantic ideology" in the Victorian period. After Byron's death, the *romance* and the *Romantic* were reduced ultimately to the debauch of Holywell Street or the kitsch of the Victorian Valentine and were thus made finally to adopt their modern sense: either amatory passion or sentimental infatuation. And the previous connection to the struggle for utopic and sans-culottic solutions to the world's injustices was forgotten in the semiotic and erotic shift. That shift would eventually leave us in our contemporary period with two dominant semantic overtones: the pure sentimentality of the Hallmark card on the one hand and the soft-core pornography of the Harlequin romance on the other.[31] Either version of the "romance" and the "romantic" serves to undercut and completely obscure the previous association of the terms with radical politics.

Perhaps the most ironic example of this transformation in the nineteenth century is the fact that both William Dugdale and William Benbow, two of the radical publishers of Byron's work in the Romantic period, would in the Victorian period become famous pornographers, soft-core and otherwise. Both publishers are closely connected to the legacy of Byron. Not only did Benbow pirate a good deal of Byron's poetry in the 1820s; after being prosecuted for obscene libel by the Society for the Suppression of Vice, Benbow also established a new bookshop in Leicester Square that he named "Byron's Head." The shop was described by Southey himself as "one of those preparatory schools for the brothel and gallows; where obscenity, sedition and blasphemy are retailed in drams for the vulgar" (McCalman 205). William Dugdale published almost the whole Byron canon in pirated editions over the course of the teens and twenties, and would go on to become, along with Benbow, one of the more famous pornographers of the Victorian period, combining these two publishing interests in the explicitly pornographic *Don Leon*, which he attributed to Byron as his rediscovered, unburnt memoir and which he published in 1866. The work included such an abundant series of explicit sex acts—sodomy, fellatio, cunnilingus, sapphism, onanism, and so on—that it was banned in England after it was reprinted in 1900 (in France).

Earlier in 1836, under the pseudonym H. Smith, Dugdale also published a porno-biography of Byron written by yet another quondam radical, John Mitford. The title is worth giving in full: *The Private Life of Lord Byron: Comprising His Voluptuous Amours, Secret Intrigues, and Close Connection with Various Ladies of Rank and Fame, in Scotland and London, at Eton, Harrow, Cambridge, Paris, Rome, Venice, &c., &c. with a Particular Account of the Countess Guiaccoli* [*sic*], *and (Never Before Published) Details of the Murder at Ravenna, which Caused his Lordship to Leave Italy, Various Singular Anecdotes of Persons and Families of the Highest Circles of Haut Ton Compiled from Authentic Sources. With Extracts from Unburnt Documents! And Familiar Letters, from his Lordship to His Friends: Being an Amusing and Interesting Expose of Fashionable Frailities* [*sic*], *Follies, and Debaucheries. With Numerous Coloured Engarvings* [*sic*]. London: H. Smith [William Dugdale], 37, Holywell Street, [1836]. Previously closely involved in the radical literature surrounding the Queen Caroline affair of 1820–21, Mitford, like Benbow and Dugdale, eventually turned to the pornographic trade to make a living.[32] Mitford begins his pornographic biography of Byron with the statement that, when it comes to the life of Byron, "there is no necessity for having recourse to invention, for the whole of Lord Byron's career, abroad and at home, is more like romance than the realities occurring to a really existent being" (3–4). And he ends by sounding the same note: "The preceding adventure had so much the appearance of romance, that many of my readers may be inclined to think it a fiction of the author's brain," adding that "it is not so, but 'a plain unvarnished tale,' without ornament or comment" (158).[33] In fact, the work proceeds very much like a Harlequin romance, divested of its domestic trappings, moving from one amorous entanglement to another (many accompanied by engravings of bare-breasted beauties in compromising positions). Making almost no mention of Byron's poetry, the biography turns the Satanic man of genius into the bawdy "man of *penetration*" (55; italics in the original) with "diabolical opinions of the fairest and best part of God's creation" (148). Any mention of Byron's military aspirations is, as Mitford explains, "purposely omitted" in favor of "his *amorous adventures*" (126). Byron's military adventures are instead reduced to nothing but a series of sex jokes: "Byron was too good a soldier in the wards of Venus to let such an advantage escape; he seized on the material requisite for a bum-bardment, battering in breech, mounting a 'chevaux de frize,' or carrying a front barbet battery by a 'coup de main' " (86). Even Byron's beloved sword-and-sheathe metaphor is shorn of all but its sexual dimension: "he . . . had a poniard which required sheathing, and was introduced harmlessly into its covering on the sofa" (164), which is to say, in this particular scene, Lady Caroline Lamb.

Such an association of Byron with the pornographic not only helped to cement the association of poets with the masturbatory but also aligned romantic passion with the fantasies and desires of adolescence. In a common move, Victorian critics identified the Romantic desire for ideal solutions to the world's problems and oppressions as mere adolescent fantasy. In essays by Thomas Love Peacock (1820) and Macaulay (1825), for example, such desires are aligned instead with childhood. Macaulay compares the mental unsoundness of the poet to the credulity of a child "affected by the story of poor Red Riding-Hood" (378). As he goes on, "Such is the despotism of the imagination over uncultivated minds" (378). Peacock expressly associates poetry with romance and thus argues that it is best performed when societies and people are still in their infancy: "Poetry was the mental rattle that awakened the attention of intellect in the infancy of civil society: but for the maturity of mind to make a serious business of the playthings of its childhood, is as absurd as for a full-grown man to rub his gums with coral, and cry to be charmed to sleep by the jingle of silver bells" (764). He explains that "[a] poet in our times is a semi-barbarian in a civilized community" (763–64), thus reiterating the association Scott helped to establish between the poet and the ancient minstrel, but with the readers of such romances now characterized not as healthful citizens but, rather, as "indolent, languid men," to echo Carlyle's similar rhetoric: "[T]here is always a multitude of listless idlers, yawning for amusement, and gaping for novelty: and the poet makes it his glory to be foremost among their purveyors" (Peacock 761). Peacock also makes it clear that he is contrasting the occupation of the poet to "the real business of life" (764):

> The highest inspirations of poetry are resolvable into three ingredients: the rant of unregulated passion, the whining of exaggerated feeling, and the cant of factitious sentiment: and can therefore serve only to ripen a splendid lunatic like Alexander, a puling driveller like Werter, or a morbid dreamer like Wordsworth. It can never make a philosopher, nor a statesman, nor in any class of life an useful or rational man. (764)

Although Peacock's main interlocutor in his essay may well be Shelley, who wrote his "Defense of Poetry" in direct response, Bulwer-Lytton in 1833 characterizes this turn from poetry as a result of the influence of Byron:

> [W]e awoke from the morbid, the passionate, the dreaming, "the moonlight and the dimness of the mind," and by a natural reaction addressed ourselves to the active and daily objects which lay before us. . . . Hence that strong attachment to the Practical, which became so visible a little time after the death of Byron, and which continues (unabated, or rather increased,) to characterize the temper of the time. Insensibly acted upon by the doctrine of the Utilitarians, we desired to see Utility in every branch of intellectual labour. . . . Politics thus gradually and commonly absorbed our attention, and we grew to identify ourselves, our feelings, and our cause, with statesmen and economists, instead of with poets and refiners. . . . [A]nd the interest usually devoted to the imaginative, was transferred to the real. (*England* 2.106–107)

For Bulwer-Lytton, even the melancholic temperament should now be recharacterized as but an adolescent phase that one must grow out of. Mentioning that "[t]his habit of mind, so unfortunate to the possessor, is not unfavourable to poetry," Bulwer-Lytton explains that "after a certain age we grow out of it; the soul becomes accustomed to the mill, and follows the track mechanically, which it commenced in disgust" (*England* 1.174). Bulwer-Lytton makes the same move a few years later in an article on the "Present State of Poetry" (1838):

> Practical life, with its social cares, its healthful struggles, and its stern experience of wisdom and passion, will work away the opiate [i.e., Byron]—for those at least whom practical life will rear to the highest callings of the poet; but still at that twilight age between youth and manhood, when imaginative minds are mostly haunted with certain melancholy and
>
> "Let their frail thoughts dally with false surmise,"
>
> the dreamer of Childe Harold will be a congenial comrade and a beloved friend—the dearer, perhaps, for the very sadness of his counsels. (*Critical* 1.339–450)

Thanks to the death of Byron, the Victorians, according to Bulwer-Lytton, are able finally to grow up. Rather than idealistically defend Luddite rebellion, the soul "becomes accustomed to the mill" and turns instead to the Victorian novel: "[T]he interest usually devoted to the imaginative, was transferred to the real" and "the more than natural distaste for poetry that succeeded the death of Byron" thus "increased the appetite for prose fictions" (*England* 1.107).

Of note is the fact that Peacock and Bulwer-Lytton are also both novelists and both in their novels famously satirized the Byronic character: Peacock in *Headlong Hall* (1816) and *Nightmare Abbey* (1818), Bulwer-Lytton in *Pelham* (1828). Indeed, though I cannot make this argument fully here, a number of prominent nineteenth-century novelists defined the novelistic concern with realism over and against the romance idealism of Byron. Jane Austen established her high-canonical credentials in opposition to not only the romance in *Northanger Abbey* (1818) but also Byron in *Persuasion* (1818). As Anne Elliot tells Captain Benwick, a lover of Byron who sports "a melancholy air" (72), "[I]t was the misfortune of poetry, to be seldom safely enjoyed by those who enjoyed it completely" since "the strong feelings which alone could estimate it truly, were the very feelings which ought to taste it but sparingly" (74). Her suggested remedy to the captain for the ill effects of too much poetry reading is "a larger allowance of prose in his daily study" (74). Isaac D'Israeli's son, Benjamin, would in *Vivian Grey* (1826) and *Venetia* (1837) follow his close friend and fellow politician, Bulwer-Lytton, in defining his identity against his own adolescent fascination with Byron. As Elfenbein explains, "Both authors followed the familiar pattern of a narrative of transition, using the model of the *Bildungsroman* to construct narratives about growing beyond Byron into what they represented as Victorian norms" (*Byron* 218). Carlyle in his own satirical and highly influential novel, *Sartor Resartus* (1831), has his main character, Diogenes Teufelsdröckh, pass through the melancholic "no" of the Romantic ideology in order to reach his philosophy of work and duty, thus establishing a peculiarly Victorian idea of the hero over and against the legacy of Byron. As he so famously exhorted his audience, "Close thy *Byron*; open thy *Goethe*" (*Carlyle Reader* 257). The Victorian novels negotiating and domesticating the Byronic hero along similar lines were legion, with Rochester in *Jane Eyre* (1847) and Heathcliff in *Wuthering Heights* (1847) being but two of the more famous examples.[34] The need for the novel to dispatch Byron continued even into the 1860s. In *Felix Holt, the Radical* (1866), George Eliot dispatches the romantic passions of Byron's poetry through the self-education of Esther Lyon while excoriating Byron's radical politics in the thinly veiled analog for Byron, Harold Transome. Even the sensation novelist, Mary Elizabeth Braddon, when she tried to establish herself as serious novelist in the Flaubert-inspired *Doctor's Wife* (1864), did so by, on the one hand, having the main female character follow Carlyle in closing her Byron and, on the other hand, having the sympathetic male sensation novelist, Sigismund Smith, who is a surrogate for Braddon, open not his Goethe but a novel, specifically "three volumes of the quiet and domestic school" (404) that he is about to author himself.[35]

MASTURBATION AND ECONOMICS

I am now ready to suggest a few reasons why the rhetoric of pathology was applied to the poet in the Victorian period, and why after 1824, the year of Byron's death, it was applied as successfully to the poet as to the novelist, who, at the end of the eighteenth century was the more common object of such sexualizing rhetoric. As the novel began to be perceived as performing a certain kind of social work, and, as the act of writing novels became associated with productive and marketable labor, poetry in the Victorian period increasingly appeared removed from the real life of culture. As one reviewer in *The British Quarterly Review* suggests in an essay on Tennyson's 1842 collection of poems, "In such an age, the maker of verse finds himself half ashamed of his vocation" and "must reason himself into the conviction that his art is not an idleness" (47–48).

A change in perception about the market can be said to have occurred between the Romantics and the Victorians. The general concern in the Romantic period was that too much was being published for an indiscriminate readership. And many therefore advised restraint in sending material out for publication. Coleridge, for example, argues in the *Biographia* that "what medical physiologists affirm of certain secretions, applies equally to our thoughts; they too must be taken up again into the circulation, and be again and again re-secreted in order to ensure a healthful vigor both to the mind and to its intellectual offspring" (1.231). Coleridge thus echoes the common wisdom of a growing body of medical literature on the evils of masturbation, citing a medical commonplace that goes back to Galen.[36] Graham is a good example of how that commonplace entered the period's popular anti-onanist tracts: the semen, he explains, is, "in a healthy state and conduct of the system, re-absorbed and mixed with the blood, of which it constitutes the most rarified and volatile part, and imparts to the body, peculiar sprightliness, vivacity, muscular strength, and general vigor and energy to the animal machine." Graham goes on to explain that this fact (that the semen "like all other secretions of the body, may, to some extent, be re-absorbed") "will not be questioned by any correct physiologist" (21). In implicitly comparing this principle to the circulatory systems of the market, Coleridge is making an explicit alignment between sexuality and textuality, between insemination and dissemination.

For Coleridge, the retention of one's private writings ensures protection against literary prostitution on the market. By the early Victorian period, however, it became clear that the market was something that had to be negotiated; Coleridge's metaphor of mental circulation was therefore extended outward to include the proper and improper circulation of texts. The "spermatic economy" was translated from the individual writer to Victorian society in general, obviating fears about the market—about economy—by turning the circulation of capital into an understandable master-trope: the circulatory systems of the Victorian social body. Through the dead and, at times, denied metaphor of the social body, fears about the market proliferation of texts were characterized instead as the diseases and temptations threatening the proper circulation of the nation's "vital power."

In such a discourse, it was precisely the solitary act of the individual poet that threatened once again to disperse that social body into so many unregulated lyrical effusions. For the majority of critics that accepted the market as a fact of life and attempted to reconceptualize it as a single, manageable entity, the solitary poet posed a double threat: writing to himself in a form and language that was more difficult than, say, the novel for the market to consume, the poet was perceived as resisting, and even questioning, the transmogrification of unregulated literary dissemination into the healthy circulation of a regulated economy. Also, and this helps to explain the shift from the Romantic concern with the mass *readership* to the Victorian concern with the solitary *writer*, the poet—in his experience of "feeling confessing itself to itself in moments of solitude"—becomes, in such rhetorical strategies, both writer and reader at once, a self-enclosed albeit exploded economy: hence, the onanist. We are still dealing with the same fear previously inspired by the rise of the novel—the diffusion of the public into an indeterminate mass of individual, private, and therefore unsupervised acts.

One can also begin to explain why the emphasis in some of the most virulent attacks is on, of all things, poetic style. Preciosity not only made poetry inaccessible to a large majority of readers but also underlined the unique, eccentric, unassimilable style of the individual author. As a result, even after the predominant figuration of England shifted from the "social body" to a "free society" of so many "responsible, disciplined individuals" (Poovey 22), the poet could still be perceived as a threat. And yet this threat could also be seen as precisely the obverse of capitalism's political foundation: bourgeois individualism. After all, one of the marks of genius was precisely its individualism. As D'Israeli states in *The Literary Character*, genius is "that creative part of art which individualises the artist, belonging to him and to no other" (408). Responding to such statements, William G. Rowland Jr. has argued in a chapter entitled "Romantic Genius and Literary Production in the Nineteenth Century" that "[i]n some ways romanticism is not an attack on capitalist culture, but rather supports capitalist and bourgeois assumptions about the ultimate value of private experience" (174–75). Elfenbein goes so far as to argue for a domestication of genius in the period:

> [A]ll respectable people have to be geniuses to the extent that they can invent themselves as unique, special, and original. The greatest fear of the domesticated genius is to be commonplace or to mouth secondhand opinions. The greatest success is to know that a special personal style infuses every aspect of one's life and gives one special prestige in the eyes of the world. (*Romantic* 67)

However, as Elfenbein explains, "The cult of the person had within it a lurking danger that masculine distinctiveness might be carried too far and cross the invisible yet critical line between acceptable difference and unacceptable deviance" (*Romantic* 69).[37] The poet of genius thus marked at once the essence within and the threat against capitalism. By 1860, Mary Poovey writes, "members of what had once seemed a social body now appear as disciplinary individuals capable of governing themselves in a society that is perfectly 'free' " (*Making* 24); to counter the tendency to anarchy in this emphasis on individualism, however, the dispersion of the social body had to be predicated on the exchangeability of these subjects and on their self-disciplined participation in the social arena: each is, in fact, an instance "of a single, self-regulating subject" (Poovey 24). The figure of the emotional, undisciplined, and eccentric as much as egocentric poet, outside the "healthy" circulation of capital, could therefore still be represented as a hard kernel sticking in the craw of market consumption, even as he represents the very individuality upon which the market's liberal foundation depends.

Could we go farther and argue that, like the homophobia that Eve Sedgwick has shown serves to screen society's actual homosocial organization, the nineteenth-century rhetoric of masturbation that gets applied to the Romantic poet of genius actually screens the masturbatory nature of the market's own supposedly balanced circulation? Homosexuality and masturbation even share homologous positions as the abjected term that resists articulation within a symbolic system. What would be termed the "invert" at the end of the nineteenth century emerged, indeed, out of a discourse about what we would now term the *pervert*, a figure that was associated less with the sodomist than the onanist throughout the nineteenth century.[38] Lord Douglas's and Oscar Wilde's "love that dare not speak its name," after all, borrows a rhetorical structure formerly applied to the masturbator: "[I]t is considered indecent even to call this vice by its proper name" (549), Kant, for example, explains one century earlier. Robert James similarly writes in his *Medicinal Dictionary* of 1743–45, under the entry "mastupratio, or manustupratio," that it is "a Vice not decent to name, but productive of the most deplorable and generally incurable Disorders."

I do not wish to deny that Byron's reference in much of his encrypted language, both in his letters and his poetry, is to sodomy. Indeed, Byron himself at one point refers to the inexpressibility of sodomitical acts. Discussing William Beckford's self-exile because of the charge of sodomy, he states in a deleted passage from *Childe Harold*: "But thou wert smitten with unhallowed thirst/ Of nameless crime" (2.18n). What I want to underline is that many of Byron's sodomitical references are supremely obscure and designed to be accessible only to a small group of individuals in the know. What is significant about such linguistic strategies for the general readership is that, as Gary Dyer has recently argued, "while the code conceals something from all but a restricted group of initiates, it advertises the concealment" (569). The language, in other words, served two functions. It allowed Byron to speak secretly to a group of individuals whose practices were outlawed and thus allowed Byron to convince himself that he was not "flatter[ing] the Million's canting in any shape" (*Letters* 6.192); on the other hand, it openly advertised to those millions a sense of naughty sexuality that could then be filled in by the reader. As Dyer explains, "In Byron's writings secrecy does not necessarily *mean* sodomy, insofar as sodomy may not be the reality behind a specific code found there (after all, Byron and his contemporaries had plenty of other secrets, with penalties that were less harsh yet still unsettling)" (563). Most readers of Byron did not have access either to the secret societies or even the language that allowed full expression of homosexual desire. However, another danger existed in the very fact of disseminated reception: anyone could read behind such passages the concealment of sexual desire; what's more, anyone had access to one kind of sexual expression that required no community and even no stable referent: only a structure of enticement, for the sexual object could be filled in at will. And both the repression and expression of such masturbatory desires was significantly more pervasive throughout the nineteenth century than either the prohibition against or exhibition of sodomy.

A good deal of scholarship has now explored the hidden homosexual clues in Byron's fiction; however, this emphasis on references to sodomy may obscure the most commonly expressed fear among critics and medics alike: the sexual dangers of the imagination and the crime that in the nineteenth century was seen as equally, if not more destructive of one's mental and physical constitution: masturbation. By the same token, as I argued in the previous chapter, the pathologization of Byron may hide a yet more deadly threat—one that can be read beyond both the rhetoric of homosexual "inversion" and that of onanistic "perversion," which is to say, the threat of revolutionary subversion. Indeed, the figuration of a *toxic* Byron is in some ways already an inoculation against Byron's unveiling of his society's beliefs as *quixotic*. The toxic and erotic body of Byron covers over another, more dangerous body: the radical, political sans-culottic body of the man whose ideas constituted a threat to more than his reader's virtue.

As we have seen, nineteenth-century critics of Byron quickly learned that the best way to combat the perceived threat from his poetry was to turn subversion into perversion. In the profusion of discourse about sexuality that followed, much of which often revolved around questions of literature's circulation and dissemination, what remained unspoken was not, in fact, a love that dare not speak its name. If anything, we are given a profusion of names—a veritable onomatology—from "self-abuse" to "the solitary vice" to "onanism" to "mastupratio" to "masturbation" to "pollution" to "spermatorrhœa" to the various terms eventually applied to the homosexual.[39] In other words, as with the love that dare not speak its name, it may be that the very perception of ineffability with regard to onanism only marks the necessary obverse of a hegemonic ideology's fiction of consistency. Ineffability, in this sense, does not foreclose but rather drives the creation of discourse to fill in the void.

As Žižek argues, "One of the most elementary definitions of ideology . . . is: a symbolic field which contains . . . a filler holding the place of some structural impossibility, while simultaneously disavowing this imposssibility" (*Plague* 76). The structural impossibility in this case may well be the fantasy that a capitalist economy can be imagined as a balanced circulatory system of exchanges: a social body. After all, as nineteenth-century worries about unregulated speculation, inequalities of wealth, urban pollution, and paper money attest, the problem with capitalist economy is that it has no real limits, for the very principle of profit making entails a structurally limitless cycle of reinvestment and expansion with no concern for the well-being of individuals or their environment.[40]

Thomas Laqueur has, to some extent, already made this argument in "Masturbation, Credit and the Novel," in which he argues that the period's anti-onanism rhetoric is not as much worried about the balancing of seminal humors as it is with an economy of surfeit, with " 'a fiery and voluptuous imagination' which had no bounds" (8).[41] The same juxtaposition between the fiction of a balanced circulatory system and the reality of a certain surplus therefore links the animal economy of the onanist and the political economy of the speculator. With both figures, the real sticking point is the very absence of the real, the fact that both the specular desire of the onanist and the monetary speculations of the economist rest on nothing more real than credulity, credence, and credit. Laqueur therefore aligns the anti-novel rhetoric of the eighteenth century with both masturbation and economics:

> By linking the fantastical elements of masturbation and the novel, I want to suggest a still broader historicist account, one which links

> autoeroticism, a new genre of imaginative literature, and a much more general and far ranging eighteenth-century debate about real versus false desire in economic life. Paper money and credit, in other words, are the same sort of fetish as the object of the autoerotic imagination. They represent, on the one hand [*sic*] the possibility of limitless growth, expansion, and desire and, on the other, the dangers of there being nothing there. ("Masturbation" 14)

By the nineteenth century, however, the novel—at least in its domestic and realist form—was no longer seen as such a threat. The question that this chapter poses is: Why is it that poetry suddenly gets fingered instead as the real danger?

As Laqueur argues, both money and the novel must rely on credit. One must believe in the fiction, the fetish of money's virtù for the capitalist system to work, even in the simple act of monetary exchange. We have returned, in other words, to the structural logic of the fetish that I explored in the last three chapters. As Žižek illustrates, the psychoanalytical fetish could be said to structure the Marxist commodity-fetish in the way suggested by Laqueur:

> When individuals use money, they know very well that there is nothing magical about it—that money, in its materiality, is simply an expression of social relations. . . . The problem is that in their social activity itself, in what they are *doing*, they are *acting* as if money, in its material reality, is the immediate embodiment of wealth as such. They are fetishists in practice not in theory. (*Sublime* 31)

The same, of course, can be said about fiction, as we saw in the chapter on Scott. When individuals read books, they know very well that there is nothing magical about them—that books, in their materiality, are simply an expression of social relations. The problem is that in their activity itself, in what they are *doing*, they are *acting* as if books, in their material reality, are the embodiment of reality as such. They are fetishists in practice not in theory. Novelistic realism perhaps most clearly functions by the logic of the fetish in this psychoanalytical sense; the realist novel maintains connection to the lost object (its referent) while also allowing the object to be lost. It is *because* readers can acknowledge yet temporarily suspend disbelief in the fictional status of the novel, that the novel, like money, like medievalism, can succeed in the popular imaginary. Indeed, it was only once the public believed in the reader's ability to disbelieve—to acknowledge at once the "truth" and the fictionality of the form—that the novel began to escape the vehement criticism directed at it around the turn of the nineteenth century when the real fear was that the naïve female and/or lower-class reader could be led to believe in those fictions not as aesthetic "truth" but as reality itself and thus to abandon their duties in the real world. The novel ceased to be seen as dangerous only once it underlined its counterfeit status thanks to the rise of real*ism*. As long as the novel could be acknowledged as but a version of reality, as a healthy because in some way "true" *diversion*, it could escape the charge of outright *perversion*. Analogy thus safeguarded against pathology.

Not so with Byron, who consistently refused this fetishizing maneuver, even finally rejecting, in the opening letter of *Childe Harold* IV, the line that separated Byron from his protagonist. This move has two equally disturbing implications. One the one hand, it abrogrates the fictionality of poetic form, insisting instead on the subjective truth of the poetic word: feeling confessing itself not only to itself, as Mill has it, but also, even more disturbingly, to the responsive reader. The most Romantic, and for the Victorians the most dangerous, of poetry refused to be read merely as entertainment but sought instead to speak directly to its readership in emotionally and politically volcanic ways, to echo Byron's favorite metaphor of the "lava of the imagination." As Byron puts it in *Don Juan*, "But I detest all fiction even in song,/ And so must tell the truth, howe'er you blame it" (6.59–60). We are no longer dealing with the mere suspension of disbelief, a formulation whose double negative perfectly mimics the logic of the fetish—but, rather, in belief *tout court*. The fear, in other words, was that people would take Byron's motto—*crede Byron*—seriously and follow him into revolutionary activity. On the other hand, such a maneuver—the collapsing of the boundary between *lego* and the *ego*—underlined precisely the fictionality of "Byron" as construct, and thus, by extension, the performative, ideological nature of "reality" at large. As we saw in chapter 3, because of this performativity and its related strategies (textualization, anthropologization, and a cold-carnival sensibility that questions all law), it was believed for a time that Byron posed a considerable threat to the status quo.

To counter this perceived threat, the nineteenth-century critic had to neutralize the radical power of Byron's poetics by reducing the Romantic poet to no more than an adolescent sexual perversity turned back upon itself: the melancholic masturbator. Many Victorians represented *themselves*, that is, as a necessary development from a romanticized adolescence to rational, heterosexual adulthood, a representation aided by the early deaths of the second-generation Romantics. The reviewers could thus be said to exorcise the Romantics by continuing to follow the logic of the fetish examined in the previous chapters: I know very well that our conventions, our laws, our beliefs are but performative fictions—Byron made that clear—but, nonetheless, I will continue to act as if I believed, or, as Ellis put it so perfectly, "These joys of triumph, it may be said, are mere illusions; but for the sake of such illusions is life chiefly worth having" (*RR* 5.1992). In other words, nineteenth-century critics infantilized the Romantics in order to protect their own childlike credulity. It may be that the relationship of the Victorian novel to Byronic poetry in general followed a similar logic. The tendency of Byron's poetry, I have argued, is to uncover the performative and narrative fictions that allow us to construct what we perceive as "reality." The Victorian novel knew full well this truth that Byron unveiled but it persisted in at once believing and not believing in its own fictions, or, to put it otherwise, it suspended its disbelief. Nineteenth-century capitalist, bourgeois ideology of course could be said to subscribe to the same fetishistic logic (*je sais bien mais quand même*), and the bourgeois subject, not surprisingly, therefore turned to the novel as her preferred artistic form.

And so, it bears remembering, did Scott after his 1814 *Waverley*, leaving the "malady" of poetic genius, as Scott put it in his 1825 journal, exclusively to Byron. Still, the opposition between a healthy poetic panacea popularized by Scott and a poetic pandemic filling "the moral world with disease" (*RR* 1.467), as Roberts characterized Byron's poetry, persisted throughout the nineteenth century as the two dominant tropes for poetry in the Victorian age. Both figurations, as the Coda argues, ultimately served to ensure poetry's eventual marginalization, but not before Tennyson made one more bid for a mass market in his own version of the romance.

CODA

Tennyson's *Idylls*, Pure Poetry, and the Market

> To generalize: it was the peculiar genius of Tennyson to light on the tired, moderate, unconscious ideologies of his time and class, and by the force of his investment in them, and his gorgeous lyric gift, to make them sound frothing-at-the-mouth mad.
>
> —Eve Sedgwick, *Between Men*

IF POETRY WAS, INDEED, PERCEIVED AS PERVERSE IN THE NINETEENTH century, as we saw in Byron, how exactly does one account for the equally pervasive tendency to represent poetry as an antidote to the ills of a prosaic age, as we saw in Scott? Why do we see such wildly opposing (if equally outrageous) claims for the poetic act? Both characterizations—curse and cure—are tied, I believe, to the nineteenth-century fantasy that one could define poetic form outside of market or political influence. Both characterizations were designed to obscure the highly politicized and *popular* maneuvers of the two poets most commonly invoked by late Romantic and early Victorian critics as the epitome of the Romantic poet of genius, Byron and Scott. Instead of acknowledging the complexity and market influence of romance poetry, an emergent Victorian ideology responded to the rise of the novel, to the implementation of a mass market, and to the political threat of an emergent lower-class readership by separating poetry altogether from market circulation.

Indeed, we could say that, as a result, a new generic preoccupation developed in perfect coincidence with, and perhaps as a direct result of, the emergent literary market of the nineteenth century. I am speaking not of those popular narrative forms that were being ingested at an ever-increasing rate by a growing body of readers and that are generally associated with the growth of a mass market—gothic tales, medieval ballads, historical romances, sensationalist fiction, the domestic novel—but of an arch-generic form that, while not so popular (even self-consciously *not* marketable), can be said to orbit popular narrative realism as the opposite that attracts it: "pure poetry."[1] Both defenders and assailants of poetry contributed to the development of this concept: defenders argued that a "perfect" or "pure" poetry, untainted by the demands of the market, provided an antidote to the enervation, sensationalism, commodification, and tastelessness of a prosaic age; assailants, on the other hand, seeking in part to refigure Byron's critique of the status quo and his influence on nineteenth-century radicals, argued that poetry, precisely insofar as it was defined against market concerns, was no longer able to have any effect in the world, that its very oppositionality divorced it from the social concerns of the day, from a public demanding a realistic representation of those concerns, and from the governing ideology of nineteenth-century society—political economy. "Purity" in this formulation is akin to onanistic self-involvement. In short, both defenders and assailants can be said to discover in verse's *versus* an inherent or natural reason for what was, in fact, a gradual if persistent historical change: poetry's sway with the reading public was decreasing, its uncertain orbit—newly caught in the growing pull of the novel—was sending it farther and farther into obscurity.[2]

Tennyson's *Idylls of the King* can be read as a last-ditch effort to accommodate the conflicting demands that were being directed at poets in the period as critics variously attacked or defended the writing of poetry. As I will show, poets were faced with an apparently paradoxical injunction in the Victorian period: realize but idealize; be like the novel, although not too sensational or "low"; at the same time, be "poetic," although not too Byronic or politically idealistic. The very fact that Tennyson managed not only to crack a difficult market but to appease critics from various journals and political affiliations suggests that, for the 1860s at least, the *Idylls* surmounted the contradictions inherent in these conflicting demands and managed to be all things to all people. I also wish to suggest, however, why Tennyson's *Idylls* could succeed so well in the sixties yet be so reviled by critics only a decade later. The reason, this chapter will argue, is that Tennyson disclosed, even while attempting to resolve, the contradictions inherent in both the dialectical injunctions directed at poets at mid-century and in the rhetorical strategies used by reviewers to contain, if only figuratively, the perceived dangers of the market.

The two main rhetorical strategies of the periodicals were as follows: 1) use the seductively "feminine" and the Satanically Byronic as the negative counters against which to define all things good; and 2) borrow the language of increasingly stable institutions such as the hospital to contain the perceived threat of a burgeoning market economy. The circulation of capital thus became reconceptualized as the circulatory systems of a single social body, with the critic as administrator, in both senses, of the cultural goods. At the same time, the reviews concerned themselves with the body and mind of the individual reader, whose unruly desires were increasingly associated not with radical ambitions but with youthful romance. According to the reviews of the 1860s, Tennyson's *Idylls* represented just the sort of tonic necessary to help heal a social body that craved the stimulants of either sensationalist, "feminized" fiction or hypersensitized Byronic romance, either of which could be read into what Tennyson calls in the epilogue of the *Idylls* that "art with poisonous honey stolen from France." The critics' rhetorical encomiums all too quickly turned into odium in the following decade, however. As this chapter argues, the very obfuscations that in the *Idylls* resolved the aesthetic conflicts of Tennyson's day—and drove the critics' panegyrics—at the same time laid bare the ideological contradictions of the period, thus setting up the dismissal of Tennyson as ineffective and ephemeral later in the century. Tennyson's own need to sweeten the bitter pill of poetry led to a double status for his *Idylls*—cure and poison both. The *Idylls*, for a time, allowed poetry to reenter the cultural mainstream, the nervous system of the social body, and thus to improve the literary tastes of the masses; however, the work also unleashed some of the poisonous contradictions inherent in both the very concept of a body social and the belief that one could in fact idealize the real or, for that matter, poeticize novelistic realism.

THE ROMANTIC LEGACY

Lionel Stevenson identifies 1825 as the year that first witnessed "a serious challenge to the primacy of poetry in the field of literature" (260). In that year, he argues, "poetry was suddenly faced with an ideological assault that gravely menaced its survival," an assault launched by Bentham in his 1825 "Rationale of Reward" ("Prejudice apart, the game of push-pin is of equal value with the arts and sciences of music and poetry"), by the "Whig intellectual," Macaulay, in his 1825 essay on Milton ("as civilisation advances, poetry almost necessarily declines"), and by Carlyle, who as early as 1825 wrote to Jane Welsh that he'd rather be a peasant than "one of these same miserable metre ballad-mongers" (Stevenson 262–64). Erickson has also marked this date as the beginning of the end of poetry's dominance in the popular imagination, basing his conclusions on an analysis of the Romantic poetry market and technological changes in the production of literature: "[I]t would seem that with the end of the reign of poetry in the literary marketplace in 1825 also came the real end of Romanticism" (40). After this date, and perhaps even more clearly after the bank panic and financial crisis of 1826, publishers simply stopped publishing first editions of poetry, until by the thirties and forties Edward Moxon was virtually the only publisher in England of new collections of poetry by individual writers; and his firm survived only because he required poets to underwrite part of the costs of publishing.[3]

We might also point to another date: 1824, the year of Byron's death, which critics and Victorian poets could retrospectively pinpoint as the beginning of the end of poetry's dominance in the popular imaginary. As Bulwer-Lytton puts it, in an article entitled the "Present State of Poetry" (1838),

> Byron died,—and poetry, like the mistress of some eastern king whose career of despotism and pomp had closed, seemed sacrificed at his tomb. When the multitude ceased to speak of Lord Byron, they ceased to talk about poetry itself. Even his contemporaries, who in his lifetime would have received a ready hearing for their most careless measures,

> would now strike their harps and sound their cymbals to empty benches. Though Mr. Leigh Hunt might write a yet better poem than his charming "Rimini," we suspect it would not, in our time, pass through seven editions, or even three. Though Mr. Moore might introduce to the world another "Lalla Rookh," yet more dazzling than her predecessor, she would never fetch three thousand guineas in the Book-Bazaar. Poetry has retired to her stronghold with her faithful few, and her empire, lately so vast, is parceled out among a hundred little principalities of prose. (*Critical* 1.335–36)[4]

Bulwer-Lytton makes it clear that the "Muse is not dead, neither does she sleep" (*Critical* 1.336), but those who hear her must find her in her "immemorial haunts" at the "old Castalian fountain" (*Critical* 1.336). Poets have turned away from Byron, according to Bulwer-Lytton, choosing Wordsworth and Shelley as their models because "[y]oung men of genius are fond of the beauties which are not for the vulgar" (*Critical* 1.338). As he continues,

> Scott, in most qualities, and Byron in some (and those his greatest,) addressed feelings and thoughts common to a very wide range of readers, however varying their pursuits, however ordinary their understandings. But Shelley and Wordsworth each address minds of philosophical or poetic temperament. They are poets for the poet—not the minstrels of bower and hall. (*Critical* 1.338)

Bulwer-Lytton even ends by exhorting the young and still little-known Tennyson to avoid imitating the Romantics, especially Byron, for, as he explains, men would not "have grown tired of hearing Byron called the Great, if there had not been Byronic homunculi in every corner of the streets" (*Critical* 1.344). Bulwer-Lytton exhorts Tennyson to avoid such influence and return to the pure source of poetry as he matures: "Streams purify themselves by running on,—especially those that come direct from Castaly" (*Critical* 1.344–45). Tennyson is exhorted, in other words, to adopt the Palace of Art's conception of purposively unmarketable and therefore unsullied high-cultural form: the fantasy of a pure poetry.

The danger was that Tennyson would feel the pull of the Byronic legacy, which, of course, in many ways he did. When he heard of Byron's death, for example, Tennyson famously carved into a rock the words "Lord Byron is dead." He himself was fascinated with the notion that poetry writing was associated with melancholic madness, an interest that was further spurred by the madness in his close family members.[5] Tennyson also consistently explored the issue of madness, melancholy, mourning, and monomania in his most famous poems, from "Mariana" to "Supposed Confessions of a Second-Rate Sensitive Mind" to "the Two Voices" to "St Simeon Stylites" to two of his major works, *In Memoriam* and Tennyson's favorite poem, *Maud*. Indeed, for a time after the publication of *Maud*, Tennyson was even placed in the Spasmodic camp, a group of Victorian poets who turned the Romantic fascination with extreme states of mind and Satanic heroes into laughable because overblown stereotype. And yet, despite this apparent alignment of Tennyson with the psychical perversities of Byron, the most common representation of Tennyson's poems in the periodical reviews of the period is as effeminate, luxurious ephemera. One reason for this tendency not to see Tennyson as dangerous is that in his own romances Tennyson turned away from any direct political overtones except those in support of empire. He even avoided the homosexual intimations of Byron's position—intimations that, as many have argued, Tennyson felt quite intimately—and turned instead to the figure of woman as his primary mastertrope.[6] In writing poetry after Byron, Tennyson found himself having to negotiate a rather fraught generic form: possibly dangerous yet laughably onanistic; culturally "high" yet recently popular; autonomously pure yet developing out of the same impure source as the novel: the romance. The conflicted position of the poetic enterprise is perhaps best exemplified by the very question that was posed incessantly in the periodical essays of the Victorian period: What is poetry?[7] The answer to that question in the reviews, as we will see, gradually sublimed poetry into ontological impossibility.

THE REAL IDEAL

As the poetry market failed, the new tendency of criticism in the nineteenth century was to value poetry's very marginality as a sign of its purity, which is to say that the literary reviews of the nineteenth century facilitated and legitimated the separation of poetry from the cultural mainstream by making a virtue of necessity, turning poetry into a high cultural product. Faced with poetry's enforced separation from an emergent mass market, the nineteenth-century critic increasingly valued that very separation.[8] As Mill put it in 1833, "A poet may write poetry with the intention of publishing it; he may write it even for the express purpose of being paid for it; that it should be poetry, being written under any such influences, is far less probable" (12–13). Though the early-Victorian "man of letters" was himself dependent on the market circulation of the periodical review, he also set the groundwork for the emergence of the university intellectual later in the century by figuring the critical enterprise as the work of a professional specialist outside the crass influence of capital. An act of honor among many critics was, then, to point out the advantages of having a specialized, albeit marginalized, sphere of culture that could heal the side effects of toiling in a material, technological world. As one *British Quarterly* reviewer exclaims, responding in the article to the Utilitarian critique of poetry, "No; the task of the poet is not a busy idleness," since it "inspires hopes which our sober and toilsome world cannot realize" (50): "If familiarity blunts the more delicate susceptibilities of social life," the reviewer explains, "literature may be said to supply an antidote to this ungracious influence" (49) and the critic, we might add, assumes in this scenario the role of culture's professional physician.

George Henry Lewes in 1842 makes the analogy perfectly clear: "Criticism is to aesthetics what the practice of medicine is to physiology. . . . Aesthetics is the *physiology of art*" (*VP* 53). Critics such as John Henry Newman in *Discourses On the Scope and Nature of University Education* (1852) and Matthew Arnold in *Essays in Criticism* (1861) or *Culture and Anarchy* (1869) were following Coleridge's lead and attempting to establish an institutional "clerisy" that would combat the ungracious influence of a material, technological world. With the disciplinary cultural doctor as its institutionalized specialist, culture acts in this rhetoric as "the true nurse of the pursuing love [of perfection]" (Arnold, *Complete* 5.145) and "living poetry," as Charles Kingsley writes in 1854, thus becomes the antidote to "the spiritual dyspepsia of an unhealthy and nerveless time" (*VS* 175). Against the epidemic influence of Byron, then, we can trace a pervasive counterdiscourse of poetic antibodies not unlike the rhetoric we saw applied to Scott's healthful romances.

This demand for an antidote that could counteract the enervating diseases of a prosaic age pervaded the poetry reviews of the Victorian age. Increasingly, the critics decried any effort simply to reproduce that "sober and toilsome world" of everyday existence and demanded instead a poetry that transcended or invigorated social existence, but a poetry that, at the same time, was understandable to any reader, regardless of class. F. W. Robertson, for example, informed a meeting of his Mechanics' Institute that poetry can "enable the man of labour to rise sometimes out of his dull, dry, hard toil, and dreary routine of daily life, into forgetfulness of his state, to breathe a higher and serener, and purer atmosphere" (Altick 198). Even Hallam claims that the "true poet" is able to "elevate inferior intellects into a higher and purer atmosphere" (851). As with the rhetoric associated with the constitution of the discipline of literary criticism—the intellect's "perfect state" (Newman 255), "more perfect conceptions" (Arnold, *Complete* 3.274), "the love and pursuit of perfection" (Arnold, *Complete* 5.145)—poetry was perceived among a certain circle of influential critics as a perfect or pure form; to quote Sidney Dobell, "a perfect Poem is the perfect expression of a Perfect Human Mind" (Starzyk 87).

For many critics, then, beginning with Hallam in his 1831 review of Tennyson's first volume of verse, it was precisely the purity of Tennyson's early poetry that distinguished him from other writers. Hallam, for example, exhorts Tennyson to continue to aspire toward a "poetry of sensation," an "art free and unalloyed" unlike the more popular compositions "which take for their primary subject the usual passions of the heart, and deal with them in a simple state, without applying the transforming powers of high imagination" (851). According to Hallam, "[A]rt should keep quite distinct from all that is not of itself"; indeed, he praises those poems by Tennyson that keep "the feeling of art . . . ascendant in our minds over distressful realities, by constant reference to images of tranquil beauty" (858). Tennyson was criticized, in fact, whenever he brought in too much of the ordinary world. This sort of critique came to a head with the publication of *The Princess*, for the introduction into *The Princess* of modern themes, particularly "talk of college and of ladies' rights," led many critics to question the obtrusion of the too-familiar into Tennyson's poetry. The problem, John Marston explains in an 1848 review of the poem, is that "the details of ordinary life are so frequently obtruded" that the "effect is similar to that which would result from investing some antique divinity with a cashmere shawl" (*VS* 167). The Palace of Art, it appears, must remain at one step removed from the real world.

If there was a dialectic at work in the period, however, the pendulum appears to have been swinging to a large extent away from the rarefied "purity" of poetic form. Tennyson therefore found himself facing conflicting advice as early as the publication of his first volume of poetry in 1830. Whereas Hallam was pushing Tennyson away from the "usual passions of the heart," John Wilson ("Christopher North") just a year later warns him that he should, like Wordsworth, "shun not the sights of common earth" (*VS* 109). As William Fox asks in his 1831 review of Tennyson's volume, "Is not the French Revolution as good as the siege of Troy?" (*VS* 73). In fact, a large number of critics criticized the very "purity" of Tennyson's early poetry. One reviewer in the *Christian Remembrancer* (1842) insists, for example, that Tennyson include, alongside " 'a baseless world of dream,' " the " 'familiar matters of today' " derived "from the ordinary fountains of mirth and woe" (*VS* 98). Unlike Hallam's demand for an "art free and unalloyed," this reviewer demands precisely "the alloy of something firmer, though it may be coarser." Because it is speech, he argues, poetry "can never be long . . . without having aims in themselves foreign to art" (*VS* 102). What we have here is a critique of the very concept of poetry as pure, all the while corroborating the belief that social realism and moral issues are "in themselves foreign to art." Indeed, the problem with Tennyson's early poetry, according to Aubrey de Vere (1849), is precisely "that of appearing poetry, distilled from poetry, rather than drawn from the living sources of life and of truth" (432). This kind of criticism, the dialectical opposite of Hallam's exhortations, reached an especial fervor with the publication of *Maud* in 1855, the poem that perhaps most clearly engaged the Byronic legacy and that, as a result, was almost universally denounced in the reviews as the result of a fevered imagination. This branch of Tennyson's poetry was seen by Walter Bagehot (1859), for example, as the kind of "mental malaria" that appeals especially to youth, that "season of semi-diseased feeling" and "susceptible imaginations" to which, he claims, the poetry of Keats and Shelley is also directed (*T* 218–19).

We should keep in mind that, following the Romantics, it was the most Romantic of the Victorians that bore the brunt of critical attacks. Tennyson's early poetry was, for example, critiqued as dangerous whenever reviewers aligned him with the second-generation Romantics or their self-proclaimed disciples, the even more reviled Spasmodics. Indeed, one of the goals of the most virulent attack on Tennyson's early poetry, according to its author John Wilson Croker, was to put Tennyson squarely in the Cockney camp. As Croker writes to John Murray, the son of the publisher of the *Quarterly* in which appeared the supposedly fatal article by Lockhart attacking Keats as an effeminate Cockney, "Tell your father and Mr. Lockhart that I undertake Tennyson and hope to make another Keats of him" (Shannon 25). Leigh Hunt, himself classed as the leader of the defamed Cockney School, felt obliged, in the hopes of proving his own knowledge of things masculine, to emasculate Tennyson in the *Church of England Quarterly Review* (1842): "[H]e runs, or rather reposes, altogether upon feelings (not to speak it offensively) too sensual. His mind lives in an atmosphere heavy with perfumes. He grows lazy by the side of his Linconshire waterlilies" (*T* 128). Even one of the Spasmodics, George Gilfillan, attacked Tennyson's perfumed and effeminate sensuality: "[H]is fancy loves, better than is manly or beseeming, the tricksy elegancies of artificial life—the 'white sofas' of his study—the trim walks of his garden—the luxuries of female dress—and all the tiny comforts and beauties which nestle round an English parlour" (Weinstein 172–73). Lolling in a sensual haze, the self-indulgent Tennyson was thus painted with the same brush that at the end of the eighteenth century daubed the female reader in such alarming colors. The same effeminacies, pathologies, and perversities would be applied to each of the poetic movements that in the Victorian period took up aspects of the Romantic ideology—from the Spasmodics of the early- to the Aesthetics of the mid- to the Decadents of the late Victorian period.

As we saw in the previous chapter, one notable effect of such criticism was the recharacterization of poetry rather than the popular novel as the "mental malaria" that must be combated. Having changed rungs on the literary hierarchy of dominant generic forms, the novel had become, in many critical evaluations of the period, not the infecting virus but the new organic totality and it was now poetry that began to be represented as the subordinated and residually viral form. As early as 1828 we find B. W. Procter defending poetry against the attacks of the Utilitarians: "The question is—whether Poetry and Art, whether all that touches our sympathies and operates upon our affections, should be rooted up and exterminated, like some long-established evil, or wide-spread disease" (196).

According to both its defenders and detractors, then, poetry was relegated to the margins of the imagined cultural sphere. Only the figuration changed: poetic forms could be represented as either pockets of bacterial infection of or islands of resistance against the market circulation of the more popular arch-generic form—narrative. In either case, poetry was no longer represented as an analogue for the social body but as a foreign body, one that could then be figured as either curse or cure. Among both defenders and detractors, a distinction was being made between poetic experience and "ordinary" experience, a distinction that, as Alan Sinfield explains, "secures in one aspect poetry's authority and in another aspect its marginality" (173). In either case, we see how poetry's figuration as it developed from the Romantics to the Victorians marginalized the poet *regardless of whether that figuration attacks or defends verse.*

Hence the debate over the very definition of poetry: Is it debilitating or invigorating, invidious or invaluable, related or unrelated to daily concerns? The poet, as a result of this debate, found himself having to negotiate apparently contradictory injunctions. Indeed, in the critical reviews of the period, a struggle occurred between critics such as Arthur Hallam, who felt that poetry should aspire toward a "purer atmosphere," and those critics such as Arthur Clough, who advised poets to follow the example of the novel (*VS* 155).[9]

And on both sides of the divide, gender was used as a tropological weapon to emasculate the opposition. According to the idealists, the simple recording of the ordinary world is a passive (and hence feminine) activity. As Mill writes in 1833, "The same persons whose time is divided between sight-seeing, gossip, and fashionable dissipation, take a natural delight in fictitious narrative; the excitement it affords is of the kind which comes from without" (8); true poetry, on the other hand, "is feeling confessing itself to itself, in moments of solitude" (12). We seek out the "true and manly poet," W. C. Roscoe writes in 1854, "not to be reminded of our shortcomings and imbecilities, but to be lifted into a clearer air which may revive our spirit and purge our eyesight" (*VS* 192).

Then again (and this qualification always seems necessary when dealing with dialectical opposites), the idealizing of a "poet of sensation" could just as commonly be represented as feminine, especially if the offended critic was advocating a return to realistic representation. John Ruskin in his essay on the pathetic fallacy, for example, criticizes Tennyson and Keats for being too easily "subdued by the feelings under which they write, hence admitting certain "modes of thought which are in some sort diseased." Ruskin attacks "reflective" or inward-turning poets as inherently susceptible to disease or madness because they tend to use the pathetic fallacy. "The temperament which admits the pathetic fallacy," Ruskin explains, "is that of a mind and body in some sort too weak to deal fully with what is before them or upon them; borne away, or over-clouded, or over-dazzled by emotion" (3.208). Such poets lack the willpower to control their emotions and lose the ability to make cognitive distinctions between the internal self and the external world. Passion, sensualism, the loss of self-control: these are the symptoms of the mind turning in on itself. The pathetic fallacy of such poets, in other words, amounts to a devouring solipsism, a masturbatory self-involvement. As Ruskin explains in *Modern Painters*, "All the diseases of the mind leading to the fatalest ruin consist primarily of [man's] isolation. They are the concentration of man upon himself" (7.263). On the other hand, the truly creative—perhaps we should read "procreative"?—poet represents a triumph of the will over fantasy, emotion, and internality. In such a poet, Ruskin writes—and listen here for the rhetoric of phallic as much as mental mastery—"the intellect also rises, until it is strong enough to assert its rule against, or together with, the utmost efforts of the passions; and the whole man stands in an iron glow, white hot, perhaps, but still strong, and in nowise evaporating; even if he melts, losing none of his weight" (*VP* 90).

Strength, firmness, fullness, weight: these were the code words for masculinity in art and, like most ideological predicates, easily circulated among critics on either side of the dialectic. The sixties represent a nodal point in that dialectic, when contradictory demands were pulling the poets of the period in opposite directions; and, as I suggested above, a resolution of the dialectic resided in the all-pervasive double injunction: realize but idealize. In the writing of the *Idylls*, Tennyson seemed to be quite conscious of the dialectical injunctions of the reviewers. J. T. Knowles reports, for example, that Tennyson told him: "When I was twenty-four I meant to write a whole great poem [on the Arthurian legend], and began it in the *Morte d'Arthur*. I said I should do it in twenty years; but the Reviews stopped me" (181–82). What stopped him may have indeed been the fear that an Arthurian romance was simply too far removed from contemporary concerns. On April 19, 1856, Emily Tennyson writes to G. S. Venables that Tennyson "troubles himself . . . that the subject has not reality enough" (Alfred Tennyson 672) and, on December 11, 1858, Tennyson writes to Ticknor and Fields: "I wish that you would disabuse your own minds and those of others, as far as you can, of the fancy that I am about an Epic of King Arthur. I should be crazed to attempt such a thing in the heart of the 19th Century" (672). The way Tennyson circumvented the criticism he apparently anticipated was to conceive of the *Idylls* as, in part, allegorical: "Of course Camelot for instance, a city of shadowy palaces, is everywhere symbolic of the gradual growth of human beliefs and institutions, and of the spiritual development of man. Yet there is no single fact or incident in the 'Idylls,' however seemingly mystical, which cannot be explained as without any mystery or allegory whatever" (Hallam Tennyson 523–24). In other words, Tennyson attempted to circumvent the Scylla and Charybdis of that Victorian dialectical injunction, realize but idealize, by having it both ways; the *Idylls* would be about both the past and the present, about individual people and "the spiritual development of man." He thus appears to repeat the fetish strategies we saw in Scott, although, as we will see, with his own distinctive twist.

The critics apparently approved of Tennyson's maneuvers, seeing in the *Idylls*, as one reviewer in the *British Quarterly Review* (1870) makes clear, an escape from both "the peculiar realism for which . . . such a hunger is now exhibited" and the "false extravagant, and perverted idealism . . . before which all health and truth is prostrated." What Tennyson has done instead, according to this reviewer, is to fix "on the legend of Arthur, as that which most readily lent itself to imposing accessories and details charged with enough of the ideal element to relieve the baldness of modern ideas" (*VS* 316). Tennyson apparently manages to have it all ways, so that, as W. E. Gladstone argues in 1859, "[t]he Arthurian Romance has every recommendation that should win its way to the homage of a great poet. . . . The distance is enough for atmosphere, not too much for detail; enough for romance, not too much for sympathy" (468), " 'The Round Table' is the world of today," the *British Quarterly* reviewer explains; indeed (and here the contradictions inherent in this ideological stance become clear), Tennyson lifts up "these half-empty forms of fancy so as to impart to them a rarer reality" (*VS* 317).

WORKING THE NOVEL OUT

Tennyson's *Idylls of the King* itself can be said to replicate the ideological strategies of nineteenth-century reviewers. On the one hand, Tennyson abstracts the heterogeneous realities of nineteenth-century Britain by presenting his readers with an idealized real—the "rarer reality" of a fantasized Camelot. On the other hand, Tennyson follows the reviewers' conservative strategies by offering up "woman" as a privileged trope defining all that is wrong with British culture. In so doing, he also protects *himself* from the charge of effeminacy that was increasingly directed at the male poet in the Victorian period. Tennyson's strategy resembles nothing less than that of his arch-enemy Alfred Austin, who writes in 1869 that the real problem with British literature and Britain in general is that women have "ceased to be domestic" and are "unrestrainedly rioting in any and every arena of life" (*Poetry* 104–5). Such a rhetorical ploy served to stabilize the "plenitude" or "health" of those literary forms and cultural formations that were, in contrast, gendered masculine—"pure poetry," the epic, nation, the institution of literary criticism. The gendering strategy and the abstracting strategy are, in fact, related: Tennyson attempts in the *Idylls* to address the complexities of the social arena and the heterogeneous demands of a burgeoning mass market by translating his fears into different registers, those of gender and sexuality, with the double effect of naturalizing (as desire) and abstracting (into determinable figures) the social and economic realities of nineteenth-century Britain. I should be clearer, however, for "woman" served both a "positive" and "negative" role in both Victorian cultural discourse and Tennyson's *Idylls*. After all, "woman" in her guise as "angel of the house" could also be said to define all that was considered proper in middle-class ideological values—self-sacrifice, devotion, hard work, compassion. In this way, "woman" functioned as a focus for Victorian culture's utopic desires to heal what was perceived as an ailing social body, while, in her dual role as angel-whore, she also served as a privileged locus for ideological contradiction. The return to "woman" as master-trope can also be read as a way to leave behind the troubling psychical and homosexual dynamics of Byron's poetry.

In certain obvious ways, Tennyson's *Idylls of the King* both legitimates and makes conspicuous criticism's tendency to present "woman" as the master-signifier of, at one and the same time, purity and putrescence. On the one hand, Tennyson argues, through Arthur, that "the maiden passion for a maid" is "what makes a man" by keeping "down the base in man"; *woman*, paradoxically enough, thus comes to focus all that is pure in *man* ("high thought, and amiable words/ And courtliness, and the desire of fame,/ And love of truth" ["Guinevere" 478–80]), all that will save Britain from the wilderness, "wherein the beast was ever more and more,/ But man was less and less" ("Coming of Arthur" 11–12). For this reason, although the "four great zones of sculpture" at Arthur's hall appear to symbolize a male phylogeny—"And in the lowest beasts are slaying men,/ And in the second men are slaying beasts,/ And on the third are warriors, perfect men,/ And on the fourth are men with growing wings" ("Holy Grail" 232–37)—it is, in fact, "woman" that provides the principle of spiritual, cultural, and mental evolution in the *Idylls*. In the youth of Camelot, for example, the knights require that the queen act as their spiritual totem: "it more beseems the perfect virgin knight/ To worship woman as true wife beyond/ All hopes of gaining, than as maiden girl" ("Merlin and Vivien" 22–24). The sublimated desire of courtly love becomes the principle of spiritual development and the knights, because of this desire, become "passionate for an utter purity/ Beyond the limit of their bond" ("Merlin and Vivien" 26–27). On the other hand, Guinevere and her evil double, Vivien, are the main causes for Camelot's fall. As spurs to erotic desire, they represent precisely the beast in man. "Woman" can be said to serve as the linchpin of Tennyson's symbolic epic romance and of his symbolic system in general because she functions as the motor of narrative, the force that determines progression and destruction both.

As a result, although the *Idylls* is purportedly about "[i]deal manhood closed in real man," as Tennyson informs Queen Victoria in the 1873 epilogue, the majority of the books are, in fact, about women; that includes all of the four books published in 1859, originally named after the female protagonists. That original collection, entitled *The True and the False*, reads like an instruction manual for proper female behavior, juxtaposing two examples of female purity—the long-suffering Enid and the ever-faithful Elaine—against two examples of dangerous womanhood—the ever-conspiring Vivien and Guinevere herself (whose sin "is all woman's grief" ["Guinevere" 216]). Indeed, Merlin could be said to speak the lesson of these original four books when he thinks to himself: "we scarce can sink as low:/ For men at most differ as Heaven and earth,/ But women, worst and best, as Heaven and Hell" ("Merlin and Vivien" 811–13).

Tennyson turned so frequently to female figures in his poetry, I believe, because the ideological contradictions determining the idea of woman was analogous to the paradoxical situation facing the poet in the mid-Victorian period. The male poet could thus deflect while addressing the attacks directed at male poets themselves in the period. As Kathy Psomiades has also argued, poetry was analogous to "woman" because it could be perceived as transcendent in its value thanks to its cultural autonomy, "like a good middle-class woman," yet tainted or perverse because of its necessary relation to a market of consumers, "like a bad, working-class prostitute" (45). Indeed, by turning so frequently to the figure of woman in his poetry, Tennyson could be said to make conspicuous the unacknowledged reason for the reviewers' own constant turn to the feminine as trope: the feminine allowed the critics to figure the paradoxes of their own cultural situation. They wished, that is, to create for themselves a transcendent realm of autonomous isolation—a disinterested Academy of cultural critics—but inevitably had to, at some point, face the exigencies of a market economy.

Women come to represent the driving force of culture and civilization in Tennyson's work because their paradoxical metaphorical status resembles the paradoxical status of poetry, of high culture, and even of literary criticism in a market economy geared to mass consumption. For this reason, the allegorical figures for spiritual development in the *Idylls* are not only figured as feminine but aligned in Tennyson's mind with religion and the arts: "The Lady of the Lake in the old romances of Lancelot," Tennyson explains, "instructs him in the mysteries of the Christian faith" (699) and the "Fairy Queens" that supposedly built the city of Camelot and the "four great zones of sculpture" in the first place represent "[t]he religions and the arts that came from the East" (701). Tennyson makes the feminine in these poems the principle of the desire to achieve some transcendent, artistic purity, a sort of antidote to the agonism of a capitalist Britain devaluing religion and the arts. Yet, at the same time that high culture becomes figured as a transcendentally pure, quasi-supernatural enterprise, the poet acknowledges both the marginality of his own cultural product and the impossible nature of the wish for high culture's transcendent autonomy.

The demands addressed to both women and high culture in the nineteenth century were impossible to materialize or, rather, the wished-for ideal could not help but be undone by the material conditions that contradicted it. Like the poet who wished to be withdrawn in his purity but must at some point be tainted by the market, the figure of woman was at once the purity of the ideal and the flesh that betrayed it. Perhaps for this reason, Tennyson has both Guinevere and his poem evoke a perfect order that is, however, already past. Like the inscription on Arthur's sword, Guinevere represents both a wish for a purity aligned with some originary or transcendent authority and the already-acknowledged impossibility of that purity within the materiality of the present. First, the description of the sword:

> on one side,
> Graven in the oldest tongue of all this world,
> "Take me," but turn the blade and ye shall see,
> And written in the speech ye speak yourself,
> "Cast me away!" ("Coming of Arthur" 300–304)

Guinevere, like the sword, is both the principle by which Arthur realizes his perfect kingdom and the materiality (in this case, of the flesh) that destroys it.

Taken, she is already presaged to be cast away. She is "the fairest under heaven" ("Coming of Arthur" 85), without whom, according to Arthur, "I seem as nothing in the mighty world,/ And cannot will my will, nor work my work/ Wholly" ("Coming of Arthur" 87–88), yet she is also "the loathsome opposite" of all Arthur had planned for his kingdom, threatening to undo all of society as she undoes the Table Round. So Arthur explains to Guinevere in the penultimate book of the *Idylls*,

> I hold that man the worst of public foes
> Who either for his own or children's sake,
> To save his blood from scandal, lets the wife
> Whom he knows false, abide and rule the house:
> For being through his cowardice allowed
> Her station, taken everywhere for pure,
> She like a new disease, unknown to men,
> Creeps, no precaution used, among the crowd,
> Makes wicked lightnings of her eyes, and saps
> The fealty of our friends, and stirs the pulse
> With devil's leaps, and poisons half the young. ("Guinevere" 509–19)

Perhaps the excessiveness of the rhetoric here is a function of Tennyson's own fears for his *Idylls*, a reaction to the attacks directed at poets themselves in the period; after all, though taken for pure, Tennyson's work may already be tainted in its materiality—its reliance on both a market economy that disseminated it to the crowd and on a straightforward narrative that stirred the pulse of its readers.

Indeed, the very structure of the work is split between the stylistic preciosity of the symbolic passages and the driving narrative of the majority of the work, just as its style vacillates between an epic language, the "oldest tongue" of literature, and "the speech ye speak yourself." Though Tennyson's poem has pretensions to epic status and though he critiques in the epilogue any "art with poisonous honey stolen from France," his *Idylls* could be said to present the reader with precisely the most suspect plot details of both Byronic romance and the nineteenth-century French novel: marriage squabbles, oath-breaking, adultery, gossip, petty scheming, intrigues, and the general pettiness of an elite class that spends its time at social gatherings, public spectacles, and love-making. The conflicting generic parameters even begin to have an effect on the very genre of traditional epic romance, as they did in Scott's romances (where, as we saw in chapter 2, Scott established his understanding of fiction's relation to moral "truth" over and against both the superstitions of the gothic and the specificities of history). As many critics have noticed, Tennyson like Scott undercuts with realistic explanations the supernatural events that are conventionally associated with the romance form.[10] The most supernatural of the books, "The Holy Grail," is placed, for example, in the mouth of an unreliable narrator, Percivale, caught up in the superstitions and false beliefs associated with the quest for the grail, and it is spoken to a reader, Ambrosius, who clearly stands in for an audience that prefers novelistic realism. As Ambrosius tells Percivale, he prefers to "Delight [himself] with gossip and old wives" (553) or "Chafferings and chatterings at the market-cross" (558) and he even asks Percivale, as if somewhat displeased by the tale to date, "Came ye on none but phantoms in your quest,/ No man, no woman?" (562–63). In such subtle ways, the very genre of epic romance, which fully authorizes the introduction of magic and the supernatural into narrative, is constantly undercut by other generic exigencies.[11] I agree with Herbert F. Tucker, who makes a similar argument about the Geraint idylls: The continual introduction of quotidian realities and the naturalistic undercuttings of the genre of epic inevitably lead the reader "to see these idylls as a trial of epic itself, in contest with the most vigorous claimant of the Victorian era to the honor of bearing the tale of the tribe: namely, the novel" (442).[12]

And, as in the critical rhetoric of the nineteenth-century periodicals, this generic battle, itself a displacement of various anxieties about the period, including anxieties about the status of the male poet, is figured, once again, in terms of gender. Through Guinevere, and the other women who drive the narratives of the individual books, Tennyson can denounce France's poisonous honey while allowing the reader a surreptitious taste. Translating his fears about the market to a sexual register also allows Tennyson both to keep his anxieties about his own work repressed and to project those fears onto a determinate figure—woman. In fact, Guinevere could be said to stand in for a number of other thus-deflected fears, since each of the evils initiated by Guinevere's faithlessness finds its parallel in contemporary Britain. The "rumour-mongering" of the peasants figures the general concerns about the growing voice of the masses and the concomitant rise in importance of journalism with its tendency to reproduce gossip, rumor, and scandal; the loss of faith in the laws of Arthur's court figures the general loss of faith in higher principles caused by the decline of religion and the rise of the values of competition and profit in a growing market economy; and, of course, the very decline of the Table Round figures the pervasive Victorian concern with the "condition of England" and the fears of England's decline.[13] These are all issues that we also saw in the romance poetry of Byron; by turning to the figure of woman, Tennyson attempted to salvage the romance from the charge of both revolutionary subversion and novelistic perversion, even as he raised many of the same issues by way of allegorical deflection. In Guinevere, Tennyson found a straw man (that is, woman) he could burn.

POETRY AS PER VERSE

Faced with the real and utterly contingent conditions that led to the marginalization of poetry in the nineteenth century (industrialism, capitalism, the education of the masses, the growth of the literary market—the point being here that there is no one determinable cause), the Victorian critic and poet managed, in the rhetoric surrounding the concept of art as cure or as curse, to confer onto the irreducible fact of marginalization the ineluctable mark of necessity. Why is poetry marginalized? Because it is driven to it by its very nature: either poetry works better from the margins in its curative role or poetry *should* be marginalized because it is inherently diseased. The explanation is tautological since it only serves to ensure poetry's separation by voiding it of all positive content: "[A]rt should keep quite distinct from all that is not of itself." This is the ideological operation that Žižek explains as Kant's concept of "formal ground," the purely "tautological gesture which only confers upon the same empirical content the universal form of law" (*Tarrying* 137). The tautology is concealed by "fill[ing] out again the empty form of ground with some fantasized imaginary content, conceived as a new, special kind of actual empirical content" (*Tarrying* 147). Herein lies the logic that led to the idolizing of Tennyson's work. The reviewers filled up the "empty form of ground"—the concept of pure or perfect art—with some fantasized content that gave it empirical weight. Hence, according to the reviews, *it is precisely through Tennyson's idealism, his "empty forms of fancy," that we can reach a "rarer reality."*

Herein also lies the logic of the gender designations Victorian critics and writers wielded to determine the positive content of "pure art": strength, firmness, fullness, weight are all terms that suggest some fantasized, empirical content to generic form. The manly poet must therefore stand "in an iron glow . . . in nowise evaporating; even if he melts, losing none of his weight." The more abstract and "rarefied" the definition of poetic form, the more the rhetoric felt the need to fill in some posited content. One might recall here the logic of the fetish that I explored in Byron and Scott. The poetic book stood in place of a doubly felt lack: on the one hand, the poet in an age of prose read his own marginalization as emasculation, which is not surprising given that critics most commonly turned to sexual tropes to make sense of the public sphere; on the other hand, poetry may also have served to uncover the performative, tautological nature of all ideologies (the lack at the heart of the symbolic order), thus running counter to the naturalizing strategies of the realist novel. One response to this double lack is to reinscribe the imagined fullness and purity of the phallus in the fetishized art object: the "whole man stand[ing] in an iron glow." We are offered an incorporation, both of the genre one wishes to purify and of those equally incorporated, now exorcised specters that threaten that very purification (the prostituted woman, the emasculated masturbator, the diseased outsider). The problem is that there is no such thing as a pure poetry. The inescapable heterogeneity of all generic forms can be denied but never eradicated by such apotropaic maneuvers.

This double lack also helps to explain how seamlessly the Decadent movement of the end of the century would be able to align the idea of pure art with "decadent" sexuality, thus collapsing the very opposition represented earlier in the century by, respectively, Scott's turn to the pure albeit barbaric medieval source of poetry to maintain the status quo and Byron's melancholic willingness to accept the decay of all generic and political forms (accompanied, of course, by his rejection of all bourgeois moral strictures as well). The reviews recast this opposition as one between panacea and pandemic; however, the opposition is itself a false one. Whether poetry was represented as cure or as curse, the position of marginality that poetry was made to occupy in either figuration is strictly homologous. As a result, the collapse of the opposition later in the century is perfectly logical, if not inevitable.

Like the notion of masculine purity or of pure masculinity, the antithetical term—the feminine—is similarly void, functioning in fact like Jacques Lacan's concept of the *point de capiton* or "quilting point": that which is constructed and perceived as some hidden cause behind the contingent, heterogeneous events of social existence and which thus serves to constitute a unified ideological field. What functions as the quilting point in the nineteenth century is the feminine, which, to quote Coleridge, threatens to "break up and scatter before it all robustness and manly vigor of intellect, all masculine fortitude of virtue" (*Friend* 24). Alfred Austin later in the century is therefore able to read in all the contingent facts of the age—"underground railways, ocean steamers, splendid carriages and horses, rare and long-kept vintages, enormous mirrors, miles of lace, new colours, exciting novels by eminent hands, newspapers without end, gorgeous spectacles, naked dancing-girls, deft cooks, and a mild religion"—one ground and cause: the age's "feminine infirmities" (*VP* 120).

Tennyson's use of "woman" as both the principle of progression and destruction only makes explicit the way the critics' ideological fantasies operate—by way of the paradox of desire: the closer one gets to the (desired) fantasy-object, the greater the chance that one will uncover the lack behind one's symbolic system, behind any ideology. In such a symbolic system, "woman," as the fantasy-object of desire, logically becomes, as in the figure of Guinevere, worst and best at once. "Woman" can thus be said to constitute not only the quilting point but also the unraveling point of Victorian cultural ideology. And desire, as ideological function, can be said both to constitute the fantasy-objects of Victorian ideological beliefs—pure poetry, high culture, the British social body—and to underscore the impossibility of ever fully realizing either a cohesive social body or a pure realm of uncommodified cultural production.

When it comes to the issue of ideological fetishization in Tennyson's *Idylls*, we may, therefore, be faced with a position between Scott and Byron: We are presented, that is, with an opposition between the fetishist and the melancholic, the former seeking to reestablish plenitude in the substituted object, the latter refusing to incorporate the object of loss. Tennyson could be said to have been caught between the two psychic economies, on the one hand invoking the possibility of a perfect order of wholeness centered in the fetishized sword, on the other hand insiting upon the impossibility of such a fantasy of plenitude. The law of the father, manifested in the sword of justice, is undercut, so to speak, by the figuration of Guinevere as desired phallic-mother-figure, for Arthur's sword is consistently associated with the feminine through the analogical alignment with Guinevere and the literal alignment with the Lady of the Lake, who both provides and takes back Arthur's sword. This fact reminds one that Freud identifies the fetish as "a substitute for the woman's (mother's) phallus which the little boy once believed in and does not wish to forego" (5.199). The purity sought by the Name-of-the-Father finds its obverse, one could say, precisely in what the Victorians perceived as perversion: the effeminacy of Tennyson's purified verse. We might be tempted, indeed, to follow Lacan and call this fraught position père-version.[14]

Because of such contradictions in Tennyson's work, various critics have described Tennyson as a "subversive reactionary" (Isobel Armstrong 3), a "reluctant revolutionary" (Christ, *Finer* 36), or, as T. S. Eliot argued, "the most instinctive rebel against the society in which he was the perfect conformist" (295).[15] As Sedgwick put it in the epigraph to this chapter, "[I]t was the peculiar genius of Tennyson to light on the tired, moderate, unconscious ideologies of his time and class, and by the force of his investment in them, and his gorgeous lyric gift, to make them sound frothing-at-the-mouth mad" (*Between Men* 119). Tennyson should perhaps be treated differently than not only radical authors such as Byron who reject all orthodoxy but also conservative authors such as Scott who at once believe and do not believe in the fetish objects they proffer to the public. Tennyson, by contrast, may be considered a "reluctant revolutionary" precisely because of his orthodoxy. He so much invests himself in the fantasy of a perfect order that he acknowledges its impossibility in the impure present. Unlike Byron, however, Tennyson continues to believe in his fantasy's value and even centrality. He could be said, that is, to "subvert the ruling ideology by taking it more literally than it is ready to take itself," the "*over*orthodox" position that Žižek identifies with such authors as Pascal, Kleist, Kierkegaard, and Brecht (*Plague* 77).

Such statements by critics of Tennyson may also begin to suggest why poetry was perceived as a threat in the Victorian period, as something that "should be rooted up and exterminated, like some long-established evil, or wide-spread disease." Unlike the realist fiction that dominated the market, poetry may have uncovered, precisely through the sorts of contradictions I have been examining, the way ideology functions in the rest of society. After all, what drives "realism" is precisely the fetishistic belief—at once acknowledged and disavowed—that some substantial reality does in fact exist behind a text's curtain of representations. As I argued in the last chapter, the novel follows the same fetishistic logic that structures the bourgeois subject: I know full well that my ideological beliefs (the referential objects of the realist plot, the reverential power of the money form, the residential inviolability of the private subject) rest on nothing more stable than constructed fictions but, nonetheless, I will act as if I believed. In the critical appreciation of Tennyson's allegorical and symbolic *Idylls,* those ideological beliefs—the "half-empty forms of fancy"—may remain all too conspicuous precisely because of Tennyson's investment in them *in all their ideality.* Because of this investment in an impossible ideal and despite the compensatory rhetoric of phallic plenitude, Tennyson's *Idylls*—in its evocation of an ideal purity always already lost—comes all too close to suggesting that any fantasy-object, be it the transcendent ideal of a perfect kingdom or the purity of poetry's self-reflexive turn or the representable real of contemporary Britain, can only ever cover over the irreducible lack of every signifying system, leaving the reader to fill in his or her own desires for plenitude, for meaning, for truth. In his very claim to be averse to perversity, Tennyson perhaps cannot help but exemplify, finally, what it has been the goal of this book to explore: the perversity of verse.

NOTES

INTRODUCTION

1. See, for other examples, Jennifer Ford, Frederick Burwick, and Alan Richardson.

2. Note that limitations of space will force me at times to refer to the "realist novel" as a "monolithic category" of sorts, much as McKeon, by necessity, treats "romance idealism." I hope, though, to redress this problem in my next book, *Byron and the Constitution of the British Novel*, to be co-written with Emily Allen.

3. To be clearer, many of the issues I will explore were in fact implemented in the eighteenth century, particularly with regard to poetry, including the opposition between a perverse sexual poetry and a "pure poetry," as Linda Zionkowski has recently explained in *Men's Work*; indeed, the term, pure poetry, was invented by the *eighteenth* century. The nineteenth century could be said, rather, to invent the aesthetic categories by which we would subsequently make sense of culture, including the contemporary sense of "culture" itself.

4. There is a large body of work on this issue. See, in particular, Ina Ferris, *Achievement* 1–78; John Taylor; Patrick Brantlinger, *Reading Lesson*; D. A. Miller, especially chapter 5; Athena Vrettos; John Mullan; Kate Flint, especially chapter 5; Jane Wood; Pamela K. Gilbert; Helen Small; and Peter Melville Logan. See also Elaine Showalter.

5. Few studies have dealt with the issue of the "nervous man" in the period. Notable exceptions include Jane Wood (chapter 2), Logan (chapter 2), and D. A. Miller 146-56, all of whom address the novel. Some studies have addressed the effeminacy of the poet, especially in terms of Keats, although these studies tend not to examine the Romantic medical discourse behind this effeminization: Marjorie Levinson's *Keats's Life of Allegory*; Susan Wolfson's "Feminizing Keats"; Christopher Ricks; and James Najarian. See also Stephen Guy-Bray on Thomas Lovell Beddoes. On the feminization of Byron, see, in particular, Sonia Hofkosh, chapter 2, and Wolfson's " 'Their She Condition.' " For the eighteenth-century precursors of this effeminization of poetry, see Zionkowski, chapter 1. Alan Richardson discusses the Romantic discourse of the nerves in relation to the Romantic poets but without significantly addressing the anxieties provoked by these discourses. Jennifer Ford addresses the fears connected to dreaming and the uncontrolled imagination in relation to the medical tracts of the day. On the pathologization of the category of genius and the relation of that pathology to Romantic literature, see Elfenbein, *Romantic Genius*.

6. On the Victorian social body, see Mary Poovey and Jon Klancher 38–46.

7. See Bourdieu's *Outline of a Theory of Practice* 72–95.

8. See Sedgwick's "Jane Austen and the Masturbating Girl." For a similar argument, see Ed Cohen, especially chapter 2. For Sedgwick's classic study of homosocial desire, see *Between Men*.

9. I have not been able to take into account many fine books that came into print after this book had been sent for review, including Jerome McGann's *Byron and Romanticism* (2002); Jane Stabler's *Byron, Poetics, and History* (2002); and Thomas Laqueur's *Solitary Sex* (2003).

CHAPTER 1. DIAGNOSING GENIUS

1. We can find the seeds of later developments even in the early works on genius. Whereas Joseph Warton sees "true genius" as the only disposition that can produce what he terms "pure poetry," he also acknowledges that such a temperament is predisposed to debauchery (1.106). Alexander Gerard is concerned throughout his *Essay on Genius* to underline that genius requires proper bounds: "In a man of genius, imagination can scarce take a single step, but judgment should attend it. The most luxuriant fancy stands most in need of being checked by judgment" (75). Although he argues that similar faculties apply to both scientific and artistic genius, Gerard also associates "genius in the arts," in particular, with strong passions, sometimes bordering on melancholy (416). Unlike genius for science, "genius for the arts can never exist where the passions have not great power over the imagination" (356). William Duff in his 1767 *Essay on Original Genius* aligns "original genius" particularly with poetry, which he in turn associates with "WILDNESS AND LUXURIANCE" (45), arguing that it is greatest when mankind is just "emerging from a state of ignorance and barbarity" (261). Duff also argues that poets are especially susceptible to passion: the poet "must himself be wrought up to a high pitch of extasy, if he expects to throw us into it. Indeed it is the peculiar felicity of an original Author to feel in the most exquisite degree every emotion, and to see every scene he describes" (177).

2. Both Wordsworth and Coleridge, for example, contest Lord Bacon's statement that knowledge is power by pointing out the relation of knowledge to disease (Wordsworth, *Prose* 1.324–25n and 1.328; Coleridge, *Constitution* 62–63).

3. According to John Mullan, Cheyne was "perhaps the most renowned popularizer of ideas of 'Nervous Distemper' " (203).

4. Cheyne may get the figure of one-third from Richard Blackmore's *Treatise of the Spleen and Vapours,* where Blackmore estimates that one-third of the English suffer from diseases arising from hysteria and hypochondria (iv). Blackmore states that the spleen "has here gained . . . a universal and tyrannical Dominion over both Sexes" (v).

5. Roy Porter makes a similar point about Cheyne in *Doctor of Society* 92. Porter also examines the eighteenth-century pathologization of civilization in his book (86–118).

6. See also Mullan 201.

7. For a widely cited examination of the one-sex model, see Thomas Laqueur's *Making Sex*. See also Michel Foucault, *History of Sexuality* 2.129. Although a one-sex model predominated, gender differences and inequalities were just as forcefully articulated, of course.

8. Hypochondria and melancholy were sometimes distinguished, as in Blackmore's *Treatise*; however, as Blackmore himself admits (154), they are often used as synonyms.

9. Aristotle also makes special mention of poets (157).

10. See Bamborough 103–18; Lawrence Babb; and Rudolf and Margot Wittkower, especially 98–107. The Wittkowers point particularly to the influence of Ficino. From Ficino on, they state, "even moderately gifted men were categorized as saturnine and, conversely, no outstanding intellectual or artistic achievement was believed possible unless its author was melancholic" (104). By the seventeenth century, according to the Wittkowers, the melancholic artist was already going out of fashion (106). One must, however, consider that we continue to witness this association throughout the eighteenth century. According to the Wittkowers, the pathologization of melancholia did not occur definitively until the nineteenth century (99).

11. See the entry for "mania" in volume 2.

12. In fact, many tracts distinguished between innate and acquired temperaments. See, for example, Cabanis 1.265–314 and 2.669–87, or Thomas Trotter's distinction between "predisposition" (197) and "acquired disposition" (288).

13. By 1807, Cheyne's estimate that one-third of the population of England was afflicted with nervous disorders was raised to two-thirds by Trotter. The reason for this increase, Trotter explains, is that "nervous ailments are no longer confined to the better ranks of life" (xvii).

14. As Jean Stengers and Anne Van Neck write, "With Tissot, we enter the circle of European celebrities" (61). *De la sante des gens de lettres* was published in 1767 with the English translation appearing in 1768. *Essai sur les maladies des gens du monde* was published in 1770 and translated into English in 1771. In 1772, the two translations were bound with a translation of Tissot's treatise on onanism and sold as *Three Essays*. I will quote from this edition throughout.

15. Note that these three terms were often used interchangeably (as many of the quotations I provide illustrate); however, some medical researchers did try to make a distinction between the irritability of the "muscular power" and the sensibility of the "nervous power." See L. S. Jacyna 67 and John D. Spillane 123–26. The distinction goes back to Albrecht von Haller.

16. See, for example, Thomas Laqueur, "Masturbation, Credit, and the Novel," and *Solitary Sex: A Cultural History of Masturbation*. Note that I come to Laqueur's book after the submission of this manuscript, too late to take full account of its argument, which does not significantly contradict his earlier published essay.

17. The medicalization of masturbation did not really exist before the eighteenth century, although the association of loss of semen with loss of strength goes back to Galen and beyond. Laqueur and others accredit the anonymous *Onania*, which appeared sometime near 1712, as the first pathologization. The author of *Onania* does, in fact, claim that "the Uncleanness with ones Self, which I write against, has never been touch'd upon yet by any able Pen" (117–18). For a history of masturbation in eighteenth- and nineteenth-century Britain, see Roy Porter's "Forbidden Pleasures"; E. H. Hare; R. P. Neuman; M. Jeanne Peterson's "Dr. Acton's Enemy"; and Robert H. MacDonald. See also Stengers and Van Neck. On the dangers of the imagination, see Vernon Rosario's *The Erotic Imagination* 13-67 and also Richard Sha.

18. As Rosario writes, "While Tissot and other anti-onanism campaigners always warned that girls could suffer the same ills as boys and even worse, and while there were even a few monographs dedicated to female 'secret habits,' antimasturbatory tracts principally concerned male seminal emissions" (*Erotic Imagination* 161). Laqueur in *Solitary Sex*, however, claims that such tracts attacked women as often as men.

Regardless, only the female half of the equation has received attention in treating the relation between masturbation and reading (Laqueur's work included).

19. See, for example, his *Onanism* (*Three Essays* 3.107). Tissot was the most influential early popularizer of onanopathology. Tissot's work was incredibly influential in the nineteenth century, receiving twenty-two known French-language editions and printings between 1813 and 1886 (Ramsey 128). The text also saw numerous English-language editions throughout the period, the first appearing in 1766, and its precepts were repeated, sometimes verbatim, in many of the nineteenth-century psychological and medical tracts that dealt with the issue of masturbation.

20. As one characteristic example among many in the nineteenth century, Sylvester Graham in his American anti-onanist tract, *A Lecture to Young Men* (1834), helps to popularize the common association of melancholy with lechery when he claims that "hypochondriacs, and those who are afflicted with nervous melancholy, are generally morbidly lecherous" (18) and that masturbators are "more liable to those depressions of spirits, and turns of melancholy, and perhaps remorse and despair; which are connected with the morbid irritability of the nervous system" (63).

21. I have slightly altered the translation. The original French is as follows: "Rien n'affoiblit autant, que cette tension continuelle de l'esprit, toujours occupé du même objet. Le masturbateur, uniquement livré à ses méditations ordurières, éprouve à cet égard les mêmes maux que l'homme de lettres qui fixe les siennes sur une seule question; & il est rare que cet excès ne nuise pas" (*L'Onanisme* 104).

22. Cabanis first presented these lectures in 1796; they would first be published in French in 1802. Although there was not an English translation and despite the controversy resulting from his association with the French *idéologues*, Cabanis' ideas were highly influential in Britain. On Cabanis's influence on Romantic writers and scientists, see, in particular, Alan Richardson 16-19. William Acton would repeat Cabanis's statement as late as 1857. Speaking of spermatorrhœa, Acton writes: "Hard study I have already mentioned more than once as predisposing to this condition" (272).

23. Wordsworth makes a similar comment in his argument against biography, *A Letter to a Friend of Robert Burns*: "[T]hat genius is not incompatible with vice, and that vice leads to misery—the more acute from the sensibilities which are the elements of genius—we needed not those communications to inform us" (*Prose* 3.123–24).

24. Note that Erasmus Darwin makes a similar move in his *Zoonomia* 1.354–60.

25. On Erasmus Darwin's "nervous fluid," see Alan Richardson 13. See also Peter Otto. Note that, on the issue of such a vital principle and the balancing of one's vital energies, the materialists and the vitalists of the Romantic period, who are often read as being in stark opposition, resembled each other more than they differed from each other. The balancing of vital energies remained a key feature of medical tracts, regardless of whether one reads this principle as a result of material organs and their organization or because of a directing spiritual or psychic force. The close connection between the body and the mind was also postulated by both sides. Cabanis and the phrenologists, Spurzheim, Gall, and Combe, are usually placed in the materialist camp since they were seeking biological explanations for mental processes. On the debates between vitalists and materialists, see Richardson (Introduction). As Richardson puts it, "A naturalistic, physiological, ecological approach to psychology and anthropology was fully compatible with the belief in a 'motion and a spirit' coursing through the body (and its mind)" (69).

26. As a reviewer in the *Edinburgh Review* sums up the situation in February 1815, "It is admitted by all, that certain changes in the bodily organs are necessary, to the production of those states of the mind which constitute Sensation, and Thought, and Volition; but the only point relative to these changes, which physiologists are unanimous in considering as established, is, that they have their seat in the Nervous System." What is more, "[r]especting their nature, nothing whatever is known;—the precise parts even of the Nervous System, in which they occur, have not been ascertained" (439).

27. Note that the absolute distinction between "moral" and "mental" phenomena began to occur largely in the Romantic period. Eighteenth-century tracts often mean by "moral" all the functions associated with mental processes, including but not limited to what we now mean by "moral concerns." By the Romantic period, the two terms were more properly distinguished.

28. It should be noted that Edinburgh's school of medicine was, nonetheless, still working to establish its own legitimacy against Cambridge and Oxford; and occasionally suffered from attacks against its generally materialist or "mechanical" philosophy of medicine. On the complicated history of the Edinburgh medical school, see Jacyna.

29. Brown, for example, writes: "The effect common to the asthenic noxious powers, upon the *functions*, is to diminish them, in such a manner, as sometimes to seem, though the appearance is fallacious, to increase them" (114). On the influence of Brunonian medicine, see de Almeida and Vickers.

30. The move toward localizing disease in specific tissues and organs was an uneven development over the course of the nineteenth century, although Edinburgh had an influence also on this development through the teachings of John Thomson. See Jacyna, chapter 4.

31. Note, however, that Rousseau had not yet read Tissot's *Onanism* when he warned against masturbation in *Emile* (1762), a passage that led Tissot to send Rousseau copies of his *Onanism*, which Rousseau then read. For more on the relationship between Tissot and Rousseau, see Rosario, *Erotic Imagination* 21–25.

32. It is worth noting here that Kant was an admirer of the Brunonian theory of medicine (Vickers 67–69).

33. Just before quoting this very passage, Russell Thacher Trall, in *Home-Treatment for Sexual Abuses*, for example, explains that "[t]he injury resulting to the constitution is not so much from the mere loss of semen, or other fluid, as from the absolute waste of vital power through the inordinate nervous excitement" (72).

34. This psychosomatic loop was aided by the understanding of pathology in the eighteenth century, which was more concerned with a patient's perceived symptoms than localized disease. The entrenched class hierarchy within the medical profession, which saw any operation on specific sites of disease as mere manual labor, further supported an unwillingness to treat illness in the body. As N. D. Jewson explains, the reliance of upper-class physicians on their aristocratic patients also put an especial importance on the *perception* of cure (378–79).

35. A similar rhetorical attack against "pedlars of medicine" (17) occurs in the second essay of Beddoes's *Hygëia* (1.2.13–49). Beddoes was particularly angered by the quackery of Samuel Solomon, perhaps because his own experiments at his Pneumatic Institute, which included Coleridge among its guinea pigs, could just as easily be seen as quackery (Porter, *Doctor of Society* 49); for Beddoes's antipathy against Solomon, see,

for example, *Hygëia* 1.1.50; Porter, *Health for Sale* 177–78; and Porter, *Doctor of Society* 145–46. Acton in 1857 argues of masturbation that "the profession should no longer shun the treatment of this class of diseases," so that "sufferers" do not feel the need "to resort to quacks or advertising firms" (303). Acton ends his work with an appendix in which he transcribes a court case that, he claims, exposes "the quack system."

36. Ivan Waddington, for example, writes: "[A]s numerous writers have pointed out, these improvements in medical science, whilst very real, did not immediately translate into significant therapeutic advances in medical practice; indeed, there is little evidence to suggest any dramatic improvements in the effectiveness of medical care until the early part of the twentieth century" (197). Roy Porter in the *Doctor of Society* (especially 30–32) helpfully lays out both the improvements in and impediments facing medicine in the late eighteenth century.

37. Logan (41) makes a similar argument in his examination of Thomas Trotter.

38. Haslam goes on to suggest that melancholy is even more dangerous than mania since the chance of recovery is much greater after the latter than the former (257–58). By comparison, Burton, referring to madness and melancholy, states that "most of our neotericks doe handle them apart," (1.132), for, he explains, melancholy's symptoms are far less noisome.

39. Haslam in his *Observations* mentions Pinel on pages 254 and 271–74. Benjamin Rush also cites this distinction in his 1812 *Medical Inquiries and Observations* 63.

40. On Erasmus Darwin's influence, see Richardson 12–16.

41. I am being quite literal here. The review of Wordsworth's 1807 *Poems, in Two Volumes* appeared right after a review of John Sinclair's *The Code of Health and Longevity*, in which the reviewer addresses the fact that medical writers must logically be affected by the same infirmities they apply to men of genius (*Edinburgh Review* [1807] 198).

42. See also David Knight and Richardson 7.

43. On the patronage system's power over medical knowledge, see Jewson.

44. A useful overview of Romantic changes in the medical profession can be found in Waddington, chapter 2. See also chapter 1 of Peterson's *The Medical Profession*.

CHAPTER 2. ROMANTICISM'S LAST MINSTREL

1. According to Freud, fetishism functions in a way that falls between neurosis and psychosis. Freud originally distinguished between neurosis and psychosis in the following way: "[I]n neurosis the ego suppresses part of the id out of allegiance to reality, whereas in psychosis it lets itself be carried away by the id and detached from a part of reality" (5.202). In analyzing a case of mourning, Freud is forced to rethink this distinction in his essay on fetishism: "In the analysis of two young men I learnt that each of them . . . had refused to acknowledge the death of his father . . . and yet neither of them had developed a psychosis. A very important piece of reality had thus been denied by the ego, in the same way as the fetishist denies the unwelcome fact of the woman's castrated condition" (5.202). To resolve the apparent contradiction, Freud turns to the formula "*je sais bien mais quand même*": "It was only one current of their mental processes that had not acknowledged the father's death; there was another which was fully aware of the fact; the one which was consistent with reality stood alongside the one which accorded with a wish" (5.202). Similarly, the fetish is able to "become the vehicle both of denying and of asseverating the fact of castration" (5.203). On the use of this conception of the fetish for ideological critique, see Žižek, especially *For They Know Not What They Do* 229–53.

2. This is not to say that pathologizations of the poet did not exist before the Romantic era, only that such attacks tended to include poetry among other forms of excessive thinking or other forms overly reliant on the market. On the eighteenth-century pathologization of the poet, see, in particular, Zionkowski.

3. An indication of how much Scott's metrical romances have been neglected in favor of his novels is the fact that I need to rely on a 1900 edition of Scott's *Poetical Works*. All reference to the poetry will cite canto and line number; reference to the prose introductions will give the relevant page numbers. Note that Peter J. Manning is currently working on a Penguin edition of the *Lay*.

4. It did not hurt that, according to the medical tracts, horseback riding was the *sine qua non* of healthy exercise. As Trotter explains, "The value of *exercise on horseback*, is so well known, that it may seem superfluous to mention it here. But in the prevention and treatment of nervous and bilious diseases, it is supereminent" (258).

5. I discuss the significance of the difference between the gentry and the peerage in chapter 3.

6. Note that in *The Achievement of Literary Authority*, Ferris does briefly discuss the juxtaposition of Scott and Byron: "Aristocratic and transgressive, the demonic masculinity of Byron served as a standard foil in the period for the healthy masculinity of the Waverley mode, replaying in male terms the female rivalry between domestic and demonic womanhood" (242).

7. See Zionkowski for Byron's eighteenth-century precursors.

8. Although the metrical romances are usually ignored, some recent work has explored the influence of Scott's novels on the political fabric of the age, particularly Bruce Beiderwell; Katie Trumpener, chapter 3; and Saree Makdisi. An important precursor, of course, is George Lukács.

9. The one exception was for individuals in Highland regiments, who were permitted to wear the plaid as their uniform.

10. On the role of the king's visit in quelling radical violence, see also Prebble 3–21.

11. On the invention of Highland costume, including Scott's knowledge of the kilt's lack of authenticity, see Hugh Trevor-Roper.

12. On the role of fiction in the construction of the bourgeois subject, see, among many others, Ian Watt, McKeon, Miller, John Bender, Nancy Armstrong, Deirdre Lynch, and Brantlinger's *Fictions of State*.

13. On the role of medievalism in political ceremony, see, in particular, Mark Girouard and Alice Chandler. Note that the monarchical appropriation of medieval themes began as early as 1787 with King George III's commissioning of historical paintings with chivalric motifs for the King's Audience Chamber at Windsor Castle.

14. Beiderwell explores a similar transition in Scott's novels: "that is, the shift *from* thinking of punishment as the infliction of pain *to* thinking of punishment as part of an elaborate administrative machinery of control" (vii).

15. For Žižek's well-known reading of the Coke campaign, see *Sublime Object* 95-97. Makdisi also examines the simulacral nature of the "real thing" in terms of Scott's Waverley. See, in particular, page 179.

16. This transformation conforms to Debord's understanding of the subject's relationship to spectacle: "The spectacle's externality with respect to the acting subject is demonstrated by the fact that the individual's own gestures are no longer his own, but rather those of someone else who represents them to him" (23).

17. On the slang meaning of "purse," see Eric Partridge's *A Dictionary of Slang*. On King George IV's sporran, see Prebble 74.

18. See endnote 1 in this chapter.

19. See Girourard and Alice Chandler for the different political affiliations medievalism could encompass. One recent work that outlines the various political instantiations of the romance as form is Miranda Burgess's *British Fiction and the Production of Social Order*.

20. Cobbett does not turn to the Radical cause until about 1804, but, as Alice Chandler explains, even "during the tumultuous agricultural uprisings of 1830, when England seemed on the brink of revolution, Cobbett kept insisting on the need for love between 'lords and gentlemen' and the 'common people,' for 'happy cottages' and 'cheerful farm-houses' " (78). For the lower-class turn to medievalism, see, in particular, Susan Zlotnick.

21. See, in particular, Alice Chandler 1–9, 46–91, and Girouard 56–86. A. Dwight Culler pinpoints three different kinds of medievalism: "the Whig view, which returned to the Anglo-Saxons; the conservative view, which returned to the feudal system of the Normans; and the radical socialist view, which returned to the brief interval between the decline of the feudal and the rise of the commercial system" (*Victorian* 155).

22. Stuart Curran also makes this point on page 140.

23. See also Marlon Ross, "Scott's Chivalric Pose" 276, and Goslee 12.

24. Of particular note on this score are Ferris, *The Achievement of Literary Authority*; Beiderwell; Trumpener, chapter 3; and Makdisi.

25. Four important articles that examine Scott's metrical romances along similar lines are Michael Gamer's "Marketing a Masculine Romance"; Celeste Langan's "Understanding Media in 1805"; and Marlon Ross's two essays, "Scott's Chivalric Pose" and "Romancing the Nation-State." See also Hermann Fischer 86–110 on Scott as the "true founder of the romantic tale in verse" (106) and Goslee. Peter T. Murphy in a chapter on Scott's metrical romances explores the ways that Scott introduces disruptive elements, such as the goblin page, only to place them "in a sort of quarantine, cordoned off and then cut away to bring peace and conclusion" (181). For Scott's publishing history, see Jane Millgate.

26. Marlon Ross makes a similar argument in "Scott's Chivalric Pose." Ross's reading of *Rokeby* in "Romancing" also dovetails nicely with my reading here, although Ross instead employs the psychoanalytical concept of transference to explain Scott's relation to the past and to the conflicts of the present. See also Manning, "Childe" 174–77; and Langan's analysis of Scott's use of allegories of technology in the *Lay*.

27. I thank Patricia Ingham for this sentence, which is extracted from a co-written talk, entitled "Incorporations of Medievalism in Scott," which was presented to the 1996 North American Society for the Study of Romanticism Conference in Boston.

28. See Marlon Ross, "Scott's Chivalric Pose" 285.

29. See, for example, Ferris, "Trope"; Poovey; Taylor; Brantlinger; and Klancher. See also chapter 1 for the medical reasoning behind this attribution.

30. For the figures on Thomas Paine, see Altick 69–72; for the circulation of novels between 1740 and 1755, see Altick 49–50.

31. The *Oxford Companion to English Literature* places the figure for More's sales at two million copies in *four* years. For my figures, see Altick 74–75. Note that both Paine and More are only *proto*-mass-market phenomena since they relied on revolutionary and Christian societies, respectively, for dissemination.

32. On the Stanhope press, see Altick 262 and Lee Erickson 27n.

33. On the prices for quarto, octavo, and small octavos between 1780 and 1810, see Altick 51. An octavo edition, for example, jumped from five or six shillings to twelve shillings and a quarto edition from ten or twelve shillings to a guinea (twenty-one shillings). Simon Eliot corroborates this trend in his quantitative analysis of the literature market (39). Eliot also makes it clear that the situation quickly changed after 1825 (39–40). See also Alan D. Boehm.

34. Note that I am not making a value judgment here about poetry and the novel but, rather, underlining the fact that reading practices are automatically caught up in questions of value. Lynch also examines this question of rereading versus consumption (130–33). See also Langan, who complicates Erickson's formulation by examining the ways Scott accommodates changes in print technology.

35. On printing-house compositors, see Altick 262.

36. For these figures, see Altick 262–63. Before and after this poetry inflation, the price of a volume of poetry was relatively steady, with the first Edinburgh edition of Burns's *Poems* selling at 5s in 1787, Arnold's *Strayed Reveller* selling at 4s.6d. in 1849, and Hardy's *Satires of Circumstance* selling at 4s.6d. in 1914 (Erickson 35). Compared to the sales of Paine or More, Scott's circulation in the first two decades of the nineteenth century seems miniscule; however, as Erickson explains, the profit margin was incredible: "Two thousand copies of a three-decker novel by, say, Bulwer-Lytton, costing thirty-one shillings sixpence, would bring his publisher £300; in contrast, 200,000 copies of a number of G. W. M. Reynolds' *Mysteries of London* (1845–46) costing a penny would produce a profit of only £83" (4).

37. For these figures, see St. Clair 3.

38. For these figures, see Altick 276.

39. See Debra Mancoff 69–76 and Kernan.

40. Langan also remarks on this word play.

41. My thanks to Patricia Ingham for this suggestion. Regarding the possible connection between Gilpin Horner and the lower classes, consider that one of the most popular lower-class journals of the period would be called *The Black Dwarf* (published from 29 January 1817 on). On the relation of the goblin to dangerous reading, see also Goslee 20 and 32–33.

42. John Keble, cited in Warren 48.

CHAPTER 3. BYRON'S SPECTROPOETICS AND REVOLUTION

1. Since Byron himself—perhaps facetiously—claimed he did not know the meaning of the term *radical*—"I don't know what it means—is it uprooting?" (*Letters* 7.81)—I should here note that I will use "radical" throughout in the general sense of "[g]oing to the root or origin; touching or acting upon what is essential and fundamental" (OED), hence the notion of "radical reform" (that is, leading to "thorough political and social change" [OED]). It may be *because* of his larger theory of radical justice that Byron rejected specific "Radicals" such as William Cobbett (whom he saw as an English Robespierre [*Letters* 7.45, 7.80]); I tend to agree with Daniel P. Watkins that "there is a real and substantive political basis for [Byron's] criticism of the new radicals that is at least as important as his emotional contempt for them" ("Byron" 100). As Byron consistently states, "pray don't *mistake* me—it is not against the *pure* principle

of reform—that I protest, but against low designing dirty levelers who would pioneer their way to a democratical tyranny" (*Letters* 7.99).

2. Friends of Byron who were imprisoned include Sir Francis Burdett (1810), Leigh Hunt (1813), John Cam Hobhouse (1819), and John Hunt (1820). Major Cartwright, whose Radical Hampden Club Byron had joined in 1812 and whose petition for reform Byron had presented to the House of Lords in that same year, was arrested in 1819. On Byron's battles against censorship, see in particular Robinson Blann. On Byron's fears about losing his rights to his daughter, see *Letters* 6.252, 6.256, and 9.104, as well as Blann 68–70 and 74.

3. Of course, there has been much debate about Byron's politics. For those critics lining up against Byron, see Malcolm Kelsall, D. M. De Silva, and Andrew Noble. For those defending Byron's politics, see Jürgen Klein, Dora Neill Raymond, Michael Foot, Daniel P. Watkins, Carl Woodring (chapter 5), and David Erdman's meticulously researched trio of papers, "Lord Byron as Rinaldo," "Byron and 'the New Force of the People,' " and "Byron and Revolt in England." For a balanced view of Byron's connections to the period's Whigs, see Manning's *Reading Romantics* 195–215. For other works that present Byron as an ambiguous political figure, see David Craig and Jonathan David Gross, especially chapter 8. On the Romantic and early Victorian dismissal of Byron's politics, see William Ruddick 26–29.

4. Kelsall, for example, writes: "Byron's political education, therefore, is not in revolution, but in disenchantment" (117).

5. On Byron's popularity with the Luddites, Ebenezer Elliott, the "Corn-Law Rhymer," and the Chartists, see Philip Collins, Keith Walker 88–111, Anne Janowitz 148–51, and Foot 387–90. For Byron's "Song for the Luddites," see *Letters* 5.149. Of interest for the argument I make in the next section is the fact that Byron sets the Luddite song next to a ditty on the Venetian Carnival. R. G. Gammage, who published his *History of the Chartist Movement* in 1854, points out how the first and largest of Chartist demonstrations, the procession at Newcastle on 27 June 1838, included numerous banners that contained inscriptions from the works of Byron (22–23). See also Crane Brinton 184–87, Erdman's "Byron and Revolt in England" 242–43, and Manning's *Reading Romantics* 206–207. Also of interest is a sequence of articles in the *Chartist Circular* from 1840 to 1841 entitled "The Politics of Poets," in which Byron is highlighted more than any other poet. On Byron's popularity among the lower classes, see Louis James 74, 201–202, and Foot 364–65. On Ryleev, see Philip Collins 21 as well as Nina Diakonova and Vadim Vacuro 145, 150–51. On the *Risorgimento*, see Giorgio Melchiori.

6. Byron also greatly admired Scott's works. See, for example, Byron, *Letters* 8.13 and 8.23. Politics, however, was a different matter. As Byron stated in an 1823 letter, even while defending Scott, "With his politics I have nothing to do; they differ from mine, which renders it difficult for me to speak of them" (*Letters* 10.189). See also *Letters* 3.220 and, for their meeting at Albemarle Street, Leslie Marchand 2.529–30. For articles documenting Byron's admiration for Scott, see P. H. Scott and Andrew Rutherford.

7. For a complementary analysis of Shelley's romances, see David Duff.

8. For Bakhtin's concept of the chronotope, see the *Dialogic Imagination* 84–258 and *Speech Genres* 10–59. For an excellent examination of Scott's chronotopes, see Ferris, *Achievement*, chapter 6. See also Makdisi's and Trumpener's examination of Scott's construction of temporalized space, as well as James Chandler's examination of temporal structures in Scott and Byron.

9. According to Foucault in *The Order of Things*, Cuvier was especially important for the emergence of historical thought at the turn of the nineteenth century, since he "introduced a radical discontinuity into the Classical scale of beings" (275). Elfenbein in *Byron and the Victorians* makes the connection to Foucault, suggesting that Byron was important for the epistemological shifts explored by Foucault (19). For the influence of Gibbon on Byron, see in particular, Ernest Giddey and Leigh Hunt 44.

10. For a different reading of Byron's nostalgia, see William Galperin. I tend to disagree that nostalgia in Byron functions merely in the conservative way Galperin suggests (257–64). Galperin comes closest to my reading in his interpretation of the Aurora passages in Canto XVI of *Don Juan* (Galperin 279–82).

11. It is worth noting that both Byron and Scott gave away their own money to form a militia, except that Scott's was designed to protect his own property while Byron's was given to another country's cause.

12. In addition to Eco, see Michael André Bernstein; Leah Marcus; and Peter Stallybrass and Allon White.

13. For a previous use of Eco's concept of cold carnival in relation to Byron, see Thomas H. Schmid's examination of *Beppo* as an example of "cold carnival." See also Anne K. Mellor's superb work, *English Romantic Irony*. For my previous use of "cold carnival" in relation to Thomas Carlyle, see "The Critic's New Clothes."

14. Sir Samuel Egerton Brydges (May 1824) echoes this distinction between humor and satire in his *Letters on the Character and Poetical Genius of Lord Byron* (*BC* 262–63). For an extended discussion of Jean Paul Richter's work, which first distinguished between humor and satire, see Schmid, particularly the introduction.

15. Jeffrey also argues that Scott, by contrast, always makes "the ludicrous itself subservient to the cause of benevolence" (*RR* 2.937).

16. For an argument along similar lines, see Watkins's "Byron and the Poetics of Revolution," especially page 102. See also his "Violence." I disagree, however, that one of "Byron's limitations" is that "he was unable to envision fully a radically and positively changed world" ("Byron" 130). On the contrary, as I explain below, this very fact *contributes* to his radical and disruptive philosophy of justice. See also Manning, *Reading* 138-41 and Jerome McGann "Byron."

17. On Byron's class snobbery, see Kelsall for an attack and Erdman's "Lord Byron and the Genteel Reformers" for a defense.

18. This image is identified as Doré's by Henri Leblanc 61–63. My version of the image is from the 1854 edition of Byron, *Oeuvres complètes de Lord Byron*.

19. Iain McCalman considers the years between 1815 and 1821 the "most insurgent and influential phase" of what he terms the "radical underworld." On Byron and the radical activities of 1816 and 1817, see Manning, *Reading*, chapter 10. On the radical activities of 1819, see James Chandler, especially the introduction. Chandler addresses Byron in chapter 6. On radicalism in general from 1817–20, see chapter 6 of J. Ann Hone's *For the Cause of Truth*.

20. Lawrence and other materialist scientists were often attacked in the early part of the nineteenth century; however, their ideas continued to gain dominance in medical circles and many of their principles (the balancing of one's vital energies, the interconnection between the body and the mind, the notion of an all-pervasive nervous system) were espoused just as commonly by the vitalists that opposed Lawrence. An indication of this increasing acceptability is the fact that, whereas in 1819 the College

of Surgeons suspended Lawrence and called on him to suppress his lectures, by 1827 he was elected to the Council of the College of Surgeons and would eventually become the sergeant-surgeon to Queen Victoria herself.

21. That the allusion is to Milton's Satan is made clear by the preface (iv).

22. Of course, the shift to a rhetoric of pathology was very much an uneven development, so that some critics would underline Byron's political threat for years to come. One author writing under the pseudonym Cato, for example, accuses Byron in 1824 of devoting "the powers of your genius to the strengthening of . . . demoralizing principles," pouring forth "a pestilential poetry which, in every page of it, unhinges society in some corner-stone or other of its majestic edifice" (124). He goes on to call Byron "a traitor to your country's peace," with "Sin and Death . . . ready to follow upon your track, to snuff the blood and to riot upon the carnage you are preparing for them" (125).

23. Note that, although Scott had many good things to say about Byron, he was consistently careful to separate Byron's person from his politics. As he explains, "Our sentiments agreed a good deal, except upon the subjects of religion and politics, upon neither of which I was inclined to believe that Lord Byron entertained very fixed opinions" (*BI* 38).

24. See previous endnote. The same strategy persists in recent scholarship, if in reverse fashion. Kelsall, for example, reduces Byron to his class identity but with the contrary goal of finding Byron guilty of complacency and collusion: "From what other basis than that of an aristocratic nineteenth-century liberal would one expect him to contemplate politics at home or abroad?" (177). Byron must have been quite amused by this common move in the periodical reviews of his own time period. As Byron, for example, responds to William Roberts's scathing criticism of his then-anonymous *Don Juan*, writing under the pseudonym Wortley Clutterbuck: "I agree with you that it is impossible Lord B. should be the author . . . because as a British peer and a British poet—it would be impracticable for him to have recourse to such facetious fiction" (*Prose* 82).

25. According to Manning, the interweaving of Byron's name with radical martyrs such as Jeremiah Brandreth "would have been apparent to any Londoner reading the newspapers at the end of 1817" (*Reading* 222). For other examples of the perception around this time that Byron could head a revolutionary movement in England, see Walker 144–45.

26. Richard Altick is not far off to state that the artisans "belonged to the aristocracy of workers" (72). As the economist Leone Levi states in 1884, mechanics and skilled artisans were "as far removed from common labourers and miners as clerks and curates are from those who have reached the highest places in the liberal professions or wealthy merchants and bankers, all of whom pass under the category of the middle classes" (Altick 82).

27. On the bound cost, see St. Clair 3, who also comments on the necessity of the binding: "If [Byron's poems] were not rebound they quickly fell to pieces and it was low tone to have unbound books on your shelves—like putting milk bottles on the table" (2). To put these figures in perspective, see chapter 2 for representative incomes in the period.

28. Given in Manning, "Childe Harold" 183. Byron soon questioned the logic of publishing in quarto form precisely because such a format necessarily reduced the number of people with access to the work. As he advised Leigh Hunt in 1815, "[D]on't

let your bookseller publish in *Quarto* it is the worst size possible for circulation" (*Letters* 4.326).

29. Note that this sale failed to take so that Newstead fell back into Byron's hands in 1814. It was then sold again in December 1817 (Marchand 362, 469, 718). Newstead Abbey was not Byron's only holding, of course, but his willingness to *sell* it while in *exile* as a *publishing poet* underscores the conflicted position in which Byron found himself. For Byron's holdings, see Erdman, "Lord Byron" 162. See Woodring 206-208 on Byron and money.

30. According to Manning ("Childe" 188–89), Byron was against the pirating of *Cain*, which was determined to be blasphemous and therefore outside the protection of copyright. Consider, however, that in a letter to Doublas Kinnaird of Feb. 6, 1822, only a couple of months after the publication of *Cain*, Byron counts precisely on anticipated piracies to circulate a projected private printing of *The Vision of Judgment*: if no publisher "is to be found—*print* fifty copies (*at my expense*) distribute them amongst my acquaintances—and you will soon see that the booksellers *will* publish them—even if we opposed them" (*Letters* 9.100). See also *Letters* 9.118.

31. See *Letters* 9.207. One might also point to Byron's desire to establish his own printing press to publish his works (see, for example, *Letters* 10.70) as well as his interest in founding a newspaper or journal, a desire that eventually led to the publication of the *Liberal* with Percy Shelley and Leigh Hunt. In this, Byron again parallels and opposes Scott, who edited the conservative *Edinburgh Annual Register*. On Scott and the *Register*, see Kenneth Curry.

32. One way John Murray tried to deal with his worries regarding the first two cantos of *Don Juan*, which he published not only anonymously but without the name of the publisher, was to charge the exorbitant price of a guinea and a half and in quarto. The high price of the book thus served as a defense against its radical dissemination, although this strategy was immediately countered by an edition published by William Hone. Titled *Don John (Murray), or Don Juan Unmasked*, it both "unmasked" the double anonymity and sold for only two shillings, with extracts from the original work.

33. On the Byronic hairstyles of Chartists, see Janowitz 148.

34. Manning too highlights the opposition between what I have termed the Cult of the Book and the Culture of the Text (*Reading* 227); however, he argues that Byron would have "keenly regretted the loss of cachet" that would result from "forsaking the respectable book trade for the popular market" (*Reading* 231), an argument that I here question. See also Walker 100–11. Walker lists pirated editions by working-class publishers on pages 110–11. Louis James lists twenty-five cheap editions of Byron before 1844 not including reprints (74, 201–202). See also William Wickwar 265–73, Joss Marsh 100–104, and McCalman 211, 288–89. Paul Thomas Murphy argues that the "working-class poetic canon" consisted primarily of three poets: Byron, Burns, and Shelley (135–36), for these were the poets "that working-class journalists most commonly cited and discussed" (138). Murphy points out, however, that more poetry by Byron than by Shelley was published in the working-class journals, the *Black Dwarf*, the *Poor Man's Advocate*, and the *Northern Star*. Walker shows how popular Byron was in the widely disseminated lower-class periodical, the *Mirror of Literature* (109–10). See also Philip Collins.

35. Note that, according to his daughter and son-in-law, Marx supposedly preferred Shelley to Byron (Edward Aveling and Eleanor Marx 105). Regardless of whether we can trust this statement (one person who distrusts it is Foot 383), the difference in

opinion between Marx and Engels can be explained perhaps by the fact that Engels concerns himself here with the radical power of Byron's poetry—Byron as corpus—whereas Marx, contemplating Byron's corpse, echoed the periodical reviews of his time and offered a prognosis of Byron's bodily self.

36. William G. Rowland Jr. makes a similar argument, as does Kurt Heinzelman in "Byron's Poetry." See also Ghislaine McDayter, especially page 44.

37. Marx, after all, uses linen—the main ingredient of paper in the Romantic period—as his main example throughout the section in *Capital* on commodities (132–63). For an exploration of how "the poem is like the circulating medium of money" (66), see Guin Batten 66–67. Heinzelman examines how one might argue that "Poetry *is* economics," in relation both to Byron ("Byron's Poetry" 378–86) and Romanticism generally (*Economics* 11–33, 196–233). For the classic example of the poststructuralist reading of Marx, see Baudrillard's *For a Critique of the Political Economy of the Sign*. Derrida offers a similar critique of the idea of use-value in *Specters of Marx* (159–63), but resists the reduction of all things to capital ("It is all capital," according to Baudrillard [82]).

38. In this I follow (and applaud) Batten's recent *Orphaned Imagination*. See, in particular, that book's "Afterword" 211–36.

39. Note, however, that in his *Economics of the Imagination* Heinzelman significantly complicates his position. For an extension (and implicit reworking) of Heinzelman's notions, see chapter 7 of Alan Liu's *Wordsworth*.

40. It may not be just a coincidence that Derrida's phrase, *il n'y a pas de hors-texte*, is formulated during his discussion of Rousseau's famous passage about masturbation (*Of Grammatology* 141–64). In the sense formulated by Derrida, Byron's alignment with such a position may have predisposed him to the sorts of rhetorical attacks I will explore in chapter 4. For positive early assessments of Byron's skepticism, see M. G. Cooke, chapter 6, especially pages 181–82, and Mellor, chapter 2.

41. For an analysis of just how conflicted such gestures by Byron can be, see Heinzelman, "Byron's Poetry" 367–73. See also Jerome Christensen, chapter 1, and Manning, "Childe" 180–81.

42. See Byron, *Letters* 10.70–71 and *Letters* 10.108. Note that Byron *did*, however, agree to receive profits from *Don Juan*, with 15 percent going to Hunt (*Letters* 10.182, 201).

43. See Derrida's *Given Time*.

44. Another example of Byron's fascination with the political force of literature is his other favorite expression, "true words are things," which Byron attributed to Mirabeau. See *Childe Harold* 3.1061; *Marino Faliero* 5.1.289; and *Don Juan* 3.793.

45. See also Christensen 332-33 and Byron, *Letters* 10.68–69.

46. I thank Karen Swann and Julie Carlson for leading me into the following discussion.

47. Freud's example when explaining fetishism is, in fact, a case of mourning (5.202–203).

48. For positive spins on Byron's melancholia, see Batten and E. D. Hirsch. See also Julia Kristeva's *Black Sun* for a psychoanalytical understanding of melancholy that resists pathologization. Note, however, Schiesari's critique of the narcissism inherent in Freud's notion of melancholia and of the tendency to value the male *melancholic* as superior to the *mourning* woman. Although I admire Schiesari's study, I also feel it necessary to point out a danger in simply pathologizing melancholia ("Melancholia is not a blessed curse; it is just a curse, one that we must all work to overturn" [Schiesari

159]). Despite Schiesari's desire to historicize the notion of melancholia, she may not be acknowledging sufficiently her debt to what I consider an equally suspect nineteenth-century pathologizing of the melancholic. See the following chapter in which I explore how this pathologization was a defense against Byron's radical acceptance of suffering as the very basis for a just relation to others.

49. For a similar argument, albeit one reached by a rather different route, see Robert F. Gleckner, especially chapter 3, chapter 9, pages 236–37 and 244–50. Jerome McGann anticipates my argument here in his discussion of the "gift of death" in Byron's poetry (*Fiery Dust* 268–73).

50. Derrida uses the term *spectropoetic* in *Specters of Marx* 45.

51. See for example, Philip W. Martin, especially 29 and 106, and John Wain. For a positive reading of Byron's performativity, see, in particular, Frank McConnell.

CHAPTER 4. POETRY AND PATHOLOGY

1. The Student's Manual saw seven editions in the two years following its publication in 1835, with a twenty-fourth edition in 1854. Todd himself estimated that he sold "not less than one hundred thousand copies" of his work "across the water" (Barker-Benfield, *Horrors* 136). As Henry Holbeach writes in the *Contemporary Review* of 1880, "There is a well-known work for students, written by an American divine, which had an immense circulation in this country a generation ago, and is still largely read" (252). So well known the work seems to be that Holbeach doesn't even feel the need to mention that divine by name, though he goes on to quote *The Student's Manual* extensively. For a discussion of Todd's *Manual*, see David Bennett 277–78 and Barker-Benfield, *Horrors*, 135–74.

2. See Tom Holland's "Undead Byron." McDayter compares this representation of Byron as vampire or specter to what Marx analyzes as the alienation of the labor-product.

3. Some previous studies have already suggested a link between the Romantic poet and the masturbator. See Levinson's *Keats's Life of Allegory*, especially her introduction (1–38). See also Guy-Bray, Steven Marcus, and Wolfson, "Feminizing Keats."

4. On the novel and the romance form, see Burgess, McKeon, Laurie Langbauer, Lennard J. Davis, Ian Duncan, Deborah Ross, and Ioan Williams. On the high novel's relationship to sensation fiction, see Ann Cvetkovich; Winifred Hughes; and Barbara Leckie, chapter 3. On the novel's relationship to the theater, see Elaine Hadley; Joseph Litvak; J. Jeffrey Franklin, chapter 3; and Emily Allen. On the British novel's relationship to the French novel, see Tim Parke.

5. In this, of course, queer theory's turn to Byron's sexuality follows a long-standing trend. See, in particular, Louis Crompton and Gross.

6. See Frances Wilson 3.

7. For a superb examination of the pathologization of Byron's genius, see Annette Wheeler Cafarelli's "Byron and the Pathology of Genius." Also of interest on this issue is her *Prose in the Age of Poets*. See also David Alan Janssen.

8. Regarding his admiration of D'Israeli's books, Byron, for example, states in a letter of November 24, 1818: "I don't know a living man's books I take up so often, or lay down more reluctantly, as *Israeli's*" (*Letters* 6.84). He makes a similar statement in the margins of D'Israeli's *Literary Character* (1818): "I have read [D'Israeli's works] oftener than perhaps those of any English Author whatever—except such as treat of Turkey" (*Prose* 219).

9. In this, D'Israeli is referring to a tradition that linked melancholy with enthusiasm, including religious enthusiasm. As André Du Laurens states in 1599, when the melancholic humour is "mixed with a certaine quantity of blood" and becomes heated, "it causeth . . . a kinde of divine ravishment, called Enthousiasma, which stirreth men up to plaie the Philosophers, Poets, and also to prophesie" (86). This passage is also quoted by Burton in his *Anatomy of Melancholy* 1.400. For a historical examination of the rhetoric of enthusiasm, see Clement Hawes and Susie Tucker.

10. James Ogden calls D'Israeli's *Curiosities of Literature* "almost embarrassingly successful" (95). Ogden's bibliography illustrates the incredible staying power of this work, which saw regular editions throughout the nineteenth and into the twentieth century (210–14).

11. For authors dealing with the issue of insanity and Romantic poetry, see Burwick, Charles Rosen, Ford, and Ekbert Faas.

12. See "Men of Letters" in *Essay* 11–24 and the reworked chapter in *Literary* 438-41.

13. Whereas in 1795 D'Israeli still tries to claim that "the pleasures of the imagination" are "conducive to health" (*Essay* 159), by 1818 such passages are removed altogether. Another good example is D'Israeli's change of position on Rousseau. Perhaps influenced by Tissot's writings, D'Israeli reworks any former praise and defense of Rousseau into admonition and warning. D'Israeli also reduces the final four chapters of his *Essay*, in which he defends and lauds the character of genius, into a single short chapter in the 1818 edition, where the encomiums are noticeably toned down.

14. See also Cafarelli *Prose*. Note, however, that Zionkowski does examine a few eighteenth-century precursors for the opposition between purity and perversity.

15. Of interest in this equation is the assocation of Methodism with radicalism in the popular imaginary. See, for example, McCalman, chapter 3 and chapter 7.

16. We find a similar comment specifically about genius in Lady Blessington's *Conversations of Lord Byron*: "The irritability of genius (continued Byron) is nothing more or less than a delicacy of organization, which gives a susceptibility to impressions to which coarser minds are never subject, and cultivation and refinement but increase it, until the unhappy victim becomes a prey to mental hypochondriasm" (129).

17. Consider also Harriette Wilson's injunction to Byron in a letter from 1820: "[T]hrow away your pen, my love, and take a little calomel" (*BC* 162).

18. We should keep in mind that the Victorians, like the Romantics, were rather well versed in scientific theories and writings. Not only did reviews of medical and psychological texts continue to appear regularly in periodical reviews but certain science journals also included reviews of volumes of poetry, particularly that of Browning and Tennyson, who were seen as fellow explorers of the mind's workings in their poetry. (See Faas 12–14, 20–33, and 46.)

19. As Spurzheim asks soon after a long chapter on, of all things, hydrocephalus acutus (in which he repeats Parry's association of hydrocephalus with the sick headache of authors), "If a poet be insane, but during intervals his imagination be unclouded, and he compose beautiful verses, shall we reject them?" (*Observations* 56).

20. Scott offers a diagnosis in his letters as well. He suggests that Byron suffers from "some strange mental malady that destroys his peace of mind and happiness, altho' it cannot quench the fire of his genius." The prognosis is also not good: "I fear the termination will be fatal in one way or other, for it seems impossible that human nature

can support the constant working of an imagination so dark and so strong. Suicide or utter insanity is not unlikely to close the scene" (*Letters* 4.297).

21. Thomas Mulock makes use of the very same metaphor in 1819 as part of a sermon that similarly cites Byron as a preeminent example of "the variform abuse of bodily gifts" (44n) and the "moody and misanthropic strain of mystic melancholy" (43n): "May we look up to that great and gracious Physician the Lord Jesus Christ" (81).

22. As George Trevelyan recalled of Macaulay, the immediate result of publishing that essay on Milton was that, "[l]ike Lord Byron, he awoke one morning and found himself famous" (116). Indeed, Trevelyan goes on to recount that "Murray declared that it would be worth the copyright of 'Childe Harold' to have Macaulay on the staff of the *Quarterly*" (117).

23. Although beyond the scope of this project, there is much to be said about how the pathologization of poetry writing affected the representation of the poetess in the period. One person who has begun this investigation is Andrew Elfenbein in *Romantic Genius*, especially chapters 4 and 5.

24. The first edition of Spurzheim's *Education* was brought out in Edinburgh in 1821 as *A View of the Elementary Principles of Education*. The first American edition was published in 1832, based on the third British edition, which was published in 1832.

25. Mill also critiques the "fashion now happily on the decline, to consider a poet as a poet, only so far as he is supposed capable of delineating the more violent passions; meaning by violent passions, states of excitement approaching to monomania" (64).

26. The original French edition was published as *Des pertes séminales involontaires* in 1836-42. The first English-language edition appears to be a translation by William Wood, entitled *On Involuntary Seminal Discharges* (Philadelphia: A. Waldie, 1839), although it first appeared under the title *A Practical Treatise* in 1847. Michael Mason suggests that Lallemand's ideas were popularized "through a series of papers (surprisingly low-key) by Benjamin Phillips in the *London Medical Gazette* between 1842 and 1845, and through Ranking's paper of 1843 in the *Lancet*, with the subsequent correspondence (which reveals that Lallemand's ideas, first published in French in 1836–42, had already influenced a number of British doctors)" (297–98). As Mason explains, "The strange tenacity of the concept in legitimate medical circles in Britain may in fact be chiefly due to this serious French treatment" (298). Officially, spermatorrhoea referred to the *involuntary* loss of semen; however, according to Lallemend, one of the main causes of this problem was, indeed, masturbation. Lallemand also contributed to the conflation of terms by deciding to "express, by the term SPERMATORRHOEA, every excessive spermatic evacuation, from whatever cause it may arise" (34). Because of the close association between spermatorrhoea and masturbation, a number of tracts used the two terms interchangeably.

27. On the popularity of Todd's work, see endnote 1.

28. My thanks go to George H. Brown for providing this translation, and to Charlie Ross and Shaun Hughes for help with the passage.

29. Todd is not the only example of the link between masturbation and the reading of Byron. According to Thomas Laqueur in *Solitary Sex: A Cultural History of Masturbation*, "Vissarion Belinsky, the founder of Russian realism, one of the towering critics of his age, and a man who examined his own private life relentlessly, confessed to the anarchist Mikhail Bakunin that reading Byron and Schiller had driven him to masturbation when he first encountered them as a nineteen-year-old student" (62). In

England, one can point to the masturbatory nature of Thomas Bailey's description of reading Byron in *A Sermon on the Death of Lord Byron*. Impassioned, ardent, rapturous, Bailey finds himself overwhelmed by a tide of excitement that threatens mental instability ("My understanding was beclouded"), sexual perversity ("my affections defiled, my passions excited"), moral transgression ("I have bowed my soul in idolatrous reverence"), and perhaps worse, for the act of reading poetry is clearly being represented here as a solitary sexual act: "[M]y hand shook with eagerness; my heart leaped with emotion as I have hurried with ardent eye through those scenes of tenderness" (27).

30. Writing of onanism, Rush argues that "madness is induced more frequently by this cause in young men, than is commonly supposed by parents and physicians. The morbid effects of intemperance in a sexual intercourse with women are feeble, and of a transient nature, compared with the train of physical and moral evils which this solitary vice fixes upon the body and mind" (33). According to Rush, the effects of masturbation include "seminal weakness, impotence, dysury, tabes dorsalis, pulmonary consumption, dyspepsia, dimness of sight, vertigo, epilepsy, hypochondriasis, loss of memory, manalgia, fatuity, and death" (347).

31. Janice Radway famously makes a distinction between romances written for a female audience and male pornography (see especially pages 66, 69–70, 83, 104, and 165); however, the romance nonetheless maintains links to sexual desire, as Radway acknowledges, and the form often does get appropriated for pornographic ends, especially in the Harlequin tradition.

32. On Mitford, see McCalman 166–67 and 205–206.

33. Novelists throughout the nineteenth century cited Shakespeare's phrase (*Othello* 1.3.90) in defending the novel's turn to realism versus romance or fabrication. Mitford may facetiously have had in mind Maria Edgeworth's statement about biography in the preface to *Castle Rackrent*: "A plain unvarnished tale is preferable to the most highly ornamented narrative" (2). In Edgeworth's case as in Mitford's, the irony of the statement is that the biography each goes on to tell is, in fact, pure fabrication.

34. See Elfenbein, *Byron*, chapters 3 and 4.

35. I plan to expand on this argument in a book that I am in the process of writing with Emily Allen, tentatively entitled *Byron and the Constitution of the British Novel*.

36. The likely source for Coleridge's statement is Albrecht von Haller's 1747 *Primae Lineae Physiologiae* (*First Lines of Physiology*), a passage that Tissot refers to in his *Onanism* (*Three Essays* 3.52). Coleridge refers to von Haller in many of his essays. This common wisdom can, however, be traced back to Hippocrates (Mason 209). The commonplace is repeated by Cabanis (1.231), Darwin (*Zoonomia* (1.285-91), and Acton (250-51), among others. Coleridge would have been well acquainted with medical knowledge regarding masturbation given his close association with Beddoes.

37. Roy Porter also makes an argument for the "pathologization of Enlightenment individualism" (*Doctor of Society* 109). As he explains, "The tensions between distinction and polite conformity bred anxieties, in turn somatized into physical complaints, which, through the manipulation of the sick-role, could be simultaneously owned and disowned. Sickliness thus provided social alibis, while suffering purchased the right to be different" (109).

38. On the invert, see chapter 3 of Vernon Rosario's *The Erotic Imagination*.

39. See also Foucault's discussion of the repressive hypothesis in the *History of Sexuality*.

40. In this paragraph, I come close to Levinson's argument in "A Question of Taste," where she associates the masturbatory logic of Keats's poetry with what she terms "the genetic code of the middle class" (204).

41. On the relationship between economics and masturbation, see also David Bennett.

CODA. TENNYSON'S IDYLLS, PURE POETRY, AND THE MARKET

1. Note that this concept was first created in the eighteenth century by Joseph Warton in his *Essay on the Genius and Writings of Pope* (1756). On the eighteenth-century construction of "pure poetry," see especially Zionkowski. See Jay Clayton for a discussion of the influence of this concept on the Romantic poets.

2. I thank Herbert F. Tucker, for this felicitous metaphor and for his superb criticism of the chapter. I also extend my gratitude to Garrett Stewart, Alan Liu, Regenia Gagnier, Paul Hernadi, and Barbara Gelpi for their comments on earlier drafts of this chapter.

3. See Erickson 36. Simon Eliot questions the importance of 1826 when he states that "the much-vaunted book trade crisis of 1826 can be seen as no more than a little, local difficulty, a slightly exaggerated version of the 'dip' that almost always followed a year of exceptionally high production" (28). Unfortunately, Eliot is calculating general market trends rather than the effects of those trends on specific generic forms. It seems safe to say that, in general, the novel was affected less adversely by such "dips" than was poetry.

4. Bulwer-Lytton begins the article by stating that "[t]he popularity of writers of prose, especially Scott, has served for a season to dislodge poetry from the familiar post it once held by the social hearth, as well as in the student's closet" (*Critical* 1.334).

5. See Ann Colley and also Barbara Herb Wright.

6. On Tennyson and homosexuality, see Alan Sinfield and Sedgwick, *Between*, chapter 7.

7. Joe Bristow's collection, *The Victorian Poet,* is an especially helpful collection of essays on this vexed question. See bibliographical information under "Abbreviations" (xi).

8. For similar comments on the elevation of the poetic enterprise despite the "anti-poetic" climate of the nineteenth century, see David J. DeLaura; Starzyk 155–82; and Sinfield 13–14, 19–21, 89–91, and 164–66.

9. The claim that Victorian poets were caught between dialectical injunctions is a commonplace of criticism on the Victorian period. As Cleanth Brooks, for example, argues, Victorian poetry "is left impaled on one of the two horns of the dilemma: poetry with a message . . . ; or, on the other hand, pure poetry, art for art's sake" (239). See also Isobel Armstrong 28–39 and 96–97; Warren 12–13; Starzyk; and Carol Christ, *Victorian and Modern Poetics* 63–73 and *The Finer Optic.* The dialectic in fact has its roots in the eighteenth century, as John Sitter makes clear (see, especially, chapters 3 and 4).

10. See Herbert Tucker; Culler, *The Poetry of Tennyson* 223–30; John Reed 58–69; and Donald S. Hair 154–68.

11. For a different but compatible reading of this book, see William Buckler 44–76.

12. Robert Pattison also comments on the affinity of the *Idylls* to the novel (138); in addition, he reminds us that lyric poetry tends to be associated in the work with the evil Vivien (142, 147).

13. For the relationship of rumor in the *Idylls of the King* to journalism, see James Eli Adams; for the relationship of the *Idylls* to British imperialism, see Victor Kiernan; and for an early discussion of the importance of religion's decline to the *Idylls*, see Jerome Buckley 192–94.

14. For Lacan's use of this same play on words, see *Feminine Sexuality* 167.

15. For similar arguments, see also Sinfield 85–86, 95–98 and Isobel Armstrong 41–67.

WORKS CITED

PRIMARY SOURCES

Acton, William. *The Functions and Disorders of the Reproductive Organs.* 3rd American from the 5th London ed. Philadelphia: Lindsay and Blakiston, 1871.

Aristotle. *Problems II and Rhetorica ad Alexandrum.* Trans. W. S. Hett. Cambridge: Harvard UP, 1957.

Arnold, Matthew. *The Complete Prose Works of Matthew Arnold.* Ed. R. H. Super. 11 vols. to date. Ann Arbor: U of Michigan P, 1960–.

———. *Lectures and Essays in Criticism.* Ed. R. H. Super. Ann Arbor: U of Michigan P, 1962.

Auden, W. H. *Selected Poems.* Ed. Edward Mendelson. New York: Vintage, 1979.

Austen, Jane. *Persuasion.* Mineola: Dover, 1997.

Austin, Alfred. "Poetry of the Period." *Temple Bar* (May 1869): 145–94.

———. *The Poetry of the Period.* London: Richard Bentley, 1870. New York: Garland, 1986.

Aveling, Edward, and Eleanor Marx. "Shelley and Socialism." *To-Day* 53 (April 1888):103–16.

Bacon, Ezekiel. "The Poetical Temperament, and Faculty." *American Journal of Insanity* 1 (April 1845): 355–64.

Bagehot, Walter. *Literary Studies.* 2 vols. Ed. Richard Holt Hutton. London: Longmans, Green, and Co., 1910.

[Bailey, Thomas.] *A Sermon on the Death of Byron.* London: Longman, Hurst, Rees, Orme, Browne, and Green, 1824.

Bailley, Matthew. *The Morbid Anatomy of Some of the Most Important Parts of the Human Body.* 1793. 2nd American edition. Walpole, NH: G. W. Nichols, 1808. In Alvin E. Rodin. *The Influence of Matthew Baillie's Morbid Anatomy: Biography, Evaluation, and Reprint.* Springfield, IL: Charles C. Thomas, 1973.

Beddoes, Thomas. *Hygëia: Or Essays Moral and Medical, on the Causes Affecting the Personal State of Our Middling and Affluent Classes.* 2 vols. Bristol: R. Phillips, 1802–03.

Bentham, Jeremy. "The Rationale of Reward." 1825. *Victorian Poetry and Poetics.* Ed. Walter E. Houghton and G. Robert Stange. 2nd ed. New York: Houghton, 1968. 843–44.

Blackmore, Richard. *Treatise of the Spleen and Vapours: or, Hypochondriacal and Hysterical Affections with Three Discourses on the Nature and Cure of the Cholick, Melancholy, and Palsies.* London: J. Pemberton, 1725.

Blessington, Marguerite, Countess of. *Lady Blessington's Conversations of Lord Byron.* Ed. Ernest J. Lovell Jr. Princeton: Princeton UP, 1969.

Braddon, Mary Elizabeth. *The Doctor's Wife.* Ed. Lyn Pykett. Oxford: Oxford UP, 1998.

British Quarterly Review 2 (August 1845): 46–71.

Brown, John. *Elements of Medicine.* Vol. 1. Portsmouth: William and Daniel Treadwell, 1804.

Browning, Elizabeth Barrett, and Robert Browning. *The Letters of Robert Browning and Elizabeth Barrett Barrett, 1845–1846.* Vol. 1. Ed. Elvan Kintner. Cambridge: Belknap, 1969

Bulwer-Lytton, Edward, Sir. *Critical and Miscellaneous Writings.* 2 vols. Philadelphia: Lea and Blanchard, 1841.

———. *England and the English.* 2 vols. London: Richard Bentley, 1833.

Burke, Edmund. *Reflections on the Revolution in France.* London: Everyman, 1912.

Burton, Robert. *The Anatomy of Melancholy.* 3 vols. Ed. Thomas C. Faulkner, Nicolas K. Kiessling, and Rhonda L. Blair. Oxford: Clarendon, 1989.

Byron, Lord. *Byron: A Critical Edition of the Major Works.* Ed. Jerome J. McGann. Oxford: Oxford UP, 1986.

———. *Byron's Letters and Journals.* 12 vols. Ed. Leslie A. Marchand. London: John Murray, 1973–82.

———. *The Complete Miscellaneous Prose.* Ed. Andrew Nicholson. Oxford: Clarendon, 1991.

———. *Oeuvres complètes de Lord Byron.* Trans. Louis Barré. Paris: J. Bry Ainé, 1854.

Cabanis, Pierre-Jean-George. *On the Relations between the Physical and Moral Aspects of Man.* 1805. 2 vols. Trans. Margaret Duggan Saidi. Ed. George Mora. Baltimore: Johns Hopkins UP, 1981.

Carlyle, Thomas. *A Carlyle Reader: Selections from the Writings of Thomas Carlyle.* Ed. G. B. Tennyson. Cambridge: Cambridge UP, 1984.

———. *Critical and Miscellaneous Essays.* Vol. 4. London: Chapman and Hall, [1899].

"Cato." *Cato to Lord Byron on the Immorality of his Writings.* London: W. Wetton, 1824.

Cheyne, George. *The English Malady: or, a Treatise of Nervous Diseases of all Kinds.* London: George Risk, George Ewing, and William Smith, 1733. Delmar, NY: Scholars' Facsimiles and Reprints, 1976.

Clarkson, Thomas. *A Portraiture of Quakerism.* Vol. 1. New York: Samuel Stansbury, 1806.

Coleridge, Samuel Taylor. *Biographia Literaria or Biographical Sketches of My Literary Life and Opinions.* 2 vols. Ed. James Engell and W. Jackson Bate. Princeton: Princeton UP, 1983.

———. *On the Constitution of the Church and State.* Ed. John Colmer. Princeton: Princeton UP, 1976.

———. *The Friend.* Ed. Barbara E. Rooke. Princeton: Princeton UP, 1969.

———. *The Notebooks of Samuel Taylor Coleridge.* 4 vols. Ed. Kathleen Coburn. London: Routledge and Kegan Paul, 1957–90.

Crichton, Alexander. *An Inquiry into the Nature and Origin of Mental Derangement.* Vol. 1. London: T. Cadell, Junior, and W. Davies, 1798. New York: AMS, 1976.

Darwin, Erasmus. *Zoonomia; or, the Laws of Organic Life.* 1794–96. 2 vols. New York: AMS, 1974.

de Vere, Aubrey. *Edinburgh Review* 90 (October 1849): 388–433.

D'Israeli, Isaac. *The Calamities and Quarrels of Authors.* Ed. Benjamin Disraeli. 2 vols. New York: A. C. Armstrong and Son, 1885.

———. *Curiosities of Literature and The Literary Character Illustrated.* New York: D. Appleton, 1846.

———. *An Essay on the Manners and Genius of the Literary Character.* London: T. Cadell and W. Davies, 1795.

———. *The Literary Character.* D'Israeli, *Curiosities* 405–46.

Don Leon: A Poem by the Late Lord Byron. London: [William Dugdale], 1866.

The Dorchester Guide; or, a House That Jack Built. Fourth Edition. London: Dean and Munday, 1820.

Duff, William. *An Essay on Original Genius.* London: Edward and Charles Dilly, 1767. New York: Garland, 1970.

Du Laurens, André. *A Discourse of the Preservation of the Sight: of Melancholike Diseases; of Rheumes, and of Old Age.* Trans. Richard Surphlet. London: Ralph Iacson, 1599.

Edgeworth, Maria. *Castle Rackrent.* Ed. George Watson. Oxford: Oxford UP, 1969.

Edinburgh Review 11 (October 1807): 195–214.

Edinburgh Review (August 1811): 379–92.

Edinburgh Review 24 (February 1815): 439–52.

Engels, Friedrich. *The Condition of the Working Class in England.* Trans. W. O. Henderson and W. H. Chaloner. New York: Macmillan, 1958.

Gammage, R. G. *History of the Chartist Movement, 1837–1854.* 1854. 2nd edition. New York: Augustus M. Kelley, 1969.

Gerard, Alexander. *An Essay on Genius.* London: W. Strahan, 1774. New York: Garland, 1970.

Gladstone, W. E. *Quarterly Review* 106 (October 1859): 454–85.

Gordon, Sir Cosmo. *The Life and Genius of Lord Byron.* London: Knight and Lacey, 1824.

Graham, Sylvester. *A Lecture to Young Men.* Providence: Weeden and Cory, 1834. New York: Arno, 1974.

Hallam, Arthur H. "On Some Characteristics of Modern Poetry." *Englishman's Magazine.* August 1831. *Victorian Poetry and Poetics.* Ed. Walter E. Houghton and G. Robert Stange. 2nd ed. New York: Houghton, 1968. 848–60.

Haslam, John. *Observations on Madness and Melancholy.* 2nd ed. London: J. Callow, 1809. New York: Arno, 1976.

Hazlitt, William. *The Complete Works of William Hazlitt.* Ed. P. P. Howe. 21 vols. London: Dent, 1930–34.

Holbeach, Henry. "The New Fiction." *Contemporary Review* 37 (January–June 1880): 247–62.

[Hone, William.] *"Don John," or Don Juan Unmasked.* London: William Hone, 1819.

———. *Don Juan, Canto the Third.* London: William Hone, 1819.

Hunt, Leigh. *Lord Byron and Some of His Contemporaries.* London: Henry Colburn, 1828. New York: AMS, 1966.

James, Robert. *A Medicinal Dictionary.* Vol. 2. London: T. Osborne, 1743–45.

Journal of Mental Science 9 (January 1864): 581–86.

Joyce, James. *A Portrait of the Artist as a Young Man.* New York: Viking, 1964.

Kant, Immanuel. *Practical Philosophy.* Trans. Mary J. Gregor. Ed. Mary J. Gregor. Cambridge: Cambridge UP, 1996.

Knowles, James T. "Aspects of Tennyson." *Nineteenth Century* 33 (January 1893): 164–88.

Lackington, James. *Memoirs of the First Forty-five Years of James Lackington, 1794.* New York: Garland, 1974.

Lallemand, Claude François. *A Practical Treatise on the Causes, Symptoms, and Treatment of Spermatorrhoea.* 1847. 4th American edition. Trans. Henry J. McDougall. Philadelphia: Blanchard and Lea, 1861.

Lockhart, John Gibson. *Memoirs of the Life of Sir Walter Scott.* Vol. 1. Boston: Houghton Mifflin, 1910.

Macaulay, Thomas Babington. "Poets and Insanity." *American Journal of Insanity* 5 (April 1849): 377–78.

Madden, R. R. *The Infirmities of Genius Illustrated by Referring the Anomalies in the Literary Character to the Habits and Constitutional Peculiarities of Men of Genius.* Vol. 2. London: Saunders and Otley, 1833.

Marx, Karl. *Capital: A Critique of Political Economy.* Vol. 1. Trans. Ben Fowkes. New York: Penguin, 1976.

Mill, John Stuart. *Essays on Poetry.* Ed. F. Parvin Sharpless. Columbia: U of South Caroliña P, 1976.

Milton, John. *Complete Poems and Major Prose.* Ed. Merritt Y. Hughes. New York: Macmillan, 1957.

Mitford, John. *The Private Life of Lord Byron.* London: H. Smith [William Dugdale], [1836].

Mulock, Thomas. *The Answer Given by the Gospel to the Atheism of all Ages; being Strictures Suggested Chiefly by the Works, Styled Theological, of the Late Thomas Paine.* London: A. A. Paris, 1819.

Newman, John Henry. *Discourses on the Scope and Nature of University Education.* Dublin: James Duffy, 1852.

The New Monthly Magazine 13 (1820): 543–48.

New Orleans Medical and Surgical Journal 11 (March 1855): 667–705.

Onania; or, the Heinous Sin of Self-Pollution. London: Thomas Crouch, 1723. New York: Garland, 1986.

"Oxonian." *The Radical Triumvirate, or, Infidel Paine, and Surgeon Lawrence, Colleaguing with the Patriotic Radicals to Emancipate Mankind from All Laws Human and Divine.* London: Francis Westley, 1820.

Parry, Caleb Hillier. *Elements of Pathology and Therapeutics.* Vol. 1. London: Underwood, 1815.

Peacock, Thomas Love. "The Four Ages of Poetry." 1820. *English Romantic Writers.* Ed. David Perkins. San Diego: Harcourt Brace Jovanovich, 1967. 758–65.

Procter, B. W. *Edinburgh Review* 47 (January 1828): 184–204.

Rousseau, Jean-Jacques. *The Confessions of Jean-Jacques Rousseau.* Trans. J. M. Cohen. London: Penguin, 1953.

Rush, Benjamin. *Medical Inquiries and Observations, upon the Diseases of the Mind.* Philadelphia: Kimber and Richardson, 1812. New York: Hafner Publishing Company, 1962.

Ruskin, John. *The Works of John Ruskin.* Ed. E. T. Cook and Alexander Wedderburn. 39 vols. New York: Longmans, 1903–12.

Scott, John. "The Author of the Scotch Novels." *London Magazine* 1 (1820): 11–22.

Scott, Walter, Sir. *The Complete Poetical Works of Sir Walter Scott.* Cambridge Edition. Boston: Houghton, 1900.

———. *Essays on Chivalry, Romance, and the Drama.* Edinburgh: Robert Cadell, 1834. Freeport: Books for Libraries, 1972.

———. *Hints Addressed to the Inhabitants of Edinburgh, and Others, in Prospect of His Majesty's Visit. By an Old Citizen.* Edinburgh: Bell and Bradfute, 1822.

———. *The Journal of Sir Walter Scott.* Ed. W. E. K. Anderson. Oxford: Clarendon, 1972.

———. *The Letters of Sir Walter Scott.* 12 vols. Ed. H. J. C. Grierson. London: Constable, 1933.

Shakespeare, William. *The Complete Works*. Ed. Alfred Harbage. New York: Viking, 1969.

Smith, Adam. *Lectures on Rhetoric and Belles Lettres*. Ed. John M. Lothian. London: Thomas Nelson, 1963.

Smith, William. *A Dissertation upon the Nerves*. London: W. Owen, 1768.

Solomon, Samuel. *A Guide to Health; or, Advice to Both Sexes, in Nervous and Consumptive Complaints: with an Essay on the Scurvy, Leprosy, and Scrofula; also, On a Certain Disease, Seminal Weakness, and a Destructive Habit of a Private Nature, to which is added, an Address to Parents, Tutors & Guardians of Youth*. 54th ed. Underbank, Stockport: J. Clarke, 1802.

Southey, Robert. *The Life and Correspondence of Robert Southey*. 6 vols. Ed. Charles Cuthbert Southey. London: Longman, Brown, Green and Longmans, 1849–50.

———. *A Vision of Judgement. Opposing Visions: Byron's and Southey's Vision of Judgment*. Ed. Henry J. Donaghy. Pocatello: Idaho State UP, 1976.

Spurzheim, Johann Christoph. *Education, Founded on the Nature of Man*. New York: Fowlers and Wells, 1847.

———. *Observations on the Deranged Manifestations of the Mind, or Insanity*. 1833. Ed. Anthony A. Walsh. Gainesville: Scholars' Facsimiles and Reprints, 1970.

[Stacy, John.] *A Critique on the Genius and Writings of Lord Byron, with Remarks on* Don Juan. Norwich: John Stacy, 1820.

Stephen, Leslie. "Wordsworth's Ethics." *Hours in a Library*. London: Smith, Elder, and Co., 1874–79.

Tennyson, Alfred. *Tennyson: A Selected Edition*. Ed. Christopher Ricks. Berkeley: U of California P, 1989.

Tennyson, Hallam. *Alfred Lord Tennyson: A Memoir*. London: Macmillan, 1906.

Tissot, Samuel Auguste David. *L'Onanisme, dissertation sur les maladies produites par la masturbation*. Troisième édition considérablement augmentée. Lausanne: François Grasset, 1764.

———. *Three Essays: First, on the Disorders of People of Fashion. Second, On Diseases Incidental to Literary and Sedentary Persons, with proper rules for preventing their fatal consequences, and instructions for their care. Third, On Onanism; or, a treatise upon the disorders produced by masturbation; or, the effect of secret and excessive venery*. Trans. Francis Bacon Lee, M. Danes, and A. Hume. Dublin: James Williams, 1772.

Todd, John. *A Remonstrance Addressed to Mr. John Murray, Respecting a Recent Publication*. London: F. C. and J. Rivington, 1822.

———. *The Student's Manual*. 1835. New Revised Edition. Northhampton: Bridgman and Childs, 1861.

Trall, Russell Thacher. *Home-Treatment for Sexual Abuses*. New York: Fowlers and Wells, 1853.

Trevelyan, G. Otto. *The Life and Letters of Lord Macaulay*. Vol. 1. New York: Harper and Brothers, 1901.

Treves, Frederick. "The Physiology of Some Phases of the Poetic Mind." *Journal of Mental Science* 24 (April 1878): 64–75, 233–43.

Trotter, Thomas. *A View of the Nervous Temperament*. London: Longman, Hurst, Rees, and Orme, 1807.

Warton, Joseph. *An Essay on the Genius and Writings of Pope*. 2 vols. 4th edition. London: J. Dodsley, 1782. New York: Garland, 1970.

Wordsworth, William, and Dorothy Wordsworth. *The Letters of William and Dorothy Wordsworth: The Early Years, 1787–1805.* 8 vols. Ed. Ernest de Selincourt. 2nd ed. Oxford: Clarendon, 1967.

———. *The Prose Works of William Wordsworth.* Ed. E. J. B. Owen and Jane W. Smyser. 3 vols. Oxford: Clarendon, 1974.

SECONDARY SOURCES

Adams, James Eli. "Harlots and Base Interpreters: Scandal and Slander in *Idylls of the King.*" *Victorian Poetry* 30 (1992): 421–39.

Allen, Emily. *Theater Figures: The Production of the Nineteenth-Century British Novel.* Columbus, OH: Ohio State UP, 2003.

Altick, Richard D. *The English Common Reader: A Social History of the Mass Reading Public 1800–1900.* Chicago: U of Chicago P, 1957.

Armstrong, Isobel. *Victorian Poetry: Poetry, Poetics, and Politics.* London: Routledge, 1993.

Armstrong, Nancy. *Desire and Domestic History: A Political History of the Novel.* New York: Oxford UP, 1987.

Babb, Lawrence. *The Elizabethan Malady: A Study of Melancholia in English Literature from 1580–1642.* East Lansing: Michigan State College P, 1951.

Bakhtin, Mikhail. *The Dialogic Imagination.* Trans. Caryl Emerson and Michael Holquist. Ed. Michael Holquist. Austin: U of Texas P, 1981.

———. *Speech Genres and Other Late Essays.* Trans. Vern W. McGee. Ed. Caryl Emerson and Michael Holquist. Austin: U of Texas P, 1986.

Bamborough, J. B. *The Little World of Man.* London: Longmans, 1952.

Barker-Benfield, G. J. *The Horrors of the Half-Known Life: Male Attitudes Toward Women and Sexuality in Nineteenth-Century America.* New York: Harper and Row, 1976.

———. "The Spermatic Economy: A Nineteenth-Century View of Sexuality." *The American Family in Social-Historical Perspective.* Ed. Michael Gordon. 2nd ed. New York: St. Martin's, 1973. 374–402.

Batten, Guinn. *The Orphaned Imagination: Melancholy and Commodity Culture in English Romanticism.* Durham: Duke UP, 1998.

Baudrillard, Jean. *For a Critique of the Political Economy of the Sign.* Trans. Charles Levin. New York: Telos, 1981.

Beer, Gillian. *The Romance.* London: Methuen, 1970.

Beiderwell, Bruce. *Power and Punishment in Scott's Novels.* Athens: U of Georgia P, 1992.

Bender, John. *Imagining the Penitentiary: Fiction and the Architecture of Mind in Eighteenth-Century England.* Chicago: U of Chicago P, 1987.

Benjamin, Walter. *Illuminations: Essays and Reflections.* Trans. Harry Zohn. Ed. Hannah Arendt. New York: Schocken Books, 1968.

Bennett, David. "Burghers, Burglars, and Masturbators: The Sovereign Spender in the Age of Consumerism." *New Literary History* 30 (1999): 269–94.

Bernstein, Michael André. *Bitter Carnival:* Ressentiment *and the Abject Hero.* Princeton: Princeton UP, 1992.

Blann, Robinson. *Throwing the Scabbard Away: Byron's Battle Against the Censors of* Don Juan. New York: Peter Lang, 1991.

Boehm, Alan D. "The 1798 Lyrical Ballads and the Poetics of Late Eighteenth-Century Book Production." *ELH* 63 (1996): 453–87.

Bourdieu, Pierre. *Outline of a Theory of Practice.* Trans. Richard Nice. Cambridge: Cambridge UP, 1977.

Brantlinger, Patrick. *Fictions of State: Culture and Credit in Britain, 1694–1994.* Ithaca: Cornell UP, 1996.

———. *The Reading Lesson: The Threat of Mass Literacy in Nineteenth-Century British Fiction.* Bloomington: Indiana UP, 1998.

Brinton, Crane. *The Political Ideas of the English Romanticists.* Oxford: Oxford UP, 1926.

Brooks, Cleanth. *Modern Poetry and the Tradition.* Oxford: Oxford UP, 1965.

Bruns, Gerald L. "The Otherness of Words: Joyce, Bakhtin, Heidegger." *Postmodernism—Philosophy and the Arts.* Ed. Hugh J. Silverman. New York: Routledge, 1990. 120–36.

Buckler, William E. *Man and His Myths: Tennyson's* Idylls of the King *in Critical Context.* New York: New York UP, 1984.

Buckley, Jerome. *Tennyson: The Growth of a Poet.* Cambridge: Harvard UP, 1960.

Burgess, Miranda J. *British Fiction and the Production of Social Order, 1740–1830.* Cambridge: Cambridge UP, 2000.

Burwick, Frederick. *Poetic Madness and the Romantic Imagination.* University Park: Pennsylvania State UP, 1996.

Butler, Marilyn. *Romantics, Rebels, and Reactionaries: English Literature and its Background, 1760-1830.* Oxford: Oxford UP, 1982.

Cafarelli, Annette Wheeler. "Byron and the Pathology of Genius." *Re-Reading Byron: Essays Selected from Hofstra University's Byron Bicentennial Conference.* Ed. Alice Levine and Robert N. Keane. New York: Garland, 1993. 205–21.

———. *Prose in the Age of Poets: Romanticism and Biographical Narrative from Johnson to De Quincey.* Philadelphia: U of Pennsylvania P, 1990.

Chandler, Alice. *A Dream of Order: The Medieval Ideal in Nineteenth-Century English Literature.* Lincoln: U of Nebraska P, 1970.

Chandler, James. *England in 1819: The Politics of Literary Culture and the Case of Romantic Historicism.* Chicago: U of Chicago P, 1998.

Christ, Carol. *The Finer Optic: The Aesthetic of Particularity in Victorian Poetry.* New Haven: Yale UP, 1975.

———. *Victorian and Modern Poetics.* Chicago: U of Chicago P, 1984.

Christensen, Jerome. *Lord Byron's Strength: Romantic Writing and Commercial Society.* Baltimore: Johns Hopkins UP, 1993.

Clayton, Jay. *Romantic Vision and the Novel.* Cambridge: Cambridge UP, 1987.

Cohen, Ed. *Talk on the Wilde Side: Toward a Genealogy of a Discourse on Male Sexualities.* New York: Routledge, 1993.

Colley, Ann C. *Tennyson and Madness.* Athens: U of Georgia P, 1983.

Collins, A. S. *The Profession of Letters: A Study of the Relation of Author to Patron, Publisher, and Public, 1780–1832.* London: Routledge, 1928.

Collins, Philip. *Thomas Cooper, the Chartist: Byron and the Poets of the Poor.* Byron Foundation Lecture 1969. Nottingham: University of Nottingham, [1970].

Cooke, M. G. *The Blind Man Traces the Circle: On the Patterns and Philosophy of Byron's Poetry.* Princeton: Princeton UP, 1969.

Craig, David. "Byron the Radical." *Byron and Scotland: Radical or Dandy?* Ed. Angus Calder. Edinburgh: Edinburgh UP, 1989. 7–22.

Crompton, Louis. *Byron and Greek Love: Homophobia in 19th-Century England.* Berkeley: U of California P, 1985.

Culler, A. Dwight. *The Poetry of Tennyson*. New Haven: Yale UP, 1977.
———. *The Victorian Mirror of History*. New Haven: Yale UP, 1985.
Curran, Stuart. *Poetic Form and British Romanticism*. New York: Oxford UP, 1986.
Curry, Kenneth. *Sir Walter Scott's* Edinburgh Annual Register. Knoxville: U of Tennessee P, 1977.
Cvetkovich, Ann. *Mixed Feelings: Feminism, Mass Culture, and Victorian Sensationalism*. New Brunswick: Rutgers UP, 1992.
Davis, Lennard J. *Factual Fictions: The Origins of the English Novel*. New York: Columbia UP, 1983.
de Almeida, Hermione. "Romantic Evolution: Fresh Perfection and Ebbing Process in Keats." *Critical Essays on John Keats*. Boston: G. K. Hall, 1990. 279–91.
Debord, Guy. *The Society of the Spectacle*. New York: Zone Books, 1995.
DeLaura, David J. "The Future of Poetry: A Context for Carlyle and Arnold." *Carlyle and His Contemporaries: Essays in Honor of Charles Richard Sanders*. Ed. John Clubbe. Durham: Duke UP, 1976. 156–80.
Derrida, Jacques. *The Gift of Death*. Trans. David Wills. Chicago: U of Chicago P, 1992.
———. *Given Time: 1. Counterfeit Money*. Trans. Peggy Kamuf. Chicago: U of Chicago P, 1992.
———. *Of Grammatology*. Trans. Gayatri Chakravorty Spivak. Baltimore: Johns Hopkins UP, 1976.
———. *Specters of Marx: The State of the Debt, the Work of Mourning, and the New International*. Trans. Peggy Kamuf. New York: Routledge, 1994.
de Silva, D. M. "Byron's Politics and the History Plays." *Byron: Poetry and Politics*. Ed. Erwin A. Stürzl and James Hogg. Salzburger Studien zur anglistik und Amerikanistik 13. Salzburg: Institut Für Anglistik und Amerikanistik, 1981. 113–36.
Diakonova, Nina and Vadim Vacuro. "Byron and Russia." Trueblood 143–59.
Duff, David. *Romance and Revolution: Shelley and the Politics of a Genre*. Cambridge: Cambridge UP, 1994.
Duncan, Ian. *Modern Romance and Transformations of the Novel: The Gothic, Scott, Dickens*. Cambridge: Cambridge UP, 1992.
Dyer, Gary. "Thieves, Boxers, Sodomites, Poets: Being Flash to Byron's *Don Juan*." *PMLA* 116 (2001): 562–78.
Eco, Umberto. "The Frames of Comic 'Freedom.' " *Carnival!* Ed. Thomas A. Sebeok. Approaches to Semiotics 64. Berlin: Mouton, 1984. 1–9.
Elfenbein, Andrew. *Byron and the Victorians*. Cambridge Studies in Nineteenth-Century Literature and Culture 4. Cambridge: Cambridge UP, 1995.
———. *Romantic Genius: The Prehistory of a Homosexual Role*. New York: Columbia UP, 1999.
Eliot, Simon. "Some Trends in British Book Production, 1800–1919." *Literature in the Marketplace: Nineteenth-Century British Publishing and Reading Practices*. Ed. John O. Jordan and Robert L. Patten. Cambridge: Cambridge UP, 1995. 19–43.
Eliot, T. S. *Selected Essays*. New York: Harcourt, Brace, and World, 1964.
Erdman, David. "Byron and 'the New Force of the People.' " *Keats-Shelley Journal* 11 (1962): 47–64.
———. "Byron and Revolt in England." *Science and Society* 11 (1947): 234–48.
———. "Lord Byron." *Romantic Rebels: Essays on Shelley and His Circle*. Ed. Kenneth Neill Cameron. Cambridge: Harvard UP, 1973. 161–202.

———. "Lord Byron and the Genteel Reformers." *PMLA* 56 (1941): 1065–94.

———. "Lord Byron as Rinaldo." *PMLA* 57 (1942): 189–231.

Erickson, Lee. *The Economy of Literary Form: English Literature and the Industrialization of Publishing, 1800–1850.* Baltimore: Johns Hopkins UP, 1996.

Faas, Ekbert. *Retreat into the Mind: Victorian Poetry and the Rise of Psychiatry.* Princeton: Princeton UP, 1988.

Felluga, Dino. "The Critic's New Clothes: *Sartor Resartus* as 'Cold Carnival.' " *Criticism* 37 (Fall 1995): 583–99.

———. " 'With a most voiceless thought': Byron and the Radicalism of Textual Culture." *European Romantic Review* 8 (Winter 2000): 148–65.

Ferris, Ina. *The Achievement of Literary Authority: Gender, History, and the Waverley Novels.* Ithaca: Cornell UP, 1991.

———. "From Trope to Code: The Novel and the Rhetoric of Gender in Nineteenth-Century Critical Discourse." *Rewriting the Victorians: Theory, History, and the Politics of Gender.* Ed. Linda M. Shires. New York: Routledge, 1992. 18–30.

Fischer, Hermann. *Romantic Verse Narrative: The History of a Genre.* Trans. Sue Bollans. Cambridge: Cambridge UP, 1991.

Flint, Kate. *The Woman Reader, 1837–1914.* Oxford: Clarendon, 1993.

Foot, Michael. *The Politics of Paradise: A Vindication of Byron.* New York: Harper and Row, 1988.

Ford, Jennifer. *Coleridge on Dreaming: Romanticism, Dreams, and the Medical Imagination.* Cambridge: Cambridge UP, 1998.

Foucault, Michel. *Discipline and Punish: The Birth of the Prison.* Trans. Alan Sheridan. New York: Vintage, 1979.

———. *History of Sexuality.* 2 vols. Trans. Robert Hurley. New York: Vintage, 1990.

———. *The Order of Things: An Archaeology of the Human Sciences.* New York: Vintage, 1970.

Franklin, J. Jeffrey. *Serious Play: The Cultural Form of the Nineteenth-Century Realist Novel.* Philadelphia: U of Pennsylvania P, 1999.

Freud, Sigmund. *Collected Papers.* 5 vols. Trans. Joan Riviere. Ed. James Strachey. New York: Basic Books, 1959.

Galperin, William H. *The Return of the Visible in British Romanticism.* Baltimore: Johns Hopkins UP, 1993.

Gamer, Michael C. "Marketing a Masculine Romance: Scott, Antiquarianism, and the Gothic." *Studies in Romanticism* 32 (1993): 523–49.

Giddey, Ernest. "Gibbon, Byron, and the Idea of Revolution." *The Byron Journal* #18 (1990): 50–60.

Gilbert, Pamela K. *Disease, Desire, and the Body in Victorian Women's Popular Novels.* Cambridge: Cambridge UP, 1997.

Girouard, Mark. *The Return to Camelot: Chivalry and the English Gentleman.* New Haven: Yale UP, 1981.

Gleckner, Robert F. *Byron and the Ruins of Paradise.* Baltimore: Johns Hopkins UP, 1967.

Goslee, Nancy Moore. *Scott the Rhymer.* Lexington: UP of Kentucky, 1988.

Gross, Jonathan David. *Byron: The Erotic Liberal.* Lanham: Rowman and Littlefield, 2001.

Guy-Bray, Stephen. "Beddoes, Pygmalion, and the Art of Onanism." *Nineteenth-Century Literature* 52 (1998): 446–70.

Hadley, Elaine. *Melodramatic Tactics: Theatricalized Dissent in the English Marketplace, 1800–1885.* Stanford: Stanford UP, 1995.

Hair, Donald S. *Domestic and Heroic in Tennyson's Poetry.* Toronto: U of Toronto P, 1981.

Hare, E. H. "Masturbatory Insanity: The History of an Idea." *The Journal of Mental Health* 108 (January 1962): 1–25.

Hawes, Clement. *Mania and Literary Style: The Rhetoric of Enthusiasm from the Ranters to Christopher Smart.* Cambridge: Cambridge UP, 1996.

Heinzelman, Kurt. "Byron's Poetry of Politics: The Economic Basis of the 'Poetical Character.' " *Texas Studies in Literature and Language* 23 (1981): 361–88.

———. *The Economics of the Imagination.* Amherst: U of Massachusetts P, 1980.

Hirsch, E. D., Jr. "Byron and the Terrestrial Paradise." *From Sensibility to Romanticism: Essays Presented to Frederick A. Pottle.* Ed. Frederick W. Hilles and Harold Bloom. New York: Oxford UP, 1965. 467–86.

Hofkosh, Sonia. *Sexual Politics and the Romantic Author.* Cambridge: Cambridge UP, 1998.

Holland, Tom. "Undead Byron." Wilson 154–65.

Hone, J. Ann. *For the Cause of Truth: Radicalism in London 1796–1821.* Oxford: Clarendon, 1982.

Hughes, Winifred. *The Maniac in the Cellar: Sensation Novels of the 1860's.* Princeton: Princeton UP, 1980.

Jacyna, L. S. *Philosophic Whigs: Medicine, Science, and Citizenship in Edinburgh, 1789–1848.* London: Routledge, 1994.

James, Louis. *Fiction for the Working Man, 1830-1850.* London: Oxford UP, 1963.

Jameson, Fredric. *The Political Unconscious: Narrative as a Socially Symbolic Act.* Ithaca: Cornell UP, 1981.

Jamison, Kay Redfield. *Touched with Fire: Manic-Depressive Illness and the Artistic Temperament.* New York: Free Press, 1993.

Janowitz, Anne. *Lyric and Labour in the Romantic Tradition.* Cambridge: Cambridge UP, 1998.

Janssen, David Alan. "Byromania: the Romantic Malady." Diss. University of Georgia, 1999.

Jewson, N. D. "Medical Knowledge and the Patronage System in 18th Century England." *Sociology* 8 [1974]: 369–85.

Kelsall, Malcolm. *Byron's Politics.* Sussex: Harvester Press, 1987.

Kernan, Alvin B. *Printing Technology, Letters, and Samuel Johnson.* Princeton: Princeton UP, 1987.

Kiernan, Victor. "Tennyson, King Arthur, and Imperialism." *Culture, Ideology, and Politics: Essays for Eric Hobsbawm.* Ed. Raphael Samuel and Gareth Stedman Jones. London: Routledge, 1983. 126–48.

Klancher, Jon P. *The Making of English Reading Audiences, 1790–1832.* Madison: U of Wisconsin P, 1987.

Klein, Jürgen. "Byron's Idea of Democracy: An Investigation into the Relationship Between Literature and Politics." *Byron: Poetry and Politics.* Ed. Erwin A. Stürzl and James Hogg. Salzburg: Institut für Anglistik und Amerikanistik, 1981. 57–87.

Knight, David. "Romanticism and the Sciences." *Romanticism and the Sciences.* Ed. Andrew Cunningham and Nicholas Jardine. Cambridge: Cambridge UP, 1990. 13–24.

Kristeva, Julia. *Black Sun: Depression and Melancholia.* Trans. Leon S. Roudiez. New York: Columbia UP, 1989.

Lacan, Jacques. *Feminine Sexuality.* Trans. Jacqueline Rose. Ed. Juliet Mitchell and Jacqueline Rose. New York: Norton, 1985.

Laclau, Ernesto, and Chantalle Mouffe. *Hegemony and Socialist Strategy: Towards a Radical Democratic Politics.* London: Verso, 1985.

Langan, Celeste. "Understanding Media in 1805: Audiovisual Hallucination in *The Lay of the Last Minstrel.*" *Studies in Romanticism* 40 (2001): 49–70.

Langbauer, Laurie. *Women and Romance: The Consolations of Gender in the English Novel.* Ithaca: Cornell UP, 1990.

Laqueur, Thomas W. *Making Sex: Body and Gender from the Greeks to Freud.* Cambridge: Harvard UP, 1990.

———. "Masturbation, Credit, and the Novel During the Long Eighteenth Century." *Qui Parle* 8 (1995): 1–19.

———. *Solitary Sex: A Cultural History of Masturbation.* New York: Zone, 2003.

Leblanc, Henri. *Catalogue de l'oeuvre complet de Gustave Doré.* Paris: Ch. Bosse, 1931.

Leckie, Barbara. *Culture and Adultery: The Novel, the Newspaper, and the Law.* Philadelphia: U of Pennsylvania P, 1999.

Levinson, Marjorie. *Keats's Life of Allegory: The Origins of a Style.* London: Blackwell, 1988.

———. "A Question of Taste: Keats and Byron." *Re-Reading Byron: Essays Selected from Hofstra University's Byron Bicentennial Conference.* Ed. Alice Levine and Robert N. Keane. New York: Garland, 1993. 187–204.

Litvak, Joseph. *Caught in the Act: Theatricality in the Nineteenth-Century English Novel.* Berkeley: U of California P, 1992.

Liu, Alan. *Wordsworth: The Sense of History.* Stanford: Stanford UP, 1989.

Logan, Peter Melville. *Nerves and Narratives: A Cultural History of Hysteria in Nineteenth-Century British Prose.* Berkeley: U of California P, 1997.

Lohmar, Brigitte. "Byron's Pilgrimage in Criticism: The Reviews of *Don Juan,* 1819–1824." *Byron.* Ed. James Hogg. Salzburg Studies in English Literature: Romantic Reassessment 81. Salzburg: Institut für Anglistik und Amerikanistik, 1982. 37–63.

Lukács, George. *The Historical Novel.* Trans. Hannah Mitchell and Stanley Mitchell. New York: Pengin, 1962.

Lynch, Deirdre Shauna. *The Economy of Character: Novels, Market Culture, and the Business of Inner Meaning.* Chicago: U of Chicago P, 1998.

MacDonald, Robert H. "The Frightful Consequences of Onanism: Notes on the History of a Delusion." *Journal of the History of Ideas* 28 (1967): 423–31.

Makdisi, Saree. "Colonial Space and the Colonization of Time in Scott's Waverley." *Studies in Romanticism* 34 (1995): 155–87.

Mancoff, Debra. *The Arthurian Revival in Victorian Art.* New York: Garland, 1990.

Manning, Peter J. "Childe Harold in the Marketplace: From Romaunt to Handbook." *Modern Language Quarterly* 52 (1991): 170–90.

———. *Reading Romantics: Texts and Contexts.* Oxford: Oxford UP, 1990.

Mannoni, Octave. "Je sais bien, mais quand même . . ." *Clefs pour l'imaginaire ou l'autre scène.* Paris: Editions du Seuil, 1969. 9–33.

Marchand, Leslie. *Byron: A Biography.* 3 vols. New York: Knopf, 1957.

Marcus, Leah. *The Politics of Mirth: Johnson, Herrick, Milton, Marvell, and the Defense of the Old Holiday Pastimes.* Chicago: U of Chicago P, 1986.

Marcus, Steven. *The Other Victorians: A Study of Sexuality and Pornography in Mid-Nineteenth-Century England.* New York: Basic Books, 1964.

Marsh, Joss. *Word Crimes: Blasphemy, Culture, and Literature in Nineteenth-Century England.* Chicago: U of Chicago P, 1998.

Martin, Loy D. *Browning's Dramatic Monologues and the Postromantic Subject.* Baltimore: Johns Hopkins UP, 1985.

Martin, Philip W. *Byron: A Poet Before His Public.* Cambridge: Cambridge UP, 1982.

Mason, Michael. *The Making of Victorian Sexuality.* Oxford: Oxford UP, 1994.

McCallum, E. L. *Object Lessons: How to Do Things with Fetishism.* New York: State U of New York P, 1999.

McCalman, Iain. *Radical Underworld: Prophets, Revolutionaries, and Pornographers in London, 1795–1840.* Cambridge: Cambridge UP, 1988.

McConnell, Frank D. "Byron's Reductions: 'Much Too Poetical.' " *ELH* 37 (1970): 415–32.

McDayter, Ghislaine. "Conjuring Byron: Byromania, Literary Commodification, and the Birth of Celebrity." Wilson 43–62.

McGann, Jerome. *Byron and Romanticism.* Ed. James Soderholm. Cambridge: Cambridge UP, 2002.

———. "Byron, Mobility, and the Poetics of Historical Ventriloquism." *Romanticism, Past and Present* 9 (1985): 66–82.

———. *Fiery Dust: Byron's Poetic Development.* Chicago: U of Chicago P, 1968.

———. *The Romantic Ideology: A Critical Investigation.* Chicago: U of Chicago P, 1983.

McKeon, Michael. *The Origins of the English Novel, 1600–1740.* Baltimore: Johns Hopkins UP, 1987.

Melchiori, Giorgio. "Byron and Italy: Catalyst of the *Risorgimento.*" Trueblood 108–21.

Mellor, Anne K. *English Romantic Irony.* Cambridge: Harvard UP, 1980.

Miller, D. A. *The Novel and the Police.* Berkeley: U of California P, 1988.

Millgate, Jane. *Scott's Last Edition: A Study in Publishing History.* Edinburgh: Edinburgh UP, 1987.

Mullan, John. *Sentiment and Sociability: The Language of Feeling in the Eighteenth Century.* Oxford: Clarendon, 1988.

Murphy, Paul Thomas. *Toward a Working-Class Canon: Literary Criticism in British Working-Class Periodicals, 1816–1858.* Columbus, OH: Ohio UP, 1994.

Murphy, Peter T. *Poetry as an Occupation and an Art in Britain, 1760-1830.* Cambridge: Cambridge UP, 1993.

Najarian, James. *Victorian Keats: Manliness, Sexuality, and Desire.* New York: Palgrave Macmillan, 2002.

Neuman, R. P. "Masturbation, Madness, and the Modern Concepts of Childhood and Adolescence." *Journal of Social History* 8 (1975): 1–27.

Noble, Andrew. "Byron: Radical, Scottish Aristocrat." *Byron and Scotland: Radical or Dandy?* Ed. Angus Calder. Edinburgh: Edinburgh UP, 1989. 23–43.

Ogden, James. *Isaac D'Israeli.* Oxford: Clarendon, 1969.

Otto, Peter. "The Regeneration of the Body: Sex, Religion, and the Sublime in James Graham's *Temple of Health* and *Hymen.*" *Romanticism on the Net* 23 (August 2001). 30 January 2002 <http://users.ox.ac.uk/~scat0385/23otto.html>.

Oxford Companion to English Literature. Ed. Margaret Drabble. Oxford: Oxford UP, 1985.

Parke, Tim. "*Flaubert devant la critique britannique,* 1857–1865." *Revue de Littérature Comparée* 59 (1985): 299–308.

Partridge, Eric. *A Dictionary of Slang and Unconventional English.* Ed. Paul Beale. New York: Macmillan, 1984.

Pattison, Robert. *Tennyson and Tradition*. Cambridge: Harvard UP, 1979.

Peterson, M. Jeanne. "Dr. Acton's Enemy: Medicine, Sex, and Society in Victorian England." *Victorian Studies* 29 (1986): 569–90.

———. *The Medical Profession in Mid-Victorian London*. Berkeley: U of California P, 1978.

Poovey, Mary. *Making a Social Body: British Cultural Formation, 1830–1864*. Chicago: U of Chicago P, 1995.

Porter, Roy. *Doctor of Socety: Thomas Beddoes and the Sick Trade in Late-Enlightenment England*. London: Routledge, 1992.

———. "Forbidden Pleasures: Enlightenment Literature of Sexual Advice." *Solitary Pleasures: The Historical, Literary, and Artistic Discourses of Autoeroticism*. Ed. Paula Bennett and Vernon A. Rosario II. New York: Routledge, 1995. 75–98.

———. *Health for Sale: Quackery in England, 1660–1850*. New York: Manchester UP, 1989.

Prebble, John. *The King's Jaunt: George IV in Scotland, August 1822*. Edinburgh: Birlinn, 2000.

Psomiades, Kathy. "Beauty's Body: Gender Ideology and British Aestheticism." *Victorian Studies* 36 (1992): 31–52.

Radway, Janice. *Reading the Romance: Women, Patriarchy, and Popular Literature*. Chapel Hill: U of North Carolina P, 1984.

Ramsey, Matthew. "The Popularization of Medicine in France, 1650–1900." *The Popularization of Medicine, 1650–1850*. Ed. Roy Porter. New York: Routledge, 1992. 97–133.

Raymond, Dora Neill. *The Political Career of Lord Byron*. New York: Henry Holt, 1924.

Reed, John. *Perception and Design in Tennyson's* Idylls of the King. Athens: Ohio UP, 1969.

Richardson, Alan. *British Romanticism and the Science of the Mind*. Cambridge: Cambridge UP, 2001.

Ricks, Christopher. *Keats and Embarrassment*. Oxford: Clarendon, 1974.

Rosario, Vernon A. *The Erotic Imagination: French Histories of Perversity*. Oxford: Oxford UP, 1997.

———. "Phantastical Pollutions: The Public Threat of Private Vice in France." *Solitary Pleasures: The Historical, Literary, and Artistic Discourses of Autoeroticism*. Ed. Paula Bennett and Vernon A. Rosario. New York: Routledge, 1995. 101–30.

Rosen, Charles. *Romantic Poets, Critics, and Other Madmen*. Cambridge: Harvard UP, 1998.

Ross, Deborah. *The Excellence of Falsehood: Romance, Realism, and Women's Contribution to the Novel*. Lexington: UP of Kentucky, 1991.

Ross, Marlon B. "Romancing the Nation-State: The Poetics of Romantic Nationalism." *Macropolitics of Nineteenth-Century Literature: Nationalism, Exoticism, Imperialism*. Ed. Jonathan Arac and Harriet Ritvo. Philadelphia: U of Pennsylvania P, 1991. 56–85.

———. "Scott's Chivalric Pose: The Function of Metrical Romance in the Romantic Period." *Genre* 18 (1986): 267–97.

Rowland, William G., Jr. *Literature and the Marketplace: Romantic Writers and Their Audiences in Great Britain and the United States*. Lincoln: U of Nebraska P, 1996.

Ruddick, William. "Byron and England: The Persistance of Byron's Political Ideas." Trueblood 25–47.

Rutherford, Andrew. "Byron, Scott, and Scotland." *Lord Byron and His Contemporaries: Essays from the Sixth International Byron Seminar.* Ed. Charles E. Robinson. Newark: U of Delaware P, 1982. 43–65.

St. Clair, William. "The Impact of Byron's Writings: An Evaluative Approach." *Byron: Augustan and Romantic.* Ed. Andrew Rutherford. London: Macmillan, 1990. 1–25.

Schiesari, Juliana. *The Gendering of Melancholia: Feminism, Pysychoanalysis, and the Symbolics of Loss in Renaissance Literature.* Ithaca: Cornell UP, 1992.

Schmid, Thomas H. *Humor and Transgression in Peacock, Shelley, and Byron: A Cold Carnival.* Lewiston: Edwin Mellen, 1992.

Scott, P. H. "Byron and Scott." *Byron and Scotland: Radical or Dandy?* Ed. Angus Calder. Edinburgh: Edinburgh UP, 1989. 51–64.

Sedgwick, Eve. *Between Men: English Literature and Male Homosocial Desire.* New York : Columbia UP, 1985.

———. "Jane Austen and the Masturbating Girl." *Solitary Pleasures: The Historical, Literary, and Artistic Discourses of Autoeroticism.* Ed. Paula Bennett and Vernon A. Rosario II. New York: Routledge, 1995. 133–53.

Sha, Richard C. "Scientific Forms of Sexual Knowledge in Romanticism." *Romanticism on the Net* 23 (August 2001). 30 January 2002 <http://users.ox.ac.uk/~scat0385/23sha.html>.

Shannon, Edgar Finley. *Tennyson and the Reviewers: A Study of His Literary Reputation and of the Influence of the Critics Upon His Poetry, 1827–1851.* Cambridge: Harvard UP, 1952.

Showalter, Elaine. *The Female Malady: Women, Madness, and English Culture, 1830–1980.* New York: Penguin, 1987.

Sinfield, Alan. *Alfred Tennyson.* Oxford: Basil Blackwell, 1986.

Sitter, John. *Literary Loneliness in Mid-Eighteenth-Century England.* Ithaca: Cornell UP, 1982.

Skinner, Basil C. "Scott as Pageant-Master—The Royal Visit of 1822." *Scott Bicentenary Essays.* Ed. Alan Bell. New York: Barnes and Noble, 1973. 228–37.

Small, Helen. *Love's Madness: Medicine, the Novel, and Female Insanity, 1800–1865.* Oxford: Clarendon, 1996.

Spillane, John D. *The Doctrine of the Nerves: Chapters in the History of Neurology.* Oxford: Oxford UP, 1981.

Stabler, Jane. *Byron, Poetics, and History.* Cambridge: Cambridge UP, 2002.

Stallybrass, Peter, and Allon White. *The Politics and Poetics of Transgression.* Ithaca: Cornell UP, 1986.

Starzyk, Lawrence J. *The Imprisoned Splendor: A Study of Victorian Critical Theory.* Port Washington: Kennikat, 1977.

Stengers, Jean, and Anne Van Neck. *Masturbation: The History of a Great Terror.* Trans. Kathryn A. Hoffman. New York: Palgrave, 2001.

Stevenson, Lionel. "The Key Poem of the Victorian Age." *Essays in American and English Literature Presented to Bruce Robert McElderry, Jr.* Ed. Max F. Schulz. Athens: Ohio UP, 1967. 260–89.

Sutherland, John. *The Life of Walter Scott: A Critical Biography.* Oxford: Blackwell, 1995.

Taylor, John Tinnon. *Early Opposition to the English Novel: The Popular Reaction from 1760–1830.* New York: King's Crown, 1943.

Trevor-Roper, Hugh. "The Invention of Tradition: The Highland Tradition of Scotland." *The Invention of Tradition.* Ed. Eric Hobsbawm and Terence Ranger. Cambridge: Cambridge UP, 1983. 15–41.

Trilling, Lionel. *The Liberal Imagination: Essays on Literature and Society.* New York: Viking, 1950.

Trueblood, Paul Graham, ed. *Byron's Political and Cultural Influence in Nineteenth-Century Europe: A Symposium.* Atlantic Highlands: Humanities Press, 1981.

Trumpener, Katie. *Bardic Nationalism: The Romantic Novel and the British Empire.* Princeton: Princeton UP, 1997.

Tucker, Herbert. "Trials of Fiction: Novel and Epic in the Geraint and Enid Episodes from *Idylls of the King.*" *Victorian Poetry* 30 (1992): 441–61.

Tucker, Susie I. *Enthusiasm: A Study in Semantic Change.* Cambridge: Cambridge UP, 1972.

Vickers, Neil. "Coleridge, Thomas Beddoes, and Brunonian Medicine." *European Romantic Review* 8 (1997): 47–94.

Vrettos, Athena. *Somatic Fictions: Imagining Illness in Victorian Culture.* Stanford: Stanford UP, 1995.

Waddington, Ivan. *The Medical Profession in the Industrial Revolution.* Dublin: Gill and Macmillan Humanities Press, 1984.

Wain, John. "The Search for Identity." *Byron: A Collection of Critical Essays.* Ed. Paul West. Englewood Cliffs: Prentice-Hall, 1963. 157–70.

Walker, Keith. *Byron's Readers: A Study of Attitudes Towards Byron 1812-1832.* Salzburg Studies in English Literature: Romantic Reassessment 88. Salzburg: Institut für Anglistik und Amerikanistik, 1979.

Warren, Alba H. *English Poetic Theory, 1825–1865.* Princeton: Princeton UP, 1950.

Watkins, Daniel P. "Byron and the Poetics of Revolution." *Keats-Shelley Journal* 34 (1985): 95–130.

———. "Violence, Class Consciousness, and Ideology in Byron's History Plays." *ELH* 48 (1981): 799–816.

Watt, Ian P. *The Rise of the Novel: Studies in Defoe, Richardson, and Fielding.* Berkeley: U of California P, 1957.

Weinstein, Mark A. *William Edmonstoune Aytoun and the Spasmodic Controversy.* Yale Studies in English 165. New Haven: Yale UP, 1968.

Wickwar, William H. *The Struggle for the Freedom of the Press, 1819–1832.* London: George Allen and Unwin, 1928.

Williams, Ioan. *Novel and Romance, 1700–1800: A Documentary Record.* New York: Barnes and Noble, 1970.

Wilson, Frances. *Byromania: Portraits of the Artist in Nineteenth- and Twentieth-Century Culture.* New York: St. Martin's, 1999.

Wittkower, Rudolf, and Margot Wittkower. *Born Under Saturn: The Character and Conduct of Artists, A Documented History from Antiquity to the French Revolution.* New York: Random House, 1963.

Wolfson, Susan J. "Feminizing Keats." *Critical Essays on John Keats.* Ed. Hermione de Almeida. Boston: G. K. Hall, 1990. 317–56.

———. " 'Their She Condition': Cross-Dressing and the Politics of Gender in Don Juan." *ELH* 54 (1987): 585–617.

Wood, Jane. *Passion and Pathology in Victorian Fiction.* Oxford: Oxford UP, 2001.

Woodring, Carl. *Politics in English Romantic Poetry*. Cambridge: Harvard UP, 1970.

Wright, Barbara Herb. "Tennyson, the Weird Seizures in *The Princess,* and Epilepsy." *Literature and Medicine* 6 (1987): 61–76.

Zionkowski, Linda. *Men's Work: Gender, Class, and the Professionalization of Poetry, 1660–1784*. New York: Palgrave, 2001.

Žižek, Slavoj. *For They Know Not What They Do: Enjoyment as a Political Factor*. London: Verso, 1991.

———. *Looking Awry: An Introduction to Jacques Lacan through Popular Culture*. Cambridge: MIT P, 1991.

———. *The Plague of Fantasies*. London: Verso, 1997.

———. *The Sublime Object of Ideology*. London: Verso, 1989.

———. "The Truth Arises from Misrecognition." *Lacan and the Subject of Language*. Ed. Ellie Ragland-Sullivan and Mark Bracher. New York: Routledge, 1991. 199–212.

Zlotnick, Susan. *Women, Writing, and the Industrial Revolution*. Baltimore: Johns Hopkins UP, 1998.

INDEX

Acton, William, 124, 125, 166n22, 167–68n35, 180n36
Adams, James Eli, 182n13
Allen, Emily, 163n2, 177n4, 180n35
Altick, Richard D., 59, 62, 148, 170–71nn30–33, 171nn35–36, 171n38, 174n26
Aristotle, 15, 16, 18, 20, 116, 118, 164n9
Armstrong, Isobel, 160, 181n9, 182n15
Armstrong, Nancy, 169n12
Arnold, Matthew, 124, 148, 171n36
Auden, W. H., 1, 8
Austen, Jane, 133
Austin, Alfred, 124, 153, 159
Aveling, Edward, 175–76n35

Babb, Lawrence, 15, 165n10
Bacon, Ezekiel, 121, 122
Bagehot, Walter, 42, 149
Bailey, Thomas, 179–80n29
Baillie, Matthew, 116
Bakhtin, Mikhail, 75, 78–79, 172n8
Bamborough, J. B., 165n10
Barker-Benfield, G. J., 23, 177n1
Barrett, Elizabeth (Elizabeth Barrett Browning), 121–22
Batten, Guin, 176nn37–38, 176–77n48
Baudrillard, Jean, 176n37
Beddoes, Thomas: and genius, 19; and masturbation, 17–18, 180n36; and nervous energy, 22–23; and novels, 17, 114, 127; and Pinel, Philippe, 30; and poetry as healthful, 113–14; and quack doctors, 167–68n35; and study, 30
Beiderwell, Bruce, 169n8, 169n14, 170n24
Benbow, William, 130–31
Bender, John, 169n12
Benjamin, Walter, 59, 60
Bennett, David, 177n1, 181n41
Bentham, Jeremy, 8, 145
Bernstein, Michael André, 173n12
Blackmore, Richard, 16–17, 20, 164n4, 164n8
Blann, Robinson, 172n2
Blessington, Lady, 178n16
Boehm, Alan D., 171n33
book, history of the: mass market, 34, 170nn30–31, 171n33; technologies of production, 53, 58–63, 66, 171nn32–33, 171n35
Bourdieu, Pierre, 7, 163n7
Braddon, Mary Elizabeth, 134
Brantlinger, Patrick, 163n4, 169n12, 170n29
Bridges, Samuel Egerton, 173n14
Brinton, Crane, 172n5
Bristow, Joe, 181n7
Brontë, Charlotte, 134
Brontë, Emily, 134
Brooks, Cleanth, 181n9
Brown, George H., 179n28
Brown, John, 22–23, 167n29, 167n32
Browning, Elizabeth Barrett. *See* Barrett, Elizabeth
Browning, Robert, 121, 178n18
Bruns, Gerald, 75
Buckler, William, 181n11
Buckley, Jerome, 182n13
Bulwer-Lytton, Edward: on Byron, Lord, 39–40, 107, 108, 132–33, 145–46; on melancholia, 132–33; on the novel, 107, 133; novels, sale of his, 171n36; *Pelham*, 133; on poetry, marginalization of, 145–46, 181n4; on poets, 125–26; on Scott, Sir Walter, 39–40, 146, 181n4; on Tennyson, 146

Burgess, Miranda, 170n19, 177n4
Burke, Edmund, 50–51
Burton, Robert, 15, 108, 168n38, 178n9
Burwick, Frederick, 163n1, 178n11
Butler, Marilyn, 108
Byron, Lady (Annabella Milbanke), 108, 114, 116–17, 120, 129
Byron, Lord (George Gordon): and the anthropologization of the present, 74–78, 80, 99, 103, 105, 117, 140, 172–73nn8–9; and book binding, 88, 91, 174–75nn27–28; *Cain*, 76, 128–29; *Childe Harold*, 9, 39, 74–106 passim, 118–19, 120, 122, 133, 137, 140, 176n44, 179n22; and class, 9, 38, 86–89, 103, 173n17, 174n24, 175n29, 175n34; and cold carnival, 71, 78–80, 86, 87, 92, 93, 103, 140, 172n5, 173nn13–14; *Deformed Transformed*, 82; D'Israeli, admiration of, 177n8; *Don Juan* 39, 76, 83, 90, 92–93, 94–95, 96, 101, 103, 140, 173n10, 174n24, 175n32, 176n42, 176n44; and the fetish, 9–10, 71, 75, 78, 80, 93, 96, 102–3, 140, 158; and genius, 2, 33, 35, 41, 81–86, 106, 108–13, 116, 123, 177n7, 178n16, 178–79n20; and gift giving, 93, 95, 100, 176nn41–42, 177n49; and homosexuality, 10, 107, 137–38, 177n5; and justice, 9, 73, 78, 80, 93, 95, 96–97, 100–103, 107, 176–77n48; and madness, 114–17; *Manfred*, 42, 117; *Marino Faliero*, 176n44; and the market, 2, 5, 71, 84, 88–96, 103, 143, 174–75n28, 175nn31–32, 175n34; and masturbation, 10, 106, 124–30, 137–38, 140, 176n40, 179–80n29; and militias, funding of, 173n11; and moral melancholia, 9, 71, 74, 82–83, 96–103, 105, 108, 176–77n48; and nostalgia, 75, 96, 99, 173n10; and the novel, 107, 133–34, 145–46; pathologizing of, 2, 3, 35, 39–42, 68, 71–72, 84–85, 106–20, 122–33 passim, 141, 144, 148, 174n22, 178n17, 178–79nn20–21; and performativity, 9, 80, 83, 93, 95, 103, 140, 177n51; and piracy, 90, 91, 130–31, 175n30, 175n34; and politics, 2, 5, 73–74, 86–87, 108, 129–30, 134, 143, 171–72n1, 172n3, 172n6, 174nn22–23, 176n44; and pornography, 117, 130–31; and revolution, 2, 5, 9, 71–75, 77, 80–108 passim, 117, 118, 120, 128–30, 134, 138, 140, 144, 159, 160, 171–72n1, 172n5, 173n16, 173n19, 174n25, 175n33; Scott, Sir Walter, evaluation of, 172n6; sexualization of, 2, 9–10, 72, 83, 106–8, 163n5; as vampire, 105–6, 177n2; *Vision of Judgment*, 175n30. *See also under* Bulwer-Lytton; Carlyle; D'Israeli, Isaac; Hunt, Leigh; Jeffrey; Manning; Marx, Karl; medievalism; Satanic hero; Scott, Sir Walter

Cabanis, Pierre-Jean-George: on the imagination, 13, 24; influence of, 166n22; and the materialists, 166n25; on men of letters, 19; on nervous energy, 22, 24, 166n25; on the nervous temperament, 20, 22, 165n12; on secretions, re-absorption of, 180n36; on the social body, 20
Cafarelli, Annette Wheeler, 177n7, 178n14
Carlson, Julie, 176n46
Carlyle, Thomas: on Byron, Lord, 68, 106, 134; and cold carnival, 173n13; against poetry, 145; on reading, 68, 132; on romanticism, 133–34; on Scott, Sir Walter, 40, 68, 106
"Cato," 174n22
Chambers, Robert, 60
Chandler, Alice, 34, 52, 169n13, 170nn19–21
Chandler, James, 4, 172n8, 173n19
Cheyne, Samuel, 14, 16, 164nn3–5, 165n13
Christ, Carol, 160, 181n9
Christensen, Jerome, 95, 176n41, 176n45
Clarkson, Thomas, 17
Clayton, Jay, 181n1
Clough, Arthur, 151
Cobbett, William, 52, 170n20, 171–72n1
Cohen, Ed, 163n8

Coleridge, Samuel Taylor: and Beddoes, 23, 167n35, 180n36; and the clerisy, 60, 148; and the Cult of the Book, 60; and the fetish, 26, 45; on knowledge as disease, 164n2; and the market, 134–35; and masturbation, 134–35, 180n36; and scholarship today, 4; and woman as master-trope, 159
Colley, Ann, 181n5
Collins, A. S., 60
Collins, Philip, 172n5, 175n34
Combe, George, 123, 166n25
Cooke, M. G., 176n40
Craig, David, 172n3
Crichton, Alexander, 21
critic. *See* man of letters; literary criticism
Croker, John Wilson, 87, 150
Crompton, Louis, 177n5
Cullen, William, 22
Culler, A. Dwight, 170n21, 181n10
Cult of the Book, 9, 58–62, 66, 71, 91, 93, 175n34. *See also under* Coleridge; Hunt, Leigh; medievalism
Culture of the Text, 9, 58–61, 66, 91, 175n34
Curran, Stuart, 170n22
Curry, Kenneth, 175n31
Cuvier, George, 76, 173n9
Cvetkovich, Ann, 177n4

Darwin, Erasmus, 21, 31, 166nn24–25, 168n40, 180n36
Davis, Lennard J., 177n4
de Almeida, Hermione, 23, 167n29
Debord, Guy, 48, 169n16
Decadents, 4, 11, 158–59
De Laura, David J., 181n8
Derrida, Jacques: on the gift, 71, 93, 95, 176n43; on justice, 73, 95, 100–101; on masturbation, 176n40; on money, 26–27, 176n37; on ontology, 100; on spectropoetics, 177n50
De Silva, D. M., 172n3
de Vere, Aubrey, 149
Diakonova, Nina, 172n5
dialectics, 2, 5, 108
Disraeli, Benjamin, 133
D'Israeli, Isaac: and Byron, Lord, 108–10, 115, 177n8; and genius, 108–13, 136; influence of, 178n10; and the man of letters, 111–12; and melancholy, 178n9; and the poet, 110–13, 125; on Rousseau, 178nn12–13
Dobell, Sidney, 148
Dorchester Guide, 84, 91
Doré, Gustave, 82, 118, 173n18
Duff, David, 172n7
Duff, William, 164n1
Dugdale, William, 130–31
Du Laurens, André, 178n9
Duncan, Ian, 177n4
Dyer, Gary, 137

Eco, Umberto, 78–79, 92, 173nn12–13
Edgeworth, Maria, 180n33
Elfenbein, Andrew: *Romantic Genius*, 10, 107, 136, 163n5, 179n23; *Byron and the Victorians*, 133, 173n9, 180n34
Eliot, George, 134
Eliot, Simon, 171n33, 181n3
Eliot, T. S., 160
Ellis, George, 80, 96, 140
Engels, Friedrich, 91, 175–76n35
Erdman, David, 172n3, 172n5, 173n17, 175n29
Erickson, Lee, 62, 145, 171n32, 171n36, 181n3

Faas, Ekbert, 178n11, 178n18

Felluga, Dino Franco, 163n2, 173n13, 180n35
Ferris, Ina: *Achievement of Literary Authority*, 68, 163n4, 169n6, 170n24, 172n8; "Trope to Code," 39, 170n29
fetishism: anthropological, 8, 26, 34, 44, 58, 59, 60, 96; commodity, 9, 26–27, 34, 50, 58, 60, 91, 96, 98, 139–40; and fiction, 10, 45–50, 58, 66–67, 114, 139–41, 160; and mourning, 96–98, 159, 168n1, 176n47; psychoanalytical, 8, 10, 34, 43–54, 57–58, 60, 63–64, 67, 68, 75, 78, 96–98, 139–40, 152, 158, 159–60, 168n1, 176n47; and

fetishism: anthropological *(continued)* the romance, 45–47, 49–53, 66, 74–75, 78, 80, 96. *See also under* Byron, Lord; Coleridge; Marx; medievalism; Scott, Sir Walter; Solomon; Tennyson; Zizek
Ficino, Marsilio, 165n10
Fischer, Hermann, 170n25
Flint, Kate, 163n4
Foot, Michael, 172n3, 172n5, 175–76n35
Ford, Jennifer, 163n1, 163n5, 178n11
Foucault, Michel, 48, 164n7, 173n9, 180n39
Fox, William, 149
Franklin, J. Jeffrey, 177n4
Freud, Sigmund, 50, 51, 168n1, 176–77n47–48

Gagnier, Regenia, 181n2
Galen, 15, 20, 134, 165n17
Gall, Franz Joseph, 166n25
Galperin, William, 173n10
Galvani, Luigi, 21
Gamer, Michael, 170n25
Gammage, R. G., 172n5
Gelpi, Barbara, 181n2
genius: and the bourgeois subject, 135–36; healthy forms of, 9, 13, 41, 81, 118; literary vs. scientific forms of, 8, 13–14, 29–30, 110–11, 118, 164n1; melancholy, relation to, 13, 18, 28–29, 81–82, 96, 108–13, 164n1; pathologizing of, 2, 3, 7, 9, 10, 13, 18, 28–29, 34–35, 38, 40, 81, 85, 106, 108–13, 118–20, 123, 124, 141, 163n5, 164n1, 166n23, 168n41, 177n7, 178n13, 178n16; poet of, 7, 10, 32, 40, 69, 82, 107, 110, 112–13, 117, 118–19, 122, 124, 136; sexualization of, 19, 106, 131. *See also under* Byron, Lord; D'Israeli, Isaac; Jeffrey; masturbation; Scott, Sir Walter; Solomon; Wordsworth
Gerard, Alexander, 164n1
Gibbon, Edward, 75–76, 173n9
Giddey, Ernest, 173n9
Gilbert, Pamela K., 163n4
Gilfillan, George, 150
Girouard, Mark, 169n13, 170n19, 170n21
Gladstone, W. E., 152–53
Gleckner, Robert F., 177n49
Gordon, Cosmo, 120
Goslee, Nancy, 46, 170n23, 170n25, 171n41
Graham, Sylvester, 21, 24–25, 134–35, 166n20
Gross, Jonathan David, 172n3, 177n5
Guy-Bray, Stephen, 163n5, 177n3

Hadley, Elaine, 177n4
Hair, Donald S., 181n10
Hallam, Arthur, 7, 148, 149, 151
Hare, E. H., 165n17
Haslam, John, 28–29, 30, 108, 110–11, 125, 168nn38–39
Hawes, Clement, 178n9
Hazlitt, William, 33, 41, 49, 114–15, 118, 127
Heinzelman, Kurt, 91–92, 176nn36–37, 176n39, 176n41
Hernadi, Paul, 181n2
Hippocrates, 180n36
Hirsch, E. D., 176–77n48
Hobhouse, John Cam, 86, 87, 89, 116, 172n2
Hofkosh, Susan, 163n5
Holbeach, Henry, 177n1
Holland, Tom, 177n2
Hone, J. Ann, 173n19
Hone, William, 83, 84, 90, 175n32
Hughes, Shaun, 179n28
Hughes, Winifred, 177n4
Hunt, John, 90, 93, 94, 172n2, 176n42
Hunt, Leigh: and Byron, Lord, 115, 173n9; and the Cult of the Book, 59; imprisonment of, 172n2; *The Liberal*, 175n31; and the market, 146, 174–75n28; and poetry, defense of, 115; and radicalism, 87; and Tennyson, 150

ideology: and the bourgeois subject, 45, 48–50, 58, 98, 107, 135–41, 144, 160, 169n12, 169n16, 180n37, 181n40; and lack, 50, 138, 158–61; and master-

tropes, 6, 7–8, 20–25, 28, 134–41, 144, 151, 153–61; materiality of, 6, 155–56; and perversion, 160–61. *See also* fetishism; social body: and bourgeois ideology; Zizek: on ideology
Ingham, Patricia C., 170n27, 171n41

Jacyna, L. S., 165n15, 167n28, 167n30
James, Louis, 172n5, 175n34
James, Robert, 16, 137
Jameson, Fredric, 54
Jamison, Kay Redfield, 97, 113
Janowitz, Anne, 172n5, 175n33
Janssen, David Alan, 177n7
Jeffrey, Francis: on Byron, Lord, 79–80, 81–82, 83, 85, 86, 118–19; on genius, 118–19; on the Satanic hero, 81–82, 85, 118; on Scott, Sir Walter, 80, 81, 173n15
Jewson, N. D., 31, 167n34, 168n43
Joyce, James, 72, 83

Kant, Immanuel, 24, 137, 158, 167n32
Keats, John: and effeminacy, 150, 163n5; and masturbation, 106, 124, 125, 181n40; pathologizing of, 124, 149, 151; and scholarship today, 4
Kebble, John, 171n42
Kelsall, Malcolm, 73–74, 78, 172nn3–4, 173n17, 174n2
Kernan, Alvin, 59, 171n39
Kiernan, Victor, 182n13
Kingsley, Charles, 148
Klancher, Jon, 163n6, 170n29
Klein, Jürgen, 172n3
Knight, David, 168n42
Knowles, J. T., 152
Kristeva, Julia, 176–77n48

Lacan, Jacques, 159–60, 182n14
Lackington, James, 59, 60
Laclau, Ernesto, 6, 88
Lallemand, François, 126–27, 179n26
Lamb, Caroline, 106, 131
Langan, Celeste, 170nn25–26, 171n34, 171n40
Langbauer, Laurie, 177n4
Laqueur, Thomas, 138–39, 164n9 (intro.), 164n7 (chap. 1), 165–66nn16–18, 179–80n29
Lawrence, William, 83, 173–74n20
Leblanc, Henri, 173n18
Leckie, Barbara, 177n4
Levi, Leone, 174n26
Levinson, Marjorie, 163n5, 177n3, 181n40
Lewes, George Henry, 148
literary criticism, legitimization of, 2, 6, 32, 60, 148, 153
Litvak, Joseph, 177n4
Liu, Alan, 176n39, 181n2
Lockhart, John Gibson, 34, 37–38, 91, 115, 150
Logan, Peter Melville, 15, 21, 163nn4–5, 168n37
Lohmar, Brigitte, 80
Lukács, George, 169n8
Lynch, Deirdre, 169n12, 171n34

Macaulay, Thomas Babington, 120, 131, 145, 179n22
MacDonald, Robert H., 165n17
Madden, R. R., 40, 108, 113, 120, 124
Makdisi, Saree, 169n8, 169n15, 170n24, 172n8
Mancoff, Debra, 171n39
Manning, Peter J.: on Byron, Lord, 75, 90, 91, 172n3, 172n5, 173n16, 173n19, 174n25, 174–75n28, 175n30, 175n34, 176n41; on the market, 53, 91, 175n34; on piracy, 175n30; on the romance, 53, 75; on Scott, Sir Walter, 169n3, 170n26
Mannoni, Octave, 34, 44
man of letters: health of, 2–3, 111; and high culture, 14, 32, 146–48, 155; and the market, 32, 111–12, 147, 155; as medic, 2–3, 8, 13–14, 32, 111–12, 117–20, 144, 148–52; pathologizing of the, 13, 16, 18, 20, 28, 32, 35, 40–41, 111, 123; and the pathologizing of imagination, 110–13; self-legitimization, 2, 111, 147, 148, 153; and specialization, 3, 8, 147. *See also under* D'Israeli, Isaac; masturbation; Tissot

Marchand, Leslie, 115, 116, 117, 172n6, 175n29
Marcus, Leah, 173n12
Marcus, Steven, 124–25, 177n3
Marsh, Joss, 175n34
Marston, John, 149
Martin, Philip W., 177n51
Marx, Eleanor, 175–76n35
Marx, Karl: on Byron, Lord, 175–76n35; and commodity fetishism, 26, 58, 60, 91, 176n37, 177n2; and psychoanalysis, 6; and simple abstraction, 5. *See also* fetishism: commodity
Mason, Michael, 179n26, 180n36
masturbation: and genius, 18, 19; history of, 165n17; and homosexuality, 10, 107, 136–38; and imagination, 14, 23–25; and the man of letters, 18–19; and the market, 10, 134–41, 144, 181n41; and melancholy, 18, 28, 166n20; and the novel, 10, 17–18, 23; pathologizing of, 5, 7, 10, 14, 17, 18–19, 23–25, 27–28, 72, 106–7, 123, 124–30, 134–37, 158, 165n17–18, 180n30; and the romance, 17, 23; and spermatorrhoea, 125, 126, 138, 166n22, 179n26; and study, 19, 166n22. *See also under* Beddoes; Byron, Lord; Coleridge; Derrida; Keats; poetry; Solomon; Tissot
McCallum, E. L., 97–98
McCalman, Iain, 130, 173n19, 175n34, 178n15, 180n32
McConnell, Frank, 177n51
McDayter, Ghislaine, 176n36, 177n2
McGann, Jerome, 1, 2, 74, 164n9, 173n16, 177n49
McKeon, Michael, 5, 163n2, 169n12, 177n4
medical profession: on civilization, 13–14, 30, 42, 164n5; on imagination, 8, 14, 16, 23–25, 29–30, 34, 40, 116, 118, 120–21, 123–24, 126, 137, 163n5, 165n17; and the market, 8, 26–27, 31–32; on the market and its pathologies, 14–15, 58, 61; pathologizing of the, 8, 13–14, 28, 121, 168n41; quack doctors, 14, 25–28, 31–32, 167–68n35; self-legitimization of the, 8, 13–14, 27–32, 110, 167n35; on study, 14–16, 19, 28–30, 111, 124, 164n2; on women, 15, 17. *See also* Byron, Lord: pathologizing of; genius: pathologizing of; man of letters: pathologizing of; masturbation; melancholy; poetry: pathologizing of
medievalism: and Byron, Lord, 9, 71, 75, 93; and the Cult of the Book, 58, 63, 66–67, 71, 93; and the fetish, 33–34, 43, 47, 50, 51, 52–54, 57–58, 63–64, 66–67, 75, 96, 139; and health, 33–34, 47, 53, 54, 56, 64, 74–75; and inefficacy, 68, 132; and the market, 52–53, 57, 64, 143; and politics, 2, 8–9, 33–34, 48–49, 50–54, 56–57, 64, 67, 80, 88, 159, 169n13, 170nn19–21; and the romance, 3, 9; and Scott, Sir Walter, 2, 9, 75–75, 80, 33–69 passim
melancholy: and adolescence, 132–33; and enthusiasm, 178n9; and hypochondria, 164n8; and mania, 168n38; and mental ability, 13, 15–16, 28–30, 82, 108, 110–11, 116, 118–19, 164n1, 165n10; and nerves, 7, 16–17, 18, 123–25; pathologizing of, 97–98, 118, 133, 146, 165n10, 176–77n48; and poetry, 10, 110–11, 116, 118–19, 123–27, 132–33; and revolution, 3, 10, 71, 83, 96, 106, 108, 118; as simple abstraction, 97; treatment of, 42, 118. *See also under* Bulwer-Lytton; Byron, Lord; D'Israeli, Isaac; genius; masturbation; Tennyson
Melchiori, Giorgio, 172n5
Mellor, Anne K., 173n13, 176n40
Mill, John Stuart, 8, 123, 140, 147, 151, 179n25
Miller, D. A., 163nn4–5, 169n12
Millgate, Jane, 170n25
Mitford, John, 130–31, 180nn32–33
More, Hannah, 61, 170n31, 171n36
Mouffe, Chantalle, 6, 88
Mullan, John, 15, 16, 163n4, 164n3, 164n6
Mulock, Thomas, 179n21
Murphy, Paul Thomas, 175n34

Murphy, Peter T., 170n25
Murray, John, 87, 90, 94, 115, 124, 128–29, 150, 175n32, 179n22

Najarian, James, 163n5
nerves: vs. humours, 16, 20; nervous disease, 13, 15, 164n3, 165n13, 169n4; nervous energy or fluid, 20–25, 27, 118, 120–27, 135, 138, 145, 163n5, 166–67nn25–26, 167n29, 167n33, 173–74n20; nervous sensibility, 15, 16–21, 30, 122, 124, 127, 165n15, 166n20; nervous temperament, 7, 16–23 passim, 40, 80, 118–27, 165n12. *See also under* melancholy; social body; Tissot
Neuman, P., 165n17
Newman, John Henry, 148
Noble, Andrew, 172n3
novels: and health, 41–42, 49; and the market, 61, 170n30; pathologizing of, 8, 10, 15, 17, 38–39, 41–42, 107, 114, 123, 127, 134, 135, 138–40, 144, 150, 157, 163n4, 165n16; rise of, 2, 3, 7, 61, 71, 107, 133, 134, 139–41, 143, 169n12; and the romance, 3, 45, 54, 107, 156–57, 177n4, 180n33; and simple abstraction, 5. *See also* Beddoes: and the novel; Byron, Lord: and the novel; fetishism: and fiction; masturbation: and the novel; poetry: and the novel

Ogden, James, 178n10
Onania, 27, 165n17
onanism. *See* masturbation
Otto, Peter, 166n25

Paine, Thomas, 61, 83, 170nn30–31, 171n36
Parke, Tim, 177n4
Parry, Caleb Hillier, 116, 178n19
Partridge, Eric, 170n17
Pattison, Robert, 182n12
Peacock, Thomas Love, 131–33
Peterson, M. Jeanne, 31, 165n17, 168n44
Pinel, Philippe, 30, 168n39. *See also under* Beddoes, Thomas
poetry: and adolescence, 4, 5, 10, 30, 67, 74, 106, 108, 131–33, 140, 149; and dialectics, 1–2, 5, 10, 144, 148–53, 181n9; and emotion, 1, 7, 132, 151, 164n1, 179n25; *genus irritabile vatum*, 35, 82; and health, 2, 39, 67, 113–14, 120, 141, 143, 147–48, 150–51, 158, 159; and idealism, 10, 72, 75, 127, 131, 132–33, 144–45, 151–52; and madness, 178n11; marginalization of, 1, 2, 3, 6, 9, 34, 67–69, 71, 74, 131–34, 141, 143–47, 150–51, 157–59, 181n4; and the market, 43, 61–65, 71, 91–92, 112, 134–41, 143–45, 147, 154–57, 159; and masturbation, 5, 7, 106, 124–28, 131, 134–41, 151, 177n3, 181n40; and the novel, 3, 10, 68, 71, 106–7, 127, 133–34, 140–41, 144–45, 150, 151, 156–58; pathologizing of, 1–7 passim, 35–41, 68–69, 71–72, 106–8, 111–28, 132–51 passim, 158, 159, 160, 163n5, 169n2, 178n19, 179n23; and purity, 3, 11, 19, 34, 67–68, 71, 143–61 passim, 163n3, 164n1, 181n1, 181nn8–9; and sexuality, 2, 72, 125, 140, 144, 151–60, 163n3. *See also* Byron, Lord; genius: poet of; Hunt, Leigh; melancholy: and poetry; Scott, Sir Walter; Tennyson
Poovey, Mary, 135–36, 163n6, 170n29
Porter, Roy, 164n5, 165n17, 167–68nn35–36, 180n37
Prebble, John, 169n10, 170n17
Procter, B. W., 150
Psomiades, Kathy, 154–55

Radical Triumvirate, 83–84, 91
Radway, Janice, 180n31
Ramsey, Matthew, 166n19
Raymond, Dora Neill, 172n3
Reed, John, 181n10
Richardson, Alan, 163n1, 163n5, 166n22, 166n25, 168n40, 168n42
Richardson, Samuel, 15
Richter, Jean Paul, 173n14
Ricks, Christopher, 163n5
Roberts, William, 39, 117–18, 120, 122, 125, 141, 174n24

Robertson, F. W., 148
romance: and adolescence, 4, 10, 30, 67, 74, 106, 108, 131–33; and chivalry, 56–57; and counter-revolution, 3–4, 9, 34, 36–37, 42–43, 51–52, 56, 64, 67, 74–75; and escapism, 3, 4, 5, 30, 74; and fiction, 45–50, 52–53, 56, 114, 131, 152, 156; and health, 33–34, 37, 41–42, 49, 54, 57, 64, 66; and idealism, 92, 115, 133; marginalization of, 4–5, 74, 106; and the market, 3, 4, 33–34, 51, 53, 57–58, 72, 147; and masculinity, 37; pathologizing of, 13, 17, 30, 35–36, 41, 58, 66, 68, 97, 147, 157; and pornography, 3, 130–31, 180n31; and revolution, 3–4, 30, 71, 78–80, 91, 92–93, 100, 105–6, 130, 157, 172n7; as simple abstraction, 5. *See also under* fetishism; Manning; masturbation; novels; Tennyson
romantic ideology, 1, 3, 9, 106, 130. *See also* ideology
Rosario, Vernon A., 19, 165nn17–18, 167n31, 180n38
Roscoe, W. C., 151
Rosen, Charles, 178n11
Ross, Charlie, 179n28
Ross, Deborah, 177n4
Ross, Marlon, 58, 170n23, 170nn25–26, 170n28
Rousseau, Jean-Jacques, 23–24, 167n31, 176n40, 178n13. *See also under* Tissot
Rowland, William G., Jr., 136, 176n36
Ruddick, William, 172n3
Rush, Benjamin, 22, 42, 129, 168n39, 180n30
Ruskin, John, 151–52
Rutherford, Andrew, 172n6

Satanic hero: and Byron, Lord, 9, 39, 71, 81–85, 120, 128, 131, 144, 169n6, 174nn21–22; and melancholy, 81–83, 98; and pathology, 3, 83–85, 120; and revolution, 3, 39, 81–85, 120, 128. *See also under* Jeffrey
Schiesari, Juliana, 15, 176–77n48
Schmid, Thomas, H., 173nn13–14
Scott, John, 42
Scott, P. H., 85, 172n6
Scott, Walter, Sir: and book binding, 63; Byron, Lord, evaluation of, 35, 85–87, 119–20, 129, 174n23; and carnival, 173n15; and chronotopes, 172n8; and class, 38, 57, 63, 66, 87–88, 171n41; and the *Edinburgh Annual Register*, 175n31; and the fetish, 8–9, 34, 43–50, 52–54, 58, 66–68, 71, 74–75, 80, 96, 102, 103, 139, 152, 158, 160; and genius, 2, 35–36, 80, 81, 85–86, 141; and George IV, 2, 9, 33, 34, 43–45, 48–50, 53, 63, 64, 67, 74, 79; and health, 2, 3, 8, 9, 33–42, 58, 68–69, 81, 106, 108, 114, 115, 120, 129, 132, 141, 148, 169n6, 178–79n20; *Lady of the Lake*, 8, 9, 37, 54–55, 56, 63; *Lay of the Last Minstrel*, 8, 33, 35, 38, 52, 53, 54, 58, 63–66, 96; marginalization of, 67–68, 106, 146, 169n3; and the market, 2, 5, 8, 34, 43, 53, 58, 61, 63–66, 88, 94, 143, 171n36, 181n4; *Marmion*, 8, 37, 45–47, 52, 55–56, 57, 63; and militias, funding of, 36–38, 63, 173n10; and mourning, 96, 105; and nostalgia, 52–54, 67, 71, 75, 96, 99, 158–59; and politics, 2, 5, 8–9, 34, 37, 42–57, 64, 67, 73–75, 77, 80, 143, 169n8, 174n23; *Rokeby*, 35, 40; sexualization of, 68. *See also under* Bulwer-Lytton; Byron, Lord; Carlyle; Jeffrey; Manning; medievalism
Sedgwick, Eve Kosovsky, 10, 107, 136, 143, 160, 163n8, 181n6
Sha, Richard, 165n17
Shannon, Edgar Finley, 150
Shelley, Percy Bysshe, 4, 132, 146, 149, 175n31, 175n34
Showalter, Elaine, 163n4
Sinclair, John, 168n41
Sinfield, Alan, 181n6, 181n8, 182n15
Sitter, John, 181n9
Skinner, Basil C., 233
Small, Helen, 163n4
Smith, Adam, 71
Smith, William, 17

social body: and the nervous system, 7, 8, 13, 22, 106, 108, 135–41, 144–45; and bourgeois ideology, 49, 51, 135–41, 159; scholarship on the, 163n6
Solomon, Samuel: and the fetish, 26, 34, 43; on genius, 19; on the market, 25–26, 98; on masturbation, 25–27, 124, 125; as quack doctor, 25–27, 167–68n35; on study, 19
Southey, Robert, 62, 85, 130
Spillane, John D., 165n15
Spurzheim, Johann Christoph, 29–30, 117–18, 123, 125, 166n25, 178n19, 179n24
Stabler, Jane, 164n9
Stacy, John, 79, 84–85, 91
Stallybrass, Peter, 173n12
Starzyk, Lawrence, 67, 148, 181nn8–9
St. Clair, William, 88, 90, 91, 171n37, 174n27
Stengers, Jean, 165n14, 165n17
Stephen, Leslie, 123
Stevenson, Lionel, 145
Stewart, Garrett, 181n2
Stukeley, William, 16
Sutherland, John, 44, 45, 50
Swann, Karen, 176n46

Taylor, John, 163n4, 170n29
Tennyson, Alfred Lord: as dialectical sublation, 2, 5, 10, 144, 148–53; and effeminacy, 147, 150, 153, 160; and the fetish, 152, 158–60; and health, 10, 144; and homosexuality, 147, 153, 181n6; *Idylls of the King*, 4, 10, 144–45, 152–57, 159–60; and the market, 4, 141, 144, 146, 157; *Maud*, 146–47, 149; and melancholy, 146–47, 181n5; and the novel, 156–57, 182n12; pathologizing of, 123, 134, 149–51; and politics, 147; and psychology, 178n18; and the romance, 10, 141, 147, 152, 156–57, 181n10; and romanticism, 10, 144, 146–47, 149–50, 153, 156, 157, 159, 160; as subversive reactionary, 3, 5, 160–61, 182n15; and woman as master-trope, 10, 144, 147, 153–60. *See also* Hunt, Leigh: and Tennyson; poetry: and purity
Tennyson, Hallam, 152
Thomson, John, 167n30
Tissot, Samuel Auguste David: on humours, 20; influence of, 126, 165n14; on masturbation, 18, 19, 23, 165–66nn18–19, 166n21, 180n36; on the man of letters, 18–19, 40, 111, 112; on the nervous system, 17, 22, 24; on the quack doctor, 27; and Rousseau, 167n31, 178n13; on study, 18, 28, 30
Todd, John, 105, 127–30, 177n1, 179n27, 179–80n29
Trall, Russell Thacher, 167n33
Trevelyan, George, 179n22
Treves, Frederick, 122
Trevor-Roper, Hugh, 169n11
Trilling, Lionel, 113
Trotter, Thomas, 18–19, 22, 165nn12–13, 168n37, 169n4
Trumpener, Katie, 169n8, 170n24, 172n8
Tucker, Herbert F., 157, 181n2, 181n10
Tucker, Susie, 178n9

Vacuro, Vadim, 172n5
Van Neck, Anne, 165n14, 165n17
Vickers, Neil, 167n29, 167n32
von Haller, Albrecht, 165n15, 180n36
Vrettos, Athena, 163n4

Waddington, Ivan, 168n36, 168n44
Wain, John, 177n51
Walker, Keith, 172n5, 174n25, 175n34
Warren, Alba H., 67, 171n42, 181n9
Warton, Joseph, 19, 164n1, 181n1
Watkins, Daniel P., 171–72n1, 172n3, 173n16
Watt, Ian, 169n12
Weinstein, Mark A., 150
White, Allon, 173n12
Whytt, Robert, 21
Wickwar, William, 175n34
Wiener, Martin, 88
Wilde, Oscar, 10, 107, 137

Williams, Ioan, 177n4
Wilson, Frances, 177n6
Wilson, Harriette, 178n17
Wilson, John (Christopher North), 149
Wittkower, Margot, 165n10
Wittkower, Rudolf, 165n10
Wolfson, Susan, 163n5, 177n3
Wood, Jane, 163nn4–5
Woodring, Carl, 172n3, 175n29
Wordsworth, William: on genius, 166n23; on knowledge, 164n2; on the market, 7; on narrative, 33; pathologizing of, 132; in periodical reviews, 31, 168n41; and purity, 146; and the real, 149; and scholarship today, 4; and Tennyson, 10
Wright, Barbara Herb, 181n5

Zionkowski, Linda, 163n3, 163n5, 169n2, 169n7, 178n14, 181n1
Zizek, Slavoj: on Coke, 169n15; on fetishism, 44–45, 48, 139, 168n1; on ideology, 6, 44, 138, 158; on nostalgia, 52; on overorthodoxy, 160
Zlotnick, Susan, 170n20